No Excuses:
Existentialism and the
Meaning of Life

Robert C. Solomon, Ph.D.

PUBLISHED BY:

THE GREAT COURSES
Corporate Headquarters
4840 Westfields Boulevard, Suite 500
Chantilly, Virginia 20151-2299
Phone: 1-800-832-2412
Fax: 703-378-3819
www.thegreatcourses.com

Copyright © The Teaching Company, 2000

Robert C. Solomon, Ph.D.

Quincy Lee Centennial
Professor of Business and Philosophy
University of Texas at Austin

Professor Robert C. Solomon is Quincy Lee Centennial Professor of Business and Philosophy at the University of Texas at Austin. Professor Solomon is also the recipient of several teaching awards and honors, including the 1973 Standard Oil Outstanding Teaching Award, the University of Texas Presidential Associates' Teaching Award (twice), a Fulbright Lecture Award, University Research and National Endowment for the Humanities grants, and the Chad Oliver Plan Iwe Teaching Award (1998). He is also a member of the Academy of Distinguished Teachers. Professor Solomon is the author of *The Passions, In the Spirit of Hegel, About Love, From Hegel to Existentialism, The Joy of Philosophy,* and *A Passion for Justice* and is the coauthor, with Kathleen M. Higgins, of *What Nietzsche Really Said.* He has authored and edited articles and books on Nietzsche, including *Nietzsche* and *Reading Nietzsche* with Kathleen M. Higgins. His most recent books, also with Kathleen Higgins, are *A Short History of Philosophy* and *A Passion for Wisdom.* His books have been translated into more than a dozen languages.

In addition, Professor Solomon writes about business ethics in such books as *Above the Bottom Line, It's Good Business, Ethics and Excellence, New World of Business,* and *A Better Way to Think about Business.* He regularly consults and provides programs for a variety of corporations and organizations concerned about business ethics. He studied biology at the University of Pennsylvania and philosophy and psychology at the University of Michigan. He is married to Kathleen M. Higgins. Professor Solomon has taught at Princeton University and the University of Pittsburgh and often teaches in New Zealand and Australia. ■

Table of Contents

Table of Contents

Table of Contents

No Excuses: Existentialism and the Meaning of Life

Scope:

Existentialism is, in my view, the most exciting and important philosophical movement of the past century and a half. Fifty years after the French philosopher Jean-Paul Sartre gave it its identity and one hundred and fifty years after the Danish philosopher Søren Kierkegaard gave it its initial impetus, existentialism continues to win new enthusiasts and, in keeping with its still exciting and revolutionary message, vehement critics.

The message of existentialism, unlike that of many more obscure and academic philosophical movements, is about as simple as can be. It is that every one of us, as an individual, is responsible—responsible for what we do, responsible for who we are, responsible for the way we face and deal with the world, responsible, ultimately, for the way the world is. It is, in a very short phrase, the philosophy of "no excuses!" Life may be difficult; circumstances may be impossible. There may be obstacles, not least of which are our own personalities, characters, emotions, and limited means or intelligence. But, nevertheless, we are responsible. We cannot shift that burden onto God, or nature, or the ways of the world. If there is a God, we choose to believe. If nature made us one way, it is up to us to decide what we are to do with what nature gives us—whether to go along or fight back, to modify or transcend nature. As the delightfully priggish Kate Hepburn says to a wonderfully vulgar Humphrey Bogart in the movie *The African Queen*, "Nature is what we are put on this earth to rise above." That is what existentialism is all about. We are responsible for ourselves.

There are no excuses.

But to say that the basic message of existentialism is quite simple and straightforward is not to say that the philosophers or the philosophies that make up the movement are simple and straightforward. The movement itself is something of a fabrication. None of the major existentialist figures, Kierkegaard, Nietzsche, Heidegger, and Camus—only excepting Sartre—

would recognize themselves as part of a "movement" at all. Kierkegaard and Nietzsche were both ferocious individualists who vehemently rejected all movements. To belong to a philosophical movement, each of them would have said, would be to show cowardice and a lack of integrity, to be simply one of the "herd." Heidegger was deeply offended when he was linked with Sartre as one of the existentialists, and he publicly denounced the association. Camus and Sartre once were friends, but they quarreled over politics and Camus also broke the association and publicly rejected it.

Many of the other writers and philosophers who have been associated with the movement would have been equally hesitant to embrace the title had they known of it. The main exceptions were those who have wanted or needed to derive some fame and notoriety by associating themselves with existentialism. In the 1950s in the United States, for example, Norman Mailer proudly took up the title, giving it his own definition, "hip."

The existentialists' writings, too, are by no means simple and straightforward. Kierkegaard and Nietzsche write beautifully but in such challenging, often disjointed, exhortations that trying to summarize or systematize their thoughts is something of a hopeless venture. Heidegger is among the most difficult writers in the entire history of philosophy, and even Sartre—a lucid literary writer when he wants to be—imitates some of the worst elements of Heidegger's notorious style. Much of the challenge of this course of lectures, accordingly, is to free the exciting and revolutionary message of existentialism from its often formidable textual enclosures.

The course begins, after a brief introduction to the historical context and the very notion of "existentialism," with a discussion of the twentieth-century writer and philosopher Albert Camus (1913–1960). Chronologically, Camus is already late in the game. (We will trace existentialist ideas as far back as Kierkegaard and Nietzsche in the mid-nineteenth century, but we will not explore those figures—say Socrates or Saint Augustine—who with some justification might be called their predecessors.) Philosophically, it is often said that Camus is more of a literary figure, a lyrical essayist, than a philosopher. But the art of persuasive personal writing rather than dry philosophical analysis is one of the earmarks of existentialism. (Even the obscure writings of Martin Heidegger [1889–1976] are remarkable in their rhetorical and emotional efficacy.)

In this sense, Camus is exemplary in his combination of deep contemplation and often poetic writing and, because his ideas are less complex than the probing and systematic works of the other existential writers before him, he makes an ideal beginning. We will start with his most famous novel, *The Stranger*, published in the early 1940s, which combines a disturbingly "flat" descriptive style with a horrifying sequence of events, introducing us to a character whose reactions to the world are indeed "strange." It is our reaction to this character, however, that makes the novel so deeply philosophical. What is it that makes him so strange? The answer to that question starts us thinking about the way we think about ourselves and each other, what we take for granted and do not normally notice.

After an analysis of *The Stranger*, I want to take us through a number of Camus's later works, beginning with a philosophical essay he wrote about the same time, *The Myth of Sisyphus*, in which he introduces his infamous concept of "The Absurd." Then, in Lectures 5 and 6, I want to examine two later novels, *The Plague* and *The Fall* (the last novel Camus published in his lifetime, although his daughter recently published an unfinished novel he was working on at the time of his death). My aim in these first half dozen lectures will be to set a certain mood for the rest of the course, a rebellious, restless, yet thoroughly conscientious mood, which I believe Camus exemplifies both in his writings and in his life.

In Lectures 7 through 9, I want to turn to the Danish philosopher Søren Kierkegaard (1813–1855) and his revolutionary work. Kierkegaard was a deeply religious philosopher—a pious Christian—and his existentialist thought was devoted to the question, "What does it mean to be—or rather, what does it mean to become—a Christian?" We should thus be advised that, contrary to some popular misunderstandings, existentialism is by no means an anti-religious or unspiritual philosophy. It can and often does embrace God, as well as a host of visions of the world that we can, without apology, call "spiritual." (We will see that Nietzsche and Heidegger both embrace such visions, although in very different ways.)

In Lectures 10 through 13, I want to consider in some detail the philosophy of Friedrich Nietzsche (1844–1900) and his role in this rather eccentric movement. Nietzsche is perhaps best known for his bold declaration "God is dead." He is also well known as a self-proclaimed "immoralist." In fact, both of these phrases are misleading. Nietzsche was by no means the first person to say that God is dead (Martin Luther had said it three centuries before), and Nietzsche himself was anything but an immoral person. He attacks morality—or rather, he attacks one conception of morality—but nevertheless he defends a profound view of ethics and human nature.

In Lecture 14, I want to turn briefly to three diverse but exemplary figures from the history of literature. All three display existentialist themes and temperaments in their works: Fyodor Dostoevsky (1821–1881), the great Russian novelist; Franz Kafka (1883–1924), the brilliant Czech novelist and story writer; and Hermann Hesse (1877–1962), a twentieth-century Swiss writer who combined a fascination with Asian philosophy with a profoundly Nietzschean interest and temperament.

In Lecture 15, I would like to briefly introduce the philosophical method of a philosopher who could not be further from the existentialist temperament but yet had a profound influence on both Heidegger and Sartre. He is the German-Czech philosopher Edmund Husserl (1859–1938), who invented a philosophical technique called "phenomenology." Both Heidegger and Sartre, at least at the beginning of their careers, thought of themselves as phenomenologists. In the rest of that lecture and in Lectures 16 and 17, I would like to consider Martin Heidegger's very difficult but extremely insightful philosophy.

Finally, in Lectures 18 through 23, I want to consider the philosophy of Jean-Paul Sartre (1905–1980), and in Lecture 24, I would like to finish with a comparison and contrast with French philosophy since his time. My suggestion will be that much of what is best in "postmodernism" is taken more or less directly from Sartre, despite the fact that he is typically attacked as the very antithesis of postmodernism. Existentialism, I want to argue, was and is not just another French intellectual fashion but a timely antidote to some of the worst self-(mis)understandings of the end of the century.

How should one approach these lectures? My advice on the lecture on *The Stranger* is a good example of how I think each lecture should be approached. Although the lectures are self-contained, it would be ideally desirable to read the "Essential Reading" (in this case, the novel) before hearing or viewing the lecture. That way, you come to the lecture ready to question and challenge with your interpretation and ideas. This will be true even for the very difficult readings from Heidegger and Sartre. It is very helpful to have contact with their style and vocabulary even if the ideas at first seem impenetrable. Initial contact is even more desirable with our other two major authors, Kierkegaard and Nietzsche. Both write in a strikingly personal, provocative style, and nothing will impress the reader more than an immediate, first-hand confrontation with their witty and sometimes shocking aphorisms and observations.

Of course, many if not most viewers of the lectures will not have the opportunity to read the material before every lecture. I do suggest, however, that some attempt be made to read the essential material soon after. (I hope the lectures entice one to do so.) The questions are designed to help the reader straighten out the ideas and vocabulary, make various comparisons, and most important, work out his or her own views regarding the material in the lectures. In general, the introductory questions presume only a hearing of the lectures and perhaps some of the essential reading. The advanced questions invite further reading and more extensive thought.

Existentialism is, first of all, a philosophy of life, a philosophy about who we are. The ultimate intent of the course, accordingly, is not only to inform the viewer about a very exciting philosophy but also to enrich his or her life and make all of us think about who we are in a very new and bold way. The main texts for the lectures can be found in Robert C. Solomon, ed., *Existentialism* (New York: McGraw Hill/Modern Library, 1974). Secondary texts that follow the perspective of the lectures can be found in Robert C. Solomon, *From Rationalism to Existentialism* (Rowman and Littlefield, 1979), and *Continental Philosophy Since 1750* (Oxford University Press, 1988). ∎

What Is Existentialism?

Lecture 1

> As for metaphysical freedom, whether there really is freedom, free will, in the very nature of things—this is a question none of these philosophers address very directly, except in the negative. Nietzsche, for example, makes fun of it and says that the very idea of a free will, of a subject who is detached from the causal nature of the universe, is really just a kind of illusion.

Existentialism is a movement, a "sensibility," not a set of doctrines. It is not, as it is too often said, a necessarily "gloomy" philosophy. It is, rather, invigorating and positive. Nor is it necessarily atheistic, a form of "secular humanism." Søren Kierkegaard, the "first" existentialist, was profoundly religious. In a world pervaded by victim psychology, existentialism offers a refreshing sense of empowerment.

Existential attitudes can be found as far back as ancient times. It is possible to trace existentialism, defined one way or another, back to Socrates and Augustine, perhaps even to Heraclitus. We will limit our examination to five definitive figures, Søren Kierkegaard, Friedrich Nietzsche, Martin Heidegger, Albert Camus, and Jean-Paul Sartre. They do not form a "school" or share any particular outlook on religion and politics. Kierkegaard is a pious Christian; Nietzsche and Sartre are atheists. Kierkegaard despised politics; Sartre was a Marxist; Camus, a humanitarian; Heidegger, a Nazi. Strictly speaking, perhaps, the only true existentialist was Sartre, who defined the term to refer to his own work during and immediately after the Second World War. He pursued the idea that "we make ourselves." Expanding our vision, however, the movement certainly includes such literary figures as Fyodor Dostoevsky and Franz Kafka, among others.

Three themes pervade existentialism:

- A strong emphasis on the individual (although this is variously defined and understood). A lot of these writers were truly eccentric. Each of them takes individuality in a different direction.

- The central role of the passions, as opposed to the usual philosophical emphasis on reason and rationality. The emphasis instead is on a passionate commitment. For the existentialist, to live is to live passionately.

- The importance of human freedom. Existentialists are concerned with personal freedom, both political freedom and free will. This is central to Kierkegaard and Sartre, but not so obviously to Nietzsche and Heidegger. The relationship between freedom and reason is particularly at issue. Traditionally, acting "rationally" is said to be free, while acting out of emotion is considered being a "slave to one's passions." The existentialists suggest that we live best and are most ourselves in terms of passion. Kierkegaard's notion of "passionate commitment" is central.

The special meaning of the central term, "existence," is first defined by Kierkegaard to refer to a life that is filled with passion, self-understanding, and commitment. For Nietzsche, to really "exist" is to manifest your talents and virtues—"becoming the person you really are." The key component of existentialism's general "sensibility" is the striking realization of one's own "contingency." One might have never been born, or been born in a different place, at a different time, as a different person, or possibly not as a person at all. Heidegger's image of "thrownness" suggests how much of our lives is given, not chosen. Kafka's "Metamorphosis," in which a very ordinary middle-class man wakes up to find himself changed into a giant cockroach, is a spectacularly unusual example of the contingency of our particular existence. Descartes's "I think, therefore I am" is a problem, not a solution to the question of existence.

Existentialism basically urges us to live our lives to the fullest, although what this means will take somewhat different forms.

The existentialists challenge the idea that human existence is so tied up with thinking. Existentialism basically urges us to live our lives to the fullest, although what this means will take somewhat different forms. Of all philosophers, it seems to me that existentialists are the most geared to our own needs and expectations. Although its origins are European, existentialism is perfectly suited to contemporary American thought. ■

Solomon, *Existentialism*, Introduction.

Any decent short overview of existentialism, e.g., many encyclopedia entries (*Collier's*, *Grolier*, *Encyclopedia Brittanica*, and so on).

For a lighter treatment, read the mock interviews in Solomon, *Introducing the Existentialists* (Hackett). For an eye-opener, there is always Kafka's "Metamorphosis."

Introductory Questions to Consider

1. What do you mean by the phrase "personal freedom"? What counts as "being free" for you?

2. What is an individual? What (if anything) makes a person an individual, even "unique"?

Advanced Questions to Consider

1. Are the passions, by their very nature, "irrational?" What is meant by the term "rationality"? Is rationality always a good thing?

2. Do you believe in fate? What would this mean? If I were to introduce you to a very good fortune teller (who had an accuracy rate of over 95%) and she offered to tell you the outcome of your marriage or the date of your death, would you be willing to ask her? Why or why not?

What Is Existentialism?

Lecture 1—Transcript

My name is Bob Solomon. I teach at The University of Texas in the wonderful city of Austin. This is going to be a series of lectures on a very exciting and still vital philosophy called "Existentialism." I call it "No Excuses," because the idea is that one of the main themes is taking responsibility.

Existentialism might be conceived of as a movement—not a "sensibility," not a series of doctrines, to be sure. One can think of it in many different ways. In the literature that has come out in the years when existentialism first became popular just after the Second World War, and ever since, it often has the connotation of being a particularly "gloomy" philosophy—one that is obsessed with the notions of anxiety and dread.

The first thing to say perhaps is that I find existentialism, actually, a very invigorating and positive-minded philosophy. The "no excuses" idea, in part, says we do have control over our own lives. It is often thought that existentialism is an atheistic philosophy. It is true that some rather notorious atheists were existentialists, most notably Jean-Paul Sartre, who gave the movement its name. Søren Kierkegaard, whom I will be talking about shortly, was also an existentialist—one might say the "first" existentialist—and he was devoutly religious—one might even say in today's terms that he would be counted as a Christian fundamentalist. He is not the only one—Martin Buber, the Jewish existentialist; and some of the more recent Christian existentialists, like Karl Barth. One finds the entire spectrum, and one can put the nature of God well within the existential tradition.

One can trace the movement as far back as one likes. I have often heard it traced back to Socrates who, after all, said famously, "One should know thyself," and took great responsibility for his own behavior, defended the virtues, and was very much the individual. I've heard it traced back to Heraclitus, before Socrates, a philosopher who defended that impermeability of life and who often delighted in contradictions and dark sayings. St. Augustine was sort of a proto-existentialist, because again his confessions are so inward looking and he is so concerned with the questions of who I am and what I am to do.

For our purposes here, I am going to restrict our attention to five figures. I am going to begin out of sequence with the philosopher Albert Camus, possibly because he is the easiest to understand, but also because I think he captures the sensibility that represents existentialist thinking. He explains why so many students over the last 50 years have become enamored with the movement. Then, I will go back in chronology and I will pick up the first existentialist, as I said, Søren Kierkegaard, a Danish philosopher who worked roughly in the middle of the 19th century. I will talk about Friedrich Nietzsche who, while he has some differences with Kierkegaard and some of the later philosophers, nevertheless fits in with this sequence. I want to talk about Martin Heidegger, a German philosopher at the beginning of this century (although he did not die until 1976) as someone who was actually very influential in terms of setting up the kind of philosophy—both existentialism and what is today called "postmodernism"—that still rules many universities today. Finally, Jean-Paul Sartre who, as I said, gave the movement its name and is probably the single most influential existentialist (and typically when people talk about existentialism, it is Sartre's ideas they have in mind).

Nevertheless, it is not a "school." There are all sorts of differences. Just to start with the obvious, I mentioned that Kierkegaard is a devout Christian. Nietzsche is famously a rather vitriolic atheist. So, you are going to get a whole spectrum of views coming from religion and so on. In the same way, if you consider politics, existentialism is often considered a kind of left-wing conspiracy. But, the truth is that while Sartre was a Marxist, Nietzsche was, if anything, a kind of reactionary. Kierkegaard was completely apolitical. Martin Heidegger by contrast was a fascist. When we talk about existentialism, I think it is very important not to try to pin it down too much to begin with; not to try to define it in terms of this or that doctrine—this or that set of beliefs. Rather, I'd like you to keep your mind open and see what these various, very individualistic figures have to say about themselves and about life, and we will come to some conclusions.

The movement is defined best of all by Jean-Paul Sartre. Sartre died just quite recently. He had a very long career in which he changed many of his ideas, but I think one of the things that he said in a very late interview captures what we are going to be talking about comes down to. He said, "I have never ceased to believe that one is and one makes oneself of whatever is made of one." The language is a bit convoluted; as you will see many of these figures tend to enjoy rather difficult language. The idea of, as he put it in his earlier writings, "We make ourselves"—that there is a sense of self-creation here—is going to be very important throughout.

I also want to expand the idea of existentialism to include not just philosophers, properly speaking—and, of course, Nietzsche, Sartre and Camus were also rather accomplished literary authors as well—but I would like to include at least a couple of novelists and poets. I am thinking in particular of Dostoevsky and Kafka, and a few others as well.

There are three themes I would like to talk about. The first is the emphasis on the individual. All of these characters were, I think we can say without insult, truly eccentric. Kierkegaard defined himself against the reigning passions and doctrines of the age. In particular, when Kierkegaard was philosophizing, much of Danish society—and certainly the whole idea of Christianity—was wrapped in the idea of collective consciousness, sometimes summarized as the Holy Spirit, or in the secular realm summarized by the term "bourgeois." Kierkegaard, by contrast, defined himself as the individual. In fact, he said what he would like written on his tombstone was simply "The Individual."

Nietzsche, of course, is another great eccentric. Nietzsche wrote pretty much in isolation. In fact, he lived in isolation for most of his mature life. He sometimes would reach out to an audience, but it is always interesting that it is a very select audience, and he dedicates his books to "the very few." One of the tricks that Nietzsche uses quite effectively (and I would say this is true of Kierkegaard as well) is he writes as if he is writing for you, the singular reader alone. He really has a kind of mini-conspiratorial tone that makes us think it is just us; we are different and we are especially different from all of them.

This notion of individuality takes different forms too. Camus, when he was in Algeria where he was born and spent most of his life, found himself very much at odds with both the French population, of which he was a member, and the Algerian population, who were fighting for independence. He gains his reputation as a courageous individual in part by taking a very independent stance, one which he continued when he was in Southern France during the occupation by the Nazis.

Jean-Paul Sartre takes individuality in a different direction. Individuality basically comes down to the idea of individual choice. It is the heart of Sartre's philosophy that we are always making choices—we make them as individuals. It doesn't matter if the whole society or the whole world makes them at the same time. The responsibility that he talks about is always the responsibility of the individual for making his or her choices and accepting the consequences that flow from it.

The second theme is the importance of the passions. If you look back through the history of philosophy, one of the things that I find striking is the fact that the passions are very often the whipping horse. Philosophy is defined as reason or the love of reason. Wisdom is often considered to be a version of reason—being reasonable. There has always been a kind of undercurrent of opposition here. I would mention Heraclitus again as someone who fully recognized the power of the passions. Of course, the Greek playwrights before him—the great tragedians—they were very keen on the power of the passions, which they sometimes demonized, but nevertheless were very clear that these are very important elements in human life.

Moving up to our area here, you might note that Kierkegaard is going to define what it means to really exist—that special notion of existence that is going to give rise to the term "existentialism." To really exist is to be passionate. In particular, it is to passionately commit oneself to a way of life; in Kierkegaard's case, to passionately commit oneself to Christianity. He talks about "passionate inwardness." So, we are not talking about passions here fully expressed and exploded on the stage so much as we are talking about passions that oneself might feel and not show. Kierkegaard makes a good deal out of talking about the truly passionate person is not the one who is dramatically visible for everyone else. The truly passionate person is the one who is quite inwardly contained and defined by his or her passions.

We often have the idea that the passions take us over, that the passions happen to us—the idea from the ancient world that the passions are often intermittent bouts of insanity. But for the existentialist, it is very clear that to live is to live passionately. Nietzsche is well known as a very passionate philosopher. When you read his work (as I hope you do), it is filled with all sorts of excitement and enthusiasm. To put it in a rather trivial way, he uses more exclamation points that probably any other philosopher in the history of the subject. He is always expounding and enthusing. He is always praising, condemning. But in his life itself it is very clear that while he was a very quiet and courteous man, his philosophy and his life were defined by some really exciting, dramatic, grand passions. He encourages us to live according to our passions.

The third theme, possibly the most famous—and possibly for the most famous (and certainly for some) philosophers, Kierkegaard and Sartre, in particular—the most central, is the concept of freedom. What freedom means is something which has been highly debated. It is one of the ironies of history that virtually every regime in every country, from the most authoritarian to the most anarchistic, has defended freedom. Freedom gets defended in many different ways. There is a distinction in philosophy between freedom in the political sphere (freedom from restraint by government, from restraint by other people; say, the majority) and freedom in a more personal way, or sometimes freedom in a more metaphysical sense. There is a so-called "free will" problem that philosophers are well concerned with. There is a sense in which neither of these is the kind of freedom that the existentialists are primarily concerned with. As for political freedom, Sartre, in particular, comes out as a vigorous defender of freedom. It is really parasitic on a much more basic note of freedom that lies at the heart of his philosophy.

As for metaphysical freedom, whether there really is freedom, free will, in the very nature of things—this is a question none of these philosophers address very directly, except in the negative. Nietzsche, for example, makes fun of it and says that the very idea of a free will, of a subject who is detached from the causal nature of the universe, is really just a kind of illusion.

The kind of freedom that they do talk about, and the kind of freedom which is absolutely essential for understanding what we are going to be doing, is that sense of personal freedom which is neither political nor metaphysical but has very much to do with how we think of ourselves, how we behave, how we think about our behavior. Kierkegaard has a nice little aphorism that sums up a good deal of this. He says, with reference to the semi-revolution in Denmark in 1848, "People hardly ever make use of the freedom that they do have, like freedom of thought. Instead, they demand freedom of speech as compensation." The idea is that freedom has to do with making choices. It has to do with deciding how you are going to live your life. Freedom also has to do with taking consequences. Once you have made your choice, you can't say, "I didn't anticipate that. I don't take responsibility for that." Having chosen, you are then responsible for what follows as well.

Freedom is often connected with reason. In much of the history of philosophy, to be free is to act rationally. What we find in the existentialists is a very different kind of thesis. In the ancient Greeks, it was often said that acting in accordance with reason makes us free; acting according to the passions makes us a slave. The Enlightenment philosopher David Hume, who will pop up every once in while in these lectures, had a very interesting reversal of this ancient wisdom. It was the ancient poet/storyteller, Aesop, who once said that the passions should be the slave of reason. Hume, in the 18th century, said that instead reason is and ought to be the slave of the passions. He was one of the eccentrics in the history of philosophy I talked about.

There are quite a few who did want to say something like, "The passions are not really the monsters that they have been portrayed to be." It is rather that passion motivates us. Without passion, there is no motivation. It is passions that give the meaning to life; without passions, life is meaningless. So, instead of talking about freedom and reason as necessarily conjoined, and passions as equivalent to a kind of slavery, what the existentialists suggest is that we think of our lives in terms of passion. This does not mean stupid passion, although that certainly has its place. But, Kierkegaard, for example, when he talks about "passionate commitment," is on to, I think, something very important. Basically, it is that passions give life meaning, and it is through passionate commitment that we give our lives the particular meaning that they have.

Another thesis that we find is based on that notion of existence that I very quickly mentioned, and I said that it is really the base of the word "existentialism." There is a sense in which all the philosophers will talk about it; put a very heavy premium on it. It starts with a distinction, a distinction which, of course, some people will find offensive. It is the distinction between really existing, or what I think we would call living your life to the fullest. Just what Kierkegaard calls so-called "existence"—just getting through/getting by, going along with the crowd, doing what you are supposed to do, being what is very blandly called "a good person." For Kierkegaard, again, existence consists of passionate commitment. Nietzsche, who doesn't use the term much, nevertheless has a very clear idea about the same concept. For Nietzsche, to be truly "existing," to really be a person, has to do with taking hold of your own life—realizing what your particular talents and virtues are, falling in love with yourself in a very important way, and understanding what your life is about is manifesting those virtues, manifesting those talents, passionately throwing yourself into the work you do, and, as he puts it (borrowing from the ancient Greeks), "Becoming the person that you really are."

There is also a thesis of "contingency." This is something that I think most of you have probably thought about at one time or another. It is the idea that our lives are, in a way, happenstance. They could be very different. We can play games. We do this all the time: If I lived in the Middle Ages, what would my life be like? Any philosopher will quickly jump in and say, "If you lived in the Middle Ages, you would not be you. You would be so different, your culture would be so different, your language would be so different, your very physical being would be so different that it doesn't make any sense to make the comparison." But, we do this all the time. You are driving down the street and you have a very close call in your automobile. You say, "If I had just arrived one minute earlier, or 10 seconds later, there would have been a horrible accident."

So too, you might ask the question, "What if I had been born five minutes earlier? Would I still be the same person, or would suddenly the contingencies of the universe be such that I would be someone quite different?" The kind of question is very important. Martin Heidegger has a rather dramatic notion, which he calls "thrown-ness." The image is that we each get thrown into the world. We don't choose the century that we are born; we don't choose our parents, the language we first learn to speak, our early friends. In fact, if you look at a good deal of your life, you realize that it is not something that you choose, but something you are thrown into. All this is going to have to be weighed against this notion of existence, the idea of passionate commitment, the idea of personal choice. What we find in all the existentialists is a very delicate balance, or I think better you might say a dialectic—a kind of active tension between, on the one hand, this sense of contingency and you are what you are because of things that you had no control over, and on the other hand, you are what you are or you become what you become because of your personal commitments and choices. That theme is going to run all the way through.

Jean-Paul Sartre is often misunderstood. He talks about something he calls "absolute freedom" and people often think that means you can do anything you want to do, regardless of circumstances. Let me begin the lectures by saying this is nonsense. It is only people who have an axe to grind, perhaps against the French, who say such things. The truth is that Sartre is very well aware of the fact that people are born in his generation into a world that is filled with war and ethnic violence. The real question is, having been born into such a world, what do you do with it?

That notion of contingency is perhaps best exemplified by one of the literary authors we will talk about briefly. That is Franz Kafka. He has a wonderful short story called "Metamorphosis," which begins with a rather startling sentence. Gregor Samsa (the hero) wakes up and finds himself turned into a giant insect. The standard interpretation—think cockroach (the most noxious insect we can think of). Samsa is born and finds himself a cockroach. In fact, before that he was a very bourgeois little man. He had his job; he had his family. He dutifully went to the job every day; he dutifully supported his family. Suddenly he wakes up and he is completely different. It is a horror story. I have never seen it adequately filmed. I don't know how you would film such a story. Reading it, what makes it so horrible is the fact that Gregor Samsa does not wake up thinking like an insect—whatever that would be. He wakes up thinking like a clerk and a family member and is somehow trying to cope with the impossibility of his new body.

There is a sense in which existentialism takes us through such metamorphoses all the time, at least in the thought experiments that it presents to us. The idea is that we find ourselves sometimes in very strange—even absurd—situations. In those absurd, strange situations, we have to figure out who we are and what we are supposed to do. There is a sense in which you might trace existentialism back to one of the keynotes of modern philosophy; that is, the French philosopher Rene Descartes who said rather famously, "I think, therefore I am." Descartes said this as part of a rather lengthy argument. This was a premise that he was to use to prove all sorts of things, but that is not of interest to us here right now. What is important is that the very statement—"I think, therefore I am"—is sort of an emblem of a certain kind of philosophy.

First of all, notice that the emphasis is on thought. As I have been stressing, for the existentialists your existence is not so much bound up with your thinking. Nietzsche, for example, will say, "You never exist quite so much as when you are not thinking." Also, there is that idea of "I am." I am, as a thinking thing, is something that is going to be challenged. For the existentialists, to exist is very much to be a being in the world; to be active, to be engaged. The very idea that "I think, therefore I am" somehow summarizes our self identity is to make it sound much simpler than it is. We don't find out who we are just by reflecting on ourselves and saying, "Here I am." Rather, you find out who you are through other things—by looking to see what you have done, what other people think of you, how you think of yourself in concrete terms.

What existentialism is really all about is how we live our lives. The reason I am so attached to it is because it seems to me, of all philosophies, it is the one that is most geared to our very real concerns, passions, and decisions. If it is complained that existentialists don't really give us enough advice about what we should do—they really just say things like: "Take responsibility for your actions"—then, I think, one might conceive of that not so much as a weakness but as a great strength and very central to the idea of existentialism itself.

You don't tell people what they should do. What is central to all these figures is what you should do—how you live is up to you. It is up to you to make the choice. It is up to you to gear up the passions to commit yourself to the choice. In someone like Nietzsche, it is up to you to discover in yourself who it is you really are, what your real talents and abilities are, the sorts of things that you love, and then commit yourself to those.

Existentialism originated, as you can tell, from these five figures. Kierkegaard is Danish. Nietzsche and Heidegger are German. Camus and Sartre are French (or in this case French-Algerian). I would argue that existentialism really has its greatest impact and power in contemporary America. The fact is that we have always been a society which has prided itself on our sense of responsibility. I think we have all noticed with a certain amount of despair in the recent decades that it has all shifted into a kind of sensibility of victimization—a sense that the world is moving too fast for us; a sense that, for example, in politics, we don't make a difference; a sense that religion has gotten somehow superficial—a mere façade, a kind of sham. We are looking for something deeper that we can call our own—a sense of empowerment (a greatly overused contemporary word).

The truth is that existentialism can give us that. What existentialism talks about and constantly hammers away is the idea that we are responsible; we do have choices, no matter how complicated or fast moving the world is, no matter how superficial those around us might be. We are in charge of our lives. We have to make the choices. We have to understand exactly how dark life can be and what to do with that, as well as figure out where joy lies and pursue that, too.

In the lectures that follow, I am going to be running through these various figures, starting with Camus. I would like to give you basically two dozen different kinds of illustrations about how these theses play out in practice.

Thanks.

Albert Camus—*The Stranger*, Part I
Lecture 2

Camus was counted as one of the "existentialists" virtually from the 1940s, when Sartre invented the term. He and Sartre were quite good friends for some time. ... They broke off around 1955 for reasons we will get to later, but basically, there was a sense in which Camus never really felt comfortable with the "existentialist" label. At one point later in his career he actively repudiated it.

Camus's novel *The Stranger* is an excellent place to begin studying the peculiar shifts of mind that best characterize existentialism. Camus resented being labeled an "existentialist," and he rejected the term. Nevertheless, *The Stranger* is the epitome of the new existentialist literature of the 1940s. The book is set in Algeria, in the middle of an intensifying civil war (which is never mentioned). It concerns the fate of a rather dull young man (Meursault), who gets caught up in a murder and is sentenced to death. Meursault is something of a Rorschach test for readers; different generations see different attributes in his peculiarities. In the 1960s, my students saw him as "cool"; in the 1980s, they saw him as a nerd.

Albert Camus (1913–1960).

United Press International; New York World-Telegram & Sun Newspaper Collection, Library of Congress, Prints and Photographs Division.

What is "strange" about Meursault is that he seems to feel nothing. He doesn't seem to think for himself or engage in reflection at all. He does not grieve the death of his mother. ("Out of sight, out of mind.") Where any of us would feel shock or abandonment, such emotions are lacking in Meursault. He has no sense of morality or morals. (He is incapable of judgment.) He is not repulsed by the activities of his neighbors (a pimp and a sleazoid). He has no ambitions. (He is offered a post in Paris and doesn't see the point.) He does not respond to love. (When Marie asks him, "Do you love me?" he doesn't understand. Love involves decisions and commitments, but Meursault understands none of that. Nor does he have any conception of what marriage entails.)

He does not respond to the fact that he has killed a man and will himself die on account of it. (Nor does he manifest any signs of fear or guilt or anxiety.) Meursault simply has no conception of the future and only an occasional fleeting thought of the past. He makes no plans and has no regrets. He lives moment by moment. He also has no feelings, except for the physical sensations of heat and light, smell and taste. A life without reason is not necessarily a life of intensified feeling. People without thoughts are often without feelings, too.

> **Meursault simply has no conception of the future and only an occasional fleeting thought of the past.**

The oddity of the murder is: Was there a murderer? The description of the murder makes it seem as though the killing "just happens." Is Meursault ever an "agent" of his own actions? The murder scene is frightening, because Meursault feels no moral qualms or anxieties. The strangeness of the trial is manifest in Part II. Was Camus politically naive? What is the author's purpose in portraying a trial of a Frenchman condemned to death for killing a "foreigner" (in self-defense)? The vicious racial tensions of the time appear nowhere.

The trial has primarily philosophical significance, as in Kafka's novel, *The Trial*. (Kafka depicts a young man who is put to death without ever knowing the charge.) The novel ends with Meursault facing his execution philosophically. The ultimate point of the novel is the nature of guilt and innocence. But it is also a celebration of life for life's sake. The point of the trial is to turn Meursault into a human being. ∎

Essential Reading

Camus, *The Stranger*, Part I, 1946 ("British" translation); 1988 ("American" translation).

Supplementary Reading

Lottman, *Camus: A Biography.*

Todd, *Albert Camus: A Life.*

Introductory Questions to Consider

1. Have you ever met someone like Meursault? What do you think of him (or her)?

2. To whom is Meursault a "stranger"? In what ways is he "strange"? Is this "lifestyle" attractive or appealing to you? Why or why not?

3. Can a person live without caring? Does the idea of a life without passions sound attractive to you? Why or why not?

Advanced Questions to Consider

1. Could a person literally live "for the moment," with no sense of past or future?

2. What is required to be the "agent" of one's actions? Is causing something to happen sufficient?

Albert Camus—*The Stranger*, Part I
Lecture 2—Transcript

A good place to begin our discussion of existentialism is with Camus's very well known novel called *The Stranger*. It captures in a bizarre kind of way some of the strange shifts in mind, in consciousness, that existentialism is going to highlight. I should add: Don't take *The Stranger* as a kind of exemplar of the existentialist standpoint. Rather, he is a kind of thought experiment in which many of the features of human nature are brought into focus.

Camus was counted as one of the "existentialists" virtually from the 1940s, when Sartre invented the term. He and Sartre were quite good friends for some time. They both hit the literary scene in Paris at the beginning of the war. Consequently, they were two young men on the make, and they were both involved in the theatre in Paris, and so on. They broke off around 1955 for reasons we will get to later, but basically, there was a sense in which Camus never really felt comfortable with the "existentialist" label. At one point later in his career he actively repudiated it. For one thing, Camus was not the Parisian that Sartre was. Camus was born and raised in Algeria. As opposed to Sartre's rather well-to-do, middle-class upbringing, Camus was brought up in rather dire poverty. He talks about that in some of his novels and letters. Algeria, at the time, was in a state of civil war. The Algerian civil war went on for decades. It wasn't a very comfortable place for a French colonial, especially one as sensitive and as politically egalitarian as the young Camus was. Algeria figures in one way or another in almost all of his novels.

The novel itself, *The Stranger*, really has to do with the fate of a dull young man who is, like Camus, a French Algerian—a *pied noir*. Strangely, the turmoil in Algeria is never mentioned throughout the entire novel. What we get is simply a kind of biography or autobiography, or more accurately, we get a kind of stream-of-consciousness, first-person report of this young man (Meursault) as he goes through his daily routines. Unfortunately, his daily routines culminate in his committing a rather senseless murder. He is arrested. He is sent to prison. He is put on trial, and he is finally condemned to execution. The novel ends as he is sitting in his cell, thinking about his impending death and becoming philosophical as a consequence.

Meursault himself is kind of like a blank screen. When writers give us a first person narrative, very often it is chocked full of reflections, moralizations, interpretations. What we get from Meursault, from Camus, is really just a very flat, matter-of-fact description of what his world looks like. Because he is such a blank screen, I have often found in the 30 years that I have been teaching this book to undergraduates, it provides a perfect Rorschach test.

Just to sort of give you some of my conclusions very quickly: When I started teaching this book back in the '60s (and you all remember the '60s), most of my students thought that this basically blank character was really "cool." He wasn't involved with anything. He never got upset about anything. He wasn't deeply engaged. He just sort of let life flow. So, he was a kind of hero. In the 1980s, by contrast (the kind of "go-go-Reagan" years), my students read this book and they all thought he was, as they put it, a nerd. He had no ambition. He didn't want to do anything with his life. He didn't take advantage of the opportunities he had. When I have done the same kind of survey in the 1990s, I am getting much more mixed signals. I don't have anything interesting to report. I do want to generalize that the nature of this novel is such that when one reads it, what one comes away with probably has as much to do with oneself as it does with the character that Camus give us.

Why is he "strange"? What makes him an outsider? There are quite a few things actually; just in my description to begin with (you can already infer if you have not read the book), that this is a character who is deficient in some basic human ways. He doesn't think. In fact, there are very few thoughts that ever appear in the book until the end. When a thought does occur, it is something like a piece of onion grass that pops up through the crack in a sidewalk. It is really out of place, very particular, and most of the time it is completely unoriginal. For example, one of his current thoughts is what his mother used to say. One of the ways that Camus sets up the novel to indicate that this character is not everything that we are is he begins with the death of his mother—I should say, if you are writing a French soap opera, if you want a tearjerker there is probably no better plot gimmick that you can use than to have a young man lose his mother.

The novel starts with Meursault reading a telegram, which says, "Mother died today." He thinks, "From the telegram, I can't tell whether it was today or yesterday." That little bit of chill indicates what is to happen for the next 30 pages. He goes to his employer and dutifully asks for the day off for the funeral and finds himself apologizing to the employer, saying, "Well, it's not my fault, you know." Thinking about his mother, he realizes that he doesn't really miss her. His explanation is that they haven't seen each other for a while anyway. She has been in a home for old people in the south. He reflects on the fact that "we really didn't have much to say to each other anymore." As the vigilant self, he orders café au lait, and sits there pretty clearly restless, obviously not moved. At the funeral, he is more affected by the heat and the flies than by the idea that his mother has died.

In short, we are, any of us, what our particular relationship with our parents happens to be. Where any of us would feel shock at the loss, in some sense abandoned in the universe, or quite simply grief, we don't get it in Meursault. The strangeness just to start is he doesn't feel the emotions that we would feel.

He has no morals. Morality requires a kind of consciousness; a kind of perspective on the world that Meursault just can't muster. I mentioned in Algeria, which was exploding with violence at the time, there is no political opinion that appears anywhere in the book. He also has some neighbors—I would almost call them friends—who are, from Camus's depiction of them, totally disgusting. He has a neighbor called Salamano who has a little dog. Salamano is pictured as the kind of guy that we would envision wearing a trench coat but nothing else. He is really a kind of sleaze, and the dog looks the way he does. At one point, Camus describes this character and says (Meursault), "I shook his hand and it was kind of reptilian." The dog is covered with mange and the relationship between the two is the old man drags this little dog along and the dog is choking and whimpering. He gets angry at the dog for making noise. He kicks it, and the dog yelps in pain. Imagine if this was your neighbor. I suspect you would be on the phone to the SPCA in a minute. Meursault just takes it as a matter of fact. He is not repulsed. He has no moral qualms. He just at one point muses about the funny relationship between the two of them.

He has another neighbor named Raymond. Raymond is actually a key figure in the novel. Raymond, not to be too polite, is a pimp. He sells Arab girls and has affairs with them himself. He treats them very badly. In one of the early scenes of the book he beats up his girlfriend rather viciously. Meursault is present at the time, does nothing, gives us no indication of any moral repulsion, and when his girlfriend (whom I will introduce in a second) says, "Why didn't you call the cops?" Meursault's only response is, "I don't like cops."

He has no ambitions. He works in an office in Algiers, and at one point his employer calls him in and asks him if he would like a promotion and transfer to Paris. Now, you don't have to be too aware of French politics or French literature to know that Paris is *the* place. A young man with ambitions, a young man who wants to get on with the job—if he is given a transfer from not just the provinces, but also the colonies into Paris for a better job—would jump at it. Meursault, he says, "Nah." Why? Well, you live one way, you live another way—it doesn't make any difference.

Most dramatic perhaps is his response to his girlfriend whom he meets very early in the novel; in fact, he meets her on the day of his mother's funeral and begins an affair. Her name is Marie, and of course, she is not described in the book in any detail. No one is described in any detail. We get the impression that she is a quite lovely French Algerian woman. She is quite fond of him. They go to a Fernandel film (French comedy). They have a few laughs. They spend time together. They go swimming. The image we get is that it is kind of a delightful period. Somewhat into the relationship, Marie turns to Meursault and asks, "Do you love me?" I suspect all of you have been on the receiving end of that question at some point in your lives. I think for anyone with blood in their veins, it suddenly raises a certain kind of excitement, whether it is a chill and, "What am I going to say now?" or perhaps it is, "I've been waiting to hear that so long. Let me answer in kind very quickly." Meursault? No response. He expresses a kind of confusion like, "what a silly question." Then when he thinks about it he says, "Well, I guess not."

When you ask, "What is love?"—an important question for all the existentialists, and for all of us, there is a huge variety of answers on the table. One answer, rather simple-minded actually, is that love is a kind of feeling, a kind of affection. I think a more detailed and perceptive answer is that love involves decisions, commitments. It involves a keen sense of yourself. In fact, I would argue what love really comes down to is learning to conceive of yourself in terms of another person. Meursault understands none of that. So, to the question "Do you love me?"—all he can think to say is, "I don't know what you mean. Probably not."

Some pages later, Marie raises the "M" question. If you don't get nervous with the "L" question, then I think all of us get nervous with the "M" question. "Do you want to get married?" But the response, again, is just kind of blasé. Basically, Meursault says, "If you want to." He doesn't have any conception of what marriage entails. He doesn't have any conception of marriage as a commitment. He doesn't have any conception of marriage as the culmination of love, since he doesn't understand what love is. So, he comments (and of course, this is all through Meursault's eyes) that suddenly Marie got a little quiet. We get the picture of her sulking. He doesn't quite understand this, but then they both start laughing and everything is okay again. He is not empathetic. He has no idea what other people are feeling. And throughout the book, there is this general sense that other people are just kind of "there" for him.

He fits in; in fact, one of the curious things about his personality is that he always takes the path of least resistance. So, when Marie asks, "Do you want to get married?"—he says, "Sure, if you want to." When Raymond the pimp asks him if he would like to be "pals," and one can imagine this sleazy character asking you, "Do you want to be friends?"—I suspect you would run the other way. But Meursault says, "Sure, if you want to."

There is a sense in which this is a really empty character. He has no emotions. He has very few thoughts. He never does what I think we would call "thinking." He doesn't reflect; he has no moral sensibilities. The net result is that we have a character who is really kind of a vacuum—a vacuum through whom we learn to see his world. This culminates at the end of the first half of the book in his murdering a man. I want to talk about that in some detail in a moment.

What is curious about the murder scene is that it doesn't look like any other murder scene you have ever read before. There is a sense in which what bothers Meursault is the fact that it is hot. He has a pistol in his pocket. In front of him is the Arab who has stabbed his friend Raymond a few hours ago. He kills the Arab, really, because he is hot. That doesn't seem to make much sense.

In response to having killed a man, of course, he is immediately whisked away to prison, and so on. What he shows again is an absence of emotion. He doesn't feel regret. He doesn't really understand what that means. He certainly doesn't feel any guilt. He doesn't understand what that means. He doesn't understand what is happening to him. Prison takes away his freedom, but he comments at one point in prison, "Why are they taking away my freedom?" The jailor explains this is part of your punishment. Again, he just accepts it.

He has no concept of the future—not just when his employer offers him this nice job in Paris and he doesn't take it, but when Marie asks about getting married, it is really just a question about doing something now; it is not a question of a lifetime together. He doesn't think about the consequences of what he does. When he puts the pistol in his pocket as he goes for a walk on the beach, it doesn't occur to him as it would occur to any of us that this is a dangerous piece of machinery. One might be called upon to use it. One could hurt oneself. One could certainly hurt other people. He doesn't make any plans. He really lives day by day, and one might almost say moment by moment. That is part of the point that Camus is trying to give us. He has no regrets about his killing. He has no feelings of almost any kind. (Let me take that back.) He has no feelings in the general sense of emotion. He doesn't feel grief at his mother's death. He doesn't feel repulsion at his rather sleazy neighbors. He doesn't feel anything that we can recognize as love with his girlfriend Marie, although you might say there is a certain kind of animal affinity there, or perhaps even affection—no more than that. He doesn't have any feeling about the people he meets all the time. He doesn't have any feeling about his job. And in the murder itself—think about how most authors would describe the scene immediately leading up to a killing—there is no tension, no fear, no anxiety, and afterwards, no regrets.

Meursault very richly feels another kind of feeling—what I think we can call "physical sensations." He appreciates—in fact, Camus's prose here can be very lyrical—the warmth of the sun, the cool of the ocean, the smell of brine that Marie leaves behind on the pillow. He has all sorts of physical sensations, which he is actually very involved in—the taste of coffee, his favorite treat—nevertheless, he doesn't have any emotions. I would say the link between emotions and thinking here is very important. Philosophers often talk as if these were two opposed matters occupying different faculties or different parts of the brain. I would argue (and I think this novel bears it out rather nicely) that people without thoughts are often without feelings too. People without feelings are often without thoughts. If you don't have emotions, what is there to think about?

Finally, the oddity of the murder. Let me talk about that. The basic story is that Meursault goes off to the beach with his friend Raymond. Because Raymond has already been stabbed in the arm by the brother of the Arab woman he has beaten up, he gives Meursault his pistol and says, "You better carry this, just in case." Why you would walk on the beach alone after an incident such as that is already a question. But, Meursault approaches what turns out to be the same Arab on the beach. The Arab pulls out a knife, which flashes in the sunlight. Meursault complains—what about? The heat of the sun, and describes, again very lyrically, the way the sun was scorching his eyelids—the way the rays of light, especially the light reflected from the blade of the knife, were gouging his eyes and scarring his eyelids, and so on. It is a very interesting literary discussion because what it has is all the metaphors of the knife but all translated into the effect of the sun.

Meursault takes a step forward, which he comments to himself is probably a foolish thing to do—not because he was coming one step closer to someone who was armed and out for him, but because he won't get out of the sun by stepping one step forward. He approaches the Arab, and the description is very graphic: His body tenses up, he says, "Like a steel spring." The trigger gave. (Notice he did not pull the trigger. The trigger gave.) The butt of the gun hits his palm. (Notice he does not fire the gun; he is rather the victim.) The bullet hits the Arab. The butt of the gun by Newton's third law hits his palm. The picture is that the killing just happens. He is there. He happens to be holding the gun (or the gun is in his hand). There is a real sense that there is no "agency" here; Meursault doesn't do anything. In fact, the first active sentence indicating that he is doing something is that he shook off the sweat that accumulated on his forehead. Then he shoots, rather pointlessly, four more shots into the body of the dead Arab.

It is a frightening scene. It is frightening because none of the emotions, none of the thoughts, none of the anxieties, and none of the moral qualms that we would certainly feel ourselves are there. That is the end of Part I. With that, we move into the second part of the book, which is entirely concerned with his imprisonment and trial.

Let's ask a question: Is Camus politically naïve? One of our best political writers who has written on Camus, Conor Cruise O'Brien, asks, "How could a man who was raised in Algeria have concocted such an absurd story?" Let me give you an analogy. Imagine a story in Faulknerian Mississippi set in the 1930s, and here is the plot: a black man stabs a white man. Later on, the white man, or one of his friends, comes across the black man who is still armed, shoots him, and kills him. Then he is arrested. He is sent to trial. He is found guilty and condemned to execution. It would never happen. You don't have to see too many Rod Steiger movies to realize he might end up having coffee with the sheriff, and then the whole incident would be quickly forgotten. That is what Algeria was certainly like in the 1940s. There was vicious racism. There was violence all around, and it is one of the less obvious parts of the book that Camus, who was writing in the midst of all this, never once mentions any of these political or racial tensions, never once talks about the cafes that were being bombed, and so on.

When he describes the trial, we are given this rather absurd picture in which a Frenchman is condemned to death for killing an Arab in self-defense. Camus was not politically naïve. He wrote voluminously on the Algerian situation and always held out for a kind of humanity. As he put it in one of his essays, "The idea is to be neither a victim, nor an executioner." Then the question is: What is the point of the trial? Why is there a trial here? I think to look at it as kind of a political show, or to look at it as many of our modern American dramas would have it—as added suspense to bring a story together—it is not that at all. I think the analogy here—and it is a very close analogy because it is one of Camus's favorite authors—is with a novel by Kafka written just several years before.

Kafka's novel, *The Trial*, has often been interpreted, in a rather dense kind of way, as a kind of parody of the Czech legal system. It is terribly inefficient. It is often obscene. In any case, it is not fair. But, I think to understand that novel as nothing but a political parody is to miss it entirely. Most perceptive readers and commentators have noted that what Kafka is really doing is capturing something basic about the human psyche. The novel begins with a note about a young man, not too unlike Meursault, who is arrested, apparently for no reason. He tries to find out: "What I am being arrested for?" And he spends the entirety of the book trying to find out what the charges are and how he can defend himself against them. He never succeeds; and at the end of the novel he too is put to death, never having figured out what the problem was. It is a novel about guilt and innocence. It is a novel which says even those of us who seem to be innocent are, in some profound sense, guilty. Try as we might to figure out what that is all about, we are not going to. More generally, to be human is to be guilty, and what Camus picks up, too, is something very much like that theme.

So, the reason for the trial in *The Stranger* is that here is Meursault—who up until this point has shown no signs of emotion, no signs of any moral sensitivity—and he is put into a situation where he is being judged by his peers; where he is being put into the spotlight of moral judgment, in particular. The point of the trial is, to put it very bluntly, to turn him into a human being. That means, in part, to teach him what it means to feel guilty.

Camus—*The Stranger*, Part II
Lecture 3

I would argue that what we call "rationality" is bounded by our emotions. What we care about, and to act rationally, is ultimately to act in line with what we care about and what our culture cares about. Finally, emotions, as a general rule, tend to be unreflective. What that means is we have them, but we don't necessarily think about the fact that we have them.

The flat, matter-of-fact portrait of Meursault in *The Stranger* captures an age-old philosophical dilemma—the role of reason and consciousness in human nature. The juxtaposition of "lived experience" and reflection raises the question of their inter- and independence. In *The Stranger*, we have the sense that consciousness sometimes interferes with life. What does it mean to be rational? Rationality requires the ability to reflect on one's life. In this sense, Meursault isn't rational. Rationality requires the ability to anticipate consequences. Rationality requires the ability to adhere to standards and values. Rationality, thus, has a social dimension.

To what extent do our emotions and moral responses depend on reason? Emotions are essentially conceptual, intentional. Emotions require the basic elements of rationality. What we call "rationality" is bounded by our emotions. Emotions are often unreflective, but many emotions depend on the ability to reflect. Emotions essentially involve values. The "rational" thing to do may be that which makes the most emotional sense. Emotions are essentially about the self.

Do experience and reflection oppose one another? Camus suggests that this is the case. When Meursault stops living his life (when he goes to prison), he begins to reflect. What he reflects on is precisely the life that he has lost. In fact, the relationship between experience and reflection is much more complicated than this simple opposition would suggest.

The notion of reflection turns on two different but related metaphors: Reflection as in one's reflection in a mirror and reflection as in introspection, a "turning in" on oneself. The first sense may be aptly compared with "seeing yourself as others see you." The second sense may be illusory, or utterly dependent on the first sense. In what sense can your consciousness be *your* consciousness? Since Hegel, it is generally agreed that self-comprehension depends on the recognition of others. Meursault becomes self-aware only with the scrutiny of the judicial process. With self-awareness comes self-identity and reflection—along with Meursault's new feelings of guilt.

What does it mean to be innocent? Meursault is innocent in the straightforward sense that he is unaware of the moral significance of his actions. The Biblical story of Adam and Eve takes innocence as the ignorance of good and evil. Meursault is incapable of being repulsed by cruelty (Salamano and Raymond). Meursault is certainly not innocent in the even more straightforward sense that he murdered a man. He is guilty in the sense that he did it; that is, he caused the death of the Arab. He is guilty in the legal sense that he is declared "guilty" by the court. What is not clear is the extent to which he is morally guilty, that he did in fact know what he was doing. To reflect is to be guilty; not to reflect is to be innocent. Camus was adamant about issues of social justice. In one sense, guilt (e.g., "original sin") affects all of us, whatever we have done, just by virtue of consciousness. Camus's experiences in wartime are clearly expressed here. Except for children, there are no innocents in war.

Camus was adamant about issues of social justice.

The Stranger ends in a meditation on the meaning of life. When the prison chaplain queries Meursault about his vision of the afterlife, "he flies into a rage and insists, 'this life is the only one that means anything!'" This is the first true emotion he has felt in the course of the book. Asked to imagine an afterlife, he can think only of living this life again. He realizes that life is so rich that after only one day of it, one could spend an eternity dwelling on the details. He thinks about how he has lived and decides that it doesn't matter how one has lived. It only matters that one has lived.

Later, in *The Myth of Sisyphus*, he will say, "there is only quantity of life." Quality of life is in some sense a bogus notion. He then opens his heart to "the benign indifference of the universe." This dramatic phrase sums up much of Camus's philosophy. We will see it again in *The Myth of Sisyphus*. The notion of "a happy death" haunts all of Camus's work. (His first novel, before *The Stranger*, was entitled *A Happy Death*.) ∎

Essential Reading

Camus, *The Stranger*, Part II.

Supplementary Reading

For a lyrical introduction to Camus's life in Algeria and his thought, see his *Notebooks*. A harshly critical but worthwhile general analysis is O'Brien, *Camus*; see also Solomon, "Camus's l'etranger and the Truth," in *From Hegel to Existentialism* (New York: Oxford University Press, 1988). A somewhat dated biography is Bree, *Camus*. More recent are Lottman and Todd (see Lecture 2).

For parallel insights, read Kafka, *The Trial*; Melville, "Billy Budd, Sailor," *Billy Budd, Sailor, and Other Stories*; Kosinski, *Being There*.

Introductory Questions to Consider

1. You will recall that Meursault shot the Arab only after the latter had drawn his knife—a knife that he had used to slash Meursault's friend a short time earlier. Why does his attorney not plead "self-defense"?

2. What is the meaning of "guilt" in Part II of *The Stranger*? Why does the jury find Meursault guilty? What is the point of this somewhat "absurd" trial? Why does the magistrate call him "Mr. Antichrist"?

3. Do you believe that Meursault's immersion in "lived experience," with its corresponding lack of reflection, is the optimal way of getting the most from life? Or does reflection play an essential and positive role in

even our most elementary experiences (feeling the warmth of the sun, the taste of chocolate, and so on)?

Advanced Questions to Consider

1. Years after *The Stranger* was published (in 1955), Camus retrospectively described Meursault as "a man who doesn't lie." Yet he does lie, as evidenced by his willingness to perjure himself for Raymond when the police came to arrest him for beating his Arab girlfriend. Can Camus's claim be reconciled with such incidents? Is it enough to be a "hero for the truth" if one simply doesn't lie—or doesn't think—about the meaning of what happens?

2. The "little robot" woman appears twice in the novel, once in the first part and once in the second part. What role does this fleeting character play for Camus? How does she illustrate the central division between Meursault's bland observations and his being "looked at" and judged?

3. Do you believe that the self (and self-consciousness) arises only with the reflection and judgment of other people?

4. In the very last line of the book, Meursault tells us that he hopes spectators at his execution greet him with "howls of execration." Why would he have such a desire? Is there anything in the logic of the novel to prepare us for this?

Camus—*The Stranger*, Part II
Lecture 3—Transcript

The flat, matter-of-fact description of Meursault's life in *The Stranger* raises some vital philosophical questions, namely the role of reason and human experience and the nature of human consciousness. There is a contrast that defines the book; in fact, defines it in a rather obvious way. On the one hand, there is what we might call "lived experience." Throughout the book, what we get from Meursault is a really moment-to-moment, very present-oriented description of what he is experiencing at the moment.

On the other hand, there is what we call "reflection." Reflection is what Meursault, throughout the first half of the book, never does. As I said, he has occasional thoughts. This hardly counts as reflection. He responds to his employer and says, "Why should I do this?" That hardly counts as a reflection. What is interesting about Camus is the way he plays these two off against each other. On the one hand, you might say Part I is all about lived experience. Meursault is quite happy, and in an important sense—which I will try to make clear—he is a complete innocent.

In Part II, when he is obviously guilty of a serious crime, he is forced to reflect. There are two different parts of the book—two different parts of a life—and Camus, now generalizing, would say, "Two very different, and sometimes opposed parts, of everyone's life." Just to take a couple of simple examples: we have all been in a situation where we really want to simply get lost in our experience, listening to a piece of music at a concert, for example. We would really love to just be one with the music. But, if you are like me, a reflective person, what you are doing is—instead of getting lost in the music—thinking, and some of the thoughts are straight distraction and irritation, such as: "I've got this essay due tomorrow"; "I've got to give a lecture on Friday." Even if you are thinking about the music, there is a sense of thinking about the music, the composer's life, whether you have heard a better rendition of the same piece. There is an interference with the experience of the music. One wants to stop this and say, "Stop thinking; just listen." The truth is, that as you do that, you are just thinking on another level. Now you are thinking about your thinking, and not the music.

Thinking sometimes interferes with the experience, whereas philosophers have generally praised thinking above all else—a life of contemplation. What is starting to become evident already is that there is a sense in which consciousness—reflection—interferes with experience and life. On the other side, I don't have to tell any of you that sometimes you are trying very hard to think seriously through a problem. More to the point, you are reflecting on your existence. You are reflecting on what you have been doing or decisions you have to make. Suddenly the appetites reach through and you find yourself just hungry or thirsty. At that point, suddenly your thinking comes to a halt or at any rate is seriously compromised.

There is a sense in which *The Stranger*, in a very blunt way, plays these two off against one another. Camus's philosophy, as we will see, has very much to do with reinvigorating the notion of lived experience, and thinking of that—not the philosophical notion of reflection—as the meaning of life.

What is "rationality"? What is "reflection"? I think the first thing to do is to tie those two together. Rationality, in the sense that we are going to be talking about it, requires reflection. That means it requires thought. It requires thinking. It requires thinking about ourselves in terms that are not geared to just the moment and what we are doing, or even decisions we have to make in the immediate future. Reflection has to do with thinking about ourselves as a whole: who we are, what our lives amount to, how we fit into the world, how we get along with other people, what other people mean in our lives. Rationality requires this kind of reflection. Consequently, we would say in this sense that Meursault in the first part of *The Stranger* isn't rational. He is not, as the Greeks would put it, a full human being.

Second, rationality is the ability to anticipate consequences. Rationality is often defined by philosophers and ethicists as appreciating means and ends; knowing how to get what you want, but also understanding what the consequences of your actions are. You are a chemist who invents a new drug, and your whole concern (one hopes) is going to be what its effects might be, how it might be abused, what side effects it might have. Of course, this is just what Meursault doesn't do. He walks out on the beach after an altercation with a gun and never gives a moment's thought to what might follow from this behavior. Rationality is also adherence to standards—

moral standards, most obviously—in most any walk of life. if you are an engineer, it is obvious that there are standards you have to appeal to. If you are a professor, there are standards you have to appeal to. If you are simply a parent, there are all sorts of standards you have to adhere to. These are going to be reflective; they are going to be given to you to a large extent by the culture. The social dimension of rationality very much has to do with fitting into your culture in a certain kind of way.

I think this is often underplayed by philosophers who think of rationality primarily in terms of rational thought. What counts as rationality is often a cultural, contextual consideration. It was rational in the 12th century to believe that the Earth was flat. That does not mean that it is true, but it means it adhered to the standards of evidence; the standards of what counted as a good theory at that time. Again, Meursault flunks. There is a sense in which, although he goes along, for example, at the trial, his employer was happy to say, "Yes, he was a good employee." He did what he was supposed to do. Nevertheless, there is a sense in which he doesn't as much adhere to standards as just fall in. He doesn't really pay much attention to moral standards, in particular. Otherwise, his neighbor Raymond, for example, would have been an object of repulsion to him.

This raises the question central to the course: To what extent do passions emotions—depend on reason? Throughout the history of philosophy these have often been opposed to one another, as some of the quotes I gave you in the first lecture would suggest. On the one hand, there is what makes us distinctively human: reason and rationality. On the other side, there is what ties us to the beasts: our residual emotional repertoire. I think the first thing to say is that emotions involve concepts. Emotions are conceptual. Emotions involve recognition. Emotions are about the world, or, a term I will introduce later in the lectures, they are "intentional," in a very specific, philosophically important way.

Emotions involve and contain rationality. Nietzsche says at one point, "As if every emotion did not contain its own quantum of reason." I would argue a stronger thesis. I would argue that what we call "rationality" is bounded by our emotions. What we care about, and to act rationally, is ultimately to act in line with what we care about and what our culture cares about. Finally, emotions, as a general rule, tend to be unreflective. What that means is we have them, but we don't necessarily think about the fact that we have them. Very often, as we all know, we have emotions and don't even recognize that we have them at all, or might deny them when we are challenged. To think of emotions as necessarily unreflective, and therefore, in some sense as not rational, is an oversimplification. Because the truth is, when we reflect on our emotions—and sometimes emotions themselves are very reflective— what we find is that there is a very dynamic exchange between what we call "emotions."

As we all know from our experience, sometimes you can talk your way out of an emotion. You can show yourself that the arguments which the emotion presupposes are not valid arguments, or you can use an argument against the emotions; for example, I have no right to be angry because he really did not do anything wrong. The connection between emotions and reflection is going to turn out to be a very complicated one. One of the things I would say about love, for example, is that love quite distinctively involves a kind of reflectiveness. French aphorist La Rochefoucauld at one point said, "How many people would never fall in love if they hadn't heard the word?" I think there is something very important by way of insight there.

Emotions involve values. It is not as if emotions are perceptions of the facts of the case. Rather, emotions always weigh things. That is why we talk about positive and negative emotions. That is why so many emotions have very strong valuations attached to them; to take the obvious: love and hatred. Love is a very positive evaluation. Hatred is a very negative one. Sadness, to take a different kind of example, is an evaluation of a certain loss. Joy is an evaluation of a certain wonderful state of affairs. If we went through the list, I would argue every emotion has this kind of value-laden nature. That, too, ties them to rationality. Often what philosophers talk about as "the rational thing to do" might even better be described as "the thing that makes the most emotional sense to do," maybe not at the moment, but in a broader span of time, looking at what it is that serves our lives.

Finally, emotions tend to be about the self. If you think about some emotions, this becomes absolutely obvious, including some emotions we are going to be talking about this lecture. Emotions like guilt, shame, embarrassment, regret, remorse, or to move to the positive side, emotions like pride. Some emotions are comparative, like envy. We are comparing what we have with what someone else has. Or jealousy, same sort of argument.

I would argue that all emotions are self-involved in some ways, which is not to say that they are selfish, and not to say they are just about the self. To understand what it means to have a self is to understand something about what it means to have our emotions.

In Camus, as I said, what we get is this play of experience and reflection in opposition. That really is what *The Stranger* is all about. Part I, what we get is Meursault's experience as he walks through everyday life, up to and including his experience of being involved in a murder. In prison, on the other hand, Meursault is forced to reflect. This has many profound implications. The philosopher Kierkegaard, whom we are going to talk about next, says at one point, "He feels like a man who is already dead." When he says that, it is because he feels that he has already lost touch with his immediate experience. He is spending too much time thinking and reflecting. When he writes about the present age (about 1850), Kierkegaard says, "The age is too reflective. It is absent with regard to passion. These days, not even a suicide acts out of despair." He, rather, basically thinks himself to death.

As you will see, this theme about reflection verses experience is going to permeate much of what we do. In prison, Meursault is forced to reflect. His life has been taken away from him. The sensual pleasures that he enjoyed— the beach, the smells, Marie—that is gone. It is hard to say what he has left. In another human being, we might say he still has his self, soul, thoughts, memories. In Meursault's case, all this is rather dubious. Of that list, that which clearly is still present in any sense is his memory, but it actually takes some time in prison before he even actually understands what that is and how important it is. He reflects a little bit to begin with on what he has lost. Again, I am a little hesitant to call it reflection. He misses Marie. It is not quite the same thing as thinking about her. In general, what we find in prison is that he is in a way trapped with his thoughts. Most important, he is not alone.

Rather, there is no doubt that people at the beginning of the novel were forming judgments and opinions about him. What is clear is he was oblivious to it. At one point, at his mother's funeral, he comments casually to us one of those thoughts: "For a second I had the absurd thought that these people were sitting in judgment of me." He immediately dismisses the thought as absurd. It turns out they were. In the second part of the novel (the trial) the same people come in, and what they are doing quite explicitly is they are there to sit in judgment of him.

What the second part of the novel is about, in a way, is other people, or what Jean-Paul Sartre will call "being for others." The idea is we don't exist by ourselves. The opinions of others are not just contingencies that we can throw off. Rather, it is the opinions of others which at least in part make us a person; allow us to have a self. In the second part, what happens with Meursault is, as other people judge him, often to his face (for example, when the prosecutor talks to him in the magistrate's office), what we see is he is being forced to consider himself as a certain sort of person. For instance, he says at one point when someone calls him "the criminal," "I never learned to think of myself that way." The truth is he had never come to think of himself in any way. He did not characterize himself as the lover of Marie, his mother's son, in terms of his job, as a French Algerian. There is a sense of self-concept, and consequently, self. That is something that he had not yet attained.

I am using the word "reflection" in a rather general way. But let me point out that we use reflection in two very different senses. As you will see, they come together rather dramatically. The French actually have two different spellings for this. The idea is, in the first place, that a reflection is something you see in a mirror, and there is a sense in which you don't see yourself, you see the reflection of yourself (or more accurately, the reflection of your body). It is a quite literal sense of reflection and it has to do with being mirrored back. We can think of all sorts of circumstances in which something like this happens. Most interesting is the sense in which we see ourselves mirrored in another person. You can take this quite literally; for example, when you are talking to someone close range and you see the reflection of your face in the pupils of their eyes, it would be pretty superficial if that is all you saw. What you see is they are looking at you, and what they are giving you back, perhaps in what they say, is a reflection of yourself. Again, more accurately, it is a reflection of how it is that you appear to them.

On the other hand, there is this philosophical notion of reflection, where reflection very generally means conceptual thought—contemplation. What we will be talking about here is reflection of a very specific sort, namely reflecting on oneself—oneself as an object of reflection. But now, take those two metaphors, and it is interesting how philosophers have collapsed them. For example, with a very simple kind of picture that when you introspect—examine yourself (as Descartes does very cursorily in "I think, therefore I am")—there is a kind of loop in which you go out of yourself and then into yourself; in which you perceive, but what you perceive is yourself. You perceive your own consciousness. This is going to raise all sorts of philosophical questions later on in what sense your consciousness can be the object of your consciousness. As a metaphor, it is quite revealing.

There is a sense in which—when we think on ourselves, reflect on ourselves—what we are doing is in some sense turning all of our perceptual, conceptual apparatus into a kind of loop and taking ourselves as the object of our perceptions and conceptions. What this means can be interpreted in lots of ways. One way of thinking about it is that it is not just as if there is an invisible mirror through which we make the loop. Rather, the mirror is something very concrete. As I just said, the concreteness is another person. It goes back to the philosopher Hegel, in the early 19th century, who had a very keen sense of the ways in which the notion of the self is dependent on other people. There is a sense in which to come to a sense of oneself is to come to see oneself through the eyes of others. It is a rather interesting psychoanalytic process which has been described in many ways and many different details, about how from that sense of socially derived selfhood we manage to get anything like an independent self—think of ourselves as individuals, rather than simply as that which other people think of in a certain way.

One way of thinking about the trial in *The Stranger* (now we give that some more detail) is that the trial is Camus supplying Meursault with not just one, but a whole town full of people looking at him, judging him, giving him a self. What Hegel had argued was basically that we come to selfhood only through the recognition of others. In Camus's novel, I think we can say Meursault comes to selfhood only through the recognition of others.

The judicial process is somewhat restricted. It is not concerned with Meursault as an overall human being. It is concerned with him with regard to one particular action which he has performed. Nevertheless, the way the trial goes—and many people have found this absolutely outrageous—is that it is not just his act of murder which is on trial, but it really is, in a sense, his whole life. What condemns him in the trial is the prosecutors making a big deal out of the fact that this is a man who did not weep at his mother's funeral. The witnesses back this up. He was rather casual. He was restless. He was complaining about the heat. He was drinking coffee. The one thing he didn't do was act like a full human being. The prosecutor here is outrageous in his own regard. He says of Meursault at one point, "I have looked into the eyes of this man, and I have found not one redeeming human trait." There is a sense in which he even goes so far as to say the next trial on the docket is someone who has killed their parents. He says as far as he is concerned, Meursault is guilty of that crime too, for not weeping at his mother's funeral.

There is a sense—if we are concerned about justice in this book—there is a sense in which Meursault is wrongly tried. I find it fascinating that his defense counsel never even once raises the defense of self-defense. Nevertheless, the result is that Meursault looks around the courtroom, he sees people in effect condemning him, and suddenly he realizes he wants to burst into tears. He is coming to the conclusion that he has a self, and there is a sense in which he is guilty.

The guilt has to be contrasted, of course, with innocence. In the first part of the book, he is innocent. He is innocent in that straight Old Testament sense. He has not eaten of the tree of knowledge of good and evil. He doesn't have any moral judgments, and consequently, when he does a horrible thing—he kills a man—one is hesitant to say that what he has done is an evil thing, or that he is guilty. As I said, there is even a problem about whether we sensibly want to talk about agency here. Throughout the trial, he remains unaware of the moral significance of what he has done. It is to him in part a matter of annoyance, because he can no longer live the life he lived. It is a matter of some confusion because he is now branded as a criminal, because he himself never thought of himself in anything like that way. In the same sense that Adam and Eve were chased out of the Garden of Eden because they ate an apple (rather, because they disobeyed God), Meursault is sent out of his rather innocent and happy existence into what most of us would consider the hellhole of prison, where he does not suffer, but what he does is gain a knowledge of good and evil.

He comes to see himself as "guilty." Let's be careful about what this means. On the one hand, guilt means he did it. You might call this causal guilt. He was the one with his finger on the trigger. That is not what this story is about. You might also note that he was legally guilty, declared guilty by the court. But that, of course, isn't relevant either. You can be declared guilty when you are innocent. You can be guilty and nevertheless be found innocent. The question is whether he is morally guilty, and that is what he comes to discover as the trial and second part of the book move on.

To be morally guilty is in one sense to be human. It is to reflect. There is a doctrine of "original sin" that lurks in the background here. You might think in the following way: We are aware of the fact that people are suffering all around us. Imagine Camus in Algeria in the midst of a civil war, in Europe during the Second World War, and there is this nagging sense that we ought to be doing something and that what we do can't possibly be enough That sense of guilt plagued Camus. It is that sense that he wants to instill in his character Meursault to make him fully human. Nevertheless, Meursault resists, because for him, despite the fact that he is forced to this recognition, he holds onto the innocence of Part I with remarkable strength.

At one point, the chaplain comes to see him after repeated rebuffs and they have a discussion in which the chaplain is pressing upon him the importance of believing in Christ, the importance of repenting for his sins, and, most important, the importance—given his execution pending—to look forward to a blissful afterlife. Meursault, for the first time in the book, loses his temper. It is the first true emotion he experiences. What he argues rather articulately is that if there is an afterlife at all, the only one that he can imagine or desire is an afterlife in which he would once again live just this life. It is experience; it is this life that counts, nothing else. And he muses that if one had just one day to live, one could spend all eternity just savoring the memories of those precious moments.

He goes back to the consideration of how he has lived. He has lived one way, not another way—did not marry Marie, did not go to Paris and so on—and comes up reflective once again with the conclusion that it doesn't matter how you live. You live one way, you live another way, but only it is just life. Later in *Myth of Sisyphus* he will advance the rather perverse conclusion that while we worry about the quality of life, the truth is there is only quantity. It is life itself that really matters.

After musing on this, he comes to what is probably the key phrase to the entire book. He considers that he is about to die, that he has lived just the way he has lived and no other, and he says, "It doesn't matter." So, he opens his heart to "the benign indifference of the universe." It is a phrase that will repeat itself in the *Myth of Sisyphus,* and he comments that it feels so "brotherly," because now, thinking back, we realize that there is a sense in which Meursault has been without meaning, and his death is without meaning too.

But, he dies happy, and this notion of dying happy ("a happy death") is one we are going to see throughout Camus's works.

Camus—*The Myth of Sisyphus*
Lecture 4

One of the themes of Camus's philosophy, and in particular his political philosophy, is the theme of rebellion. Rebellion here is a very curious notion because it is not full-fledged revolt in the sense that we typically think of it. ... Sisyphus rebels, but what is interesting is he does not do what we would expect him to do as a member of his own labor union; that is, to drop the rock and refuse to push it any further. ... He rebels in the sense that he refuses to accept the absurdity that has been imposed upon him by the gods.

In *The Myth of Sisyphus*, Camus gives us a philosophical theory, or rather, perhaps, a vision, to accompany the odd and disturbing view of the world of *The Stranger*. Sisyphus was condemned by the Olympian gods to spend all eternity in fruitless labor, rolling a rock up a mountain until it would roll back down of its own weight, again and again and again. Nothing could be more absurd, Camus tells us, than a life of such futility.

The "absurd" is this vision, this sensibility that has come to preoccupy the modern mind. Camus defines the absurd as a confrontation between "rational" human beings and an "indifferent" universe. It is the view that, despite our hopes and expectations (for justice, for salvation, for peace and harmony), the world does not deliver or care. Meursault accepts the indifference of the universe as "brotherly" in *The Stranger*. Camus is an atheist. (But he also says that if there were a God, it would not matter—life would still be absurd.)

In *The Stranger*, Camus suggests that death makes life absurd. This view has been around since ancient times. The character of Sisyphus makes it painfully clear that an eternity of futility is more absurd than a mere lifetime of futility. Death, then, is a kind of blessing, an escape from perennial boredom. *Sisyphus* and Ecclesiastes both suggest the absurdity that our lives amount to nothing.

One of Camus's targets in the *Myth* is the contemporary glorification of science and "objectivity." Galileo's retractions before the threats of the Church were more comic than tragic, Camus suggests, because it is life, not truth, that really counts. The absurd is born, Camus suggests, of the impersonal, abstract, scientific view of the world and what one contemporary philosopher has called "the view from nowhere." Ultimately, only personal experience is meaningful.

Reason is characterized by the question "why?" This is a quest for explanation, for justification, for an account that makes an action or an event comprehensible. But every "why?" leads to another "why?" All series of "why?" questions end nowhere. In terms of understanding as well as satisfaction, life is essentially absurd. Understanding does not give us satisfaction. The absurd is a confrontation between our rational minds and an "indifferent" universe. Sisyphus can be interpreted in two ways in this context. He devotes himself to his labor so completely that he must be considered happy. Thus, the role of reflection, of reason, is a problem. It leads to a question—"what does this amount to?"—to which the answer is "nothing." He undertakes his task with resentment, and his resentment of the gods thereby makes his life meaningful. Sisyphus rebels by refusing to accept the absurdity imposed on him.

Camus defines the absurd as a confrontation between "rational" human beings and an "indifferent" universe.

Camus presents reason as a problem. "Rationality" has different meanings. It refers to "consciousness" on the one hand. Only human consciousness can see absurdity in a repeated pattern. It refers to the intelligibility (comprehensibility and justice) of the world on the other. In this, Camus reminds us of some characters invented by the Russian novelist Fyodor Dostoevsky, in particular, Ivan Karamazov and the spiteful figure in *Notes from Underground*.

In what sense is Meursault an absurd hero? For him, there is no commitment. In the first part of the novel, he doesn't rebel. In the second part, he rebels when he rebuffs the priest. Either we find the meaning of life *in* our lives,

Camus seems to be saying, or not at all. From *The Stranger* and *Sisyphus*, the answer is that life is its own meaning; philosophical reflection does not give us meaning. In Camus, only insofar as we are engaged in our lives do our lives make sense. ■

Essential Reading

Camus, *The Myth of Sisyphus*; partially reprinted in Solomon, *Existentialism*, pp. 177–188).

Supplementary Reading

Camus's later elaborations on the *Myth* are in his book *The Rebel*; for a more "metaphysical" perspective on "the absurd," see Schopenhauer, *The World as Will and Representation*. For a somewhat larger interpretation of Camus's philosophy, see Sprintzen, *Camus*.

Introductory Questions to Consider

1. Camus begins *The Myth of Sisyphus* with the assertion that "there is but one truly serious philosophical problem, and that is suicide." Do you agree with him? Why would he make such a seemingly outrageous suggestion?

2. What is "the absurd"? Camus gives us several possible ways of living in the face of "the absurd." What are they? Do you think that they are equally meritorious? What is "philosophical suicide"?

3. Do you agree with Camus when he asserts that our existence is no less absurd than that of Sisyphus? Explain.

1. Camus characterizes a man gesturing behind a glass partition while he speaks on the telephone as a "dumb show," which leads us to ask why he is alive. We can appreciate this characterization—at least at first blush. But ask yourself: Would we also consider the scene a dumb show and question why the man is alive if we could hear his conversation—if we could hear that his gestures flow from his just having been told that his house is on fire? Consider your own telephone conversations. Aren't they also merely "dumb shows" that would lead an observer to question the significance of your existence? What does this tell you about the relationship between vantage point or perspective and meaning?

2. Camus, who considered himself a political moderate and a humanist, states that "to abolish conscious revolt is to elude the problem." Elsewhere, he emphasizes the need for "metaphysical revolt." Who or what is Camus, an avowed atheist, revolting against?

3. Would "the absurd" simply disappear in the face of irrefutable evidence that God exists?

Camus—*The Myth of Sisyphus*
Lecture 4—Transcript

In *The Stranger*, Camus gives us a character who is forced to reflect on his life, and utterly reflect on the meaning of life. To put the conclusion rather bluntly, life is the meaning of life. It is not anything outside of life, and it is not necessarily any content of life or way of life. It is just life itself.

About the same time the Camus wrote *The Stranger*, he wrote a philosophical essay which one might take as a theory that accompanies *The Stranger* and perhaps explains it. It is called *The Myth of Sisyphus*, and just to remind you, Sisyphus was a character in Greek mythology. He was condemned by the gods to a truly pointless task. He had to roll a rock up a mountain and when it got to the top it would roll down of its own weight, and he would have to do it again and again and again. This is a kind of symbol of what Camus refers to famously as "the absurd." He points it out in his retelling of the story of Sisyphus, though I can't think of anything more absurd than a lifetime filled with futile labor.

The notion of the absurd is a special notion. It is not particularly technical, but it is important to distinguish it from many of the absurdities we find in life. Silly things happen; ridiculous things happen. One thinks, for example, of a *Three Stooges* short. That is not the absurd—the absurd which Camus says has overtaken modern sensibilities—which is really obsession with the way we see the world today. The absurd is really a metaphysical thesis. It is, to put it very bluntly, a confrontation. It is a confrontation between the rational human mind—the mind that deserves and demands justice, then expects the universe to be comprehensible—and what Camus calls, in a phrase he borrows straight from *The Stranger*, "an indifferent universe." The truth is, the world doesn't care.

You might say that as part of our human nature—not something that we learn from society, but part of our nature itself—that we care about each other. As many philosophers have argued, we are born with a sense of compassion, sympathy, or pity. Perhaps, we are even born with this sense of justice; some sense of fairness—even in small children, when they are not treated as they would like to be treated. Without having a choice in the matter, we project this sense on the universe, and we expect the universe to fulfill our demands.

We think, for example, that evil should be punished. We think that goodness should be rewarded. The problem that goes all the way back to the early Middle Ages, often called the "problem of evil"—the obvious fact that virtue is not always rewarded, the obvious fact that the evil ones sometimes get away with what they do—has always been a deep problem for theological thinkers. Without even reference to religion, it is a problem for all of us. The absurd is this recognition that we have a demand of the world and the world just doesn't care.

In *The Stranger*, interestingly, Meursault accepts this when he opens his heart to the universe and says it feels so "brotherly." What he is saying is that the universe itself is indifferent; it just is what it is, and he himself has always been. On reflection, he simply is who he is, and he accepts that.

There is a sense in which you might say there would cease to be a problem if we believe in God. Camus, of course, is an atheist. But, the truth is that the absurd would exist even if there were a god. The problem of evil, as it goes back through history, is very much a problem in the face of God—that we have these expectations and the world doesn't seem to deliver. At one point, Camus said, "Even if there were a god, it wouldn't matter." In *The Stranger* it is often said (Meursault says) that it is death that makes life absurd. There is a long soliloquy where he considers his death penalty and the ways in which it might be less absurd; for example, if they gave him a one-in-a-million chance to escape. But, the idea that death makes life absurd, which, of course, is an ancient view (it goes all the way back to the Greeks), is countermanded by the story of Sisyphus himself.

Sisyphus is immortal. What makes his life absurd is the fact that he is condemned to a lifetime of futility. But if that lifetime of futility is an immortal lifetime, going on for all eternity, I think we would agree that that makes it not less absurd, but more absurd. One might say that it is a kind of blessing in life that we don't get a chance to get totally bored. There have been several interesting attempts to draw sketches of immortality, in which the almost inevitable outcome is at a certain point boredom; futility—a sense that it is just the same thing over and over again—a thesis that we will see come again when we talk about Nietzsche.

The idea that death leads to the absurd gives rise to another consideration, too: that there is a sense in which we expect our lives to add up to something. As Ecclesiastes in the Old Testament tells us quite bluntly, this is "the vanity of vanities." It doesn't. What Sisyphus and Ecclesiastes both give us is a picture of life where we have all of our aspirations and ambitions, our joys and our achievements, but, ultimately, in the end it amounts to nothing. That is the absurd.

There is another sense in which Camus takes as his target the whole of the scientific worldview—the idea of objectivity. The thesis, basically, is that it is only life—only one's personal experience—that really counts. He points, for example, to Galileo—a funny figure in the history of science (one of its great geniuses) but in terms of his turmoil and opposition to the Church, about which a great deal has been written, Camus says in a way he did the obvious; he was justified. Given a choice between life and truth, the obvious choice is going to be life. What's more, science in general gives us a view which one recent philosopher called "the view from nowhere." It is the idea of the impersonal, objective truth.

I remember when I was in elementary school on the bulletin board of my classroom there was a picture of the Solar System. This made me very excited. In retrospect, I now ask myself: From where was this picture depicted? What is the perspective? The answer, I think, is from nowhere in particular. When you look at this picture of the Solar System (I remember as a little kid), someone would point to the third rock from the sun and say, "That's us." Even on a poster six feet wide, it was virtually a dot with this vast expanse surrounding it. Even then, I remember the feeling that it makes you feel awfully small. Then I learned about galaxies. Now, we have these marvelous photographs of our galaxy and galaxies beyond. There is a sense in which, taking up this picture of the world, one feels infinitesimally insignificant.

Looking at a timeline of the universe: 15 billion years, of which nine to 10 billion there has been some form of life. The dinosaurs were a mere 165 million years ago. Human beings (it depends exactly what you measure from), a couple hundred thousand years. What we call history, at most 5,000 years. America, 200 years. My generation, 50 years. You look at a list, a timeline of the universe, and you feel so insignificant. I am just a dot on a dot on a dot on a very small space.

If you take a scientific worldview—what you are supposed to do is take an objective view—you are supposed to, in a sense, erase yourself. Scientific papers always proceed, "In this paper it is proven that..." or something like that. It is not "I feel that such and such..." because how you feel and who you are doesn't really matter; isn't supposed to matter. Yet, Camus says the only thing that matters—that is truly meaningful—is personal experience.

There is another way he approaches the absurd (and, of course, this fits the Sisyphus story quite nicely). We are rational, and part of what it means to be rational is that we ask the question, "Why?" Sometimes this is a quest for an explanation—in science, for example. Sometimes, it is a quest for a justification—for example, in ethics. But the interesting and upsetting thing about why-type questions, as anyone who has a three-year-old child knows very well, is that the questions keep coming. "Why is this?" Here is an answer. "Well, why is that?" Here's an answer. And, as any parent knows, a parent's knowledge gives in long before the child has finished with the "Whys."

The reason is this chain of reasoning, this chain of explanation—or in ethics, the chain of justification—has no final anchor. If you are thinking about why you do what you do, you might come up with an answer: if I do this, it will help me get that. Why do you want that? If I get that, that will help me along to getting this. The questions go on until finally you are driven to some endpoint, seemingly, where you say, "Because it gives me pleasure," or "Because it will make me happy." Then the fatal question is: What is important about pleasure? Why do you want to be happy? And you're stuck.

There are lots of philosophers, particularly in the Christian tradition, who have asked very seriously about why pleasure or happiness should be a final end. There is a sense in which justification runs out. So too, in science: understanding runs out. Understanding the universe, contrary to the view of a great many Enlightenment philosophers, will never ultimately give us satisfaction, because the truth is, the absurd is with us. The absurd is the confrontation between our rational demands and the indifferent universe. Within that context, reason itself becomes a problem.

Going back to the Sisyphus story itself, I think one should ask, "How does Sisyphus cope with the absurd?" Camus makes it very clear, in his telling of the story, that Sisyphus is what he calls "the absurd hero." While we might readily agree that the situation is absurd, what is it that makes him a hero? Looking back to *The Stranger*, there is a very important question to ask. Does the notion of the absurd hero refer back to Meursault as well? Is he an absurd hero, or is he simply, as I said in the last lecture, not yet a human being?

The Sisyphus story might be interpreted in two different ways. Camus gives us his toward each. The first interpretation, which I think is very close to Camus's best thinking, is this. He says in language which is a bit archaic and which I am using now, "Sisyphus makes his rock his thing." He puts himself into his labor, and one can imagine Sisyphus as he rolls the rock up the mountain coming to notice, appreciate, and even love the various contours and markings on the rock itself. He comes to study and appreciate, and even become very fond of, the various bumps and levels that the rock has to proceed along. There is a sense in which what he does is throws himself into his labor. The consequence of this, Camus tells us, is that Sisyphus must be considered happy.

One thinks about being given a somewhat routine chore to do at the office or at home, and there is a way of doing it that is guaranteed to cause you a bad time. That is, if you are always looking at your watch and seeing how much more time you have to go—or looking at the task itself and saying, "I'm only a third through," as you reflect on what you are doing—what you do, in an important sense, is you undermine it. The reflection poisons the experience.

Going back to *The Stranger*, there is a sense in which insofar as we get into what we do—make ourselves simply love every moment of it; love the process, even though it might be painful or tedious in portions—to that extent we live our lives to the fullest and we are happy. What is interesting here is that the role of reflection—reason—is a problem insofar as that reflection has to do with asking yourself the question, "What does this amount to?" the answer is always going to be deeply unsatisfying. You go back to Ecclesiastes again—it all amounts essentially to "nothing."

The second answer that Camus gives us is a little more difficult to stomach. It is the idea that Sisyphus takes on his task because he has to, but he does it with resentment. He resents the gods who have so condemned him. There is an irony here, of course, because Camus was an atheist, as he wants to ask what the gods are doing there. The basic idea is that what keeps Sisyphus afloat—what keeps him feeling that his life is meaningful—is that he shakes his fist at the gods as he is doing his task with, as Camus tells us, "scorn and defiance"—in other words, resentment.

One of the themes of Camus's philosophy, and in particular his political philosophy, is the theme of rebellion. Rebellion here is a very curious notion because it is not full-fledged revolt in the sense that we typically think of it. With regard to the Algerian war, he was very clear that rebellion meant refusing to go along with the science of cruelty. So, too, in the years following the Second World War when a good many of his colleagues were avid Marxists and Communists, he said to rebel was to refuse to go along with these sometimes very cruel policies. Sisyphus rebels, but what is interesting is he does not do what we would expect him to do as a member of his own labor union; that is, to drop the rock and refuse to push it any further. He continues to push the rock. It is his fate. As he does it, he rebels in the sense that he refuses to accept the absurdity that has been imposed upon him by the gods.

There is a way of interpreting this: Camus himself is prone to this interpretation in the novel we will talk about in a couple of lectures called *The Fall*. It is also something that Nietzsche talks about at great length when he talks about the morals of resentment. It is a reactive gesture. It is a way of giving meaning to your life, but in reaction—in rejection of something else. I think this is a problem, and it is very much at odds with the more positive view that Camus presents of the value of life as life itself—the kind of picture that we get in the first solution to Sisyphus's problem when he simply throws himself into his work and says, "This is what I do, and I am not going to think about the fact that in the end of eternity it has added up to nothing."

The notion of rationality and reflection here refers, on the one hand, to consciousness. I think it is important to realize that with Camus, before him with Kierkegaard, with some other figures that we are going to talk about—Dostoevsky—consciousness is not a blessing. Consciousness is not necessarily an achievement. Consciousness is a problem. Camus says of Sisyphus: "If his story is tragic, it is tragic because the hero is conscious." Here what he means is self-conscious; reflective.

One can imagine, for example, one of those wasps that has a certain ritual hard-wired: checking its larva, coming up, checking its prey, going through a kind of ritual, in which evil-minded biologists will sometimes move the prey a little bit and cause the wasp to repeat this performance indefinitely. One imagines a cockroach trying to get a raisin across the floor, but it keeps hitting a bump and rolling back down. The cockroach does it again and again and again. One imagines a machine whose very nature is to perform the same movement over and over again.

None of this is absurd; it only becomes absurd when there is a human being or some conscious creature involved who sees that this is repetition and it is futile. It is by contrast with the expectation that this will amount to something that life is absurd. The notion of rationality also refers to intelligibility—the idea that we understand the universe. As I said, Camus doesn't give a whole lot of attention to science, so it is not so much scientific explanation he is concerned with so much as it simply a matter of trying to understand why life is as it is; why things happen as they happen. The truth is that is just what our understanding won't allow us, because the universe is absurd—not just in the sense that it does not satisfy our moral demands, but it doesn't satisfy our demands for understanding either.

We are going to see these themes repeated in many different authors. They all precede Camus. I mentioned Dostoevsky, and many of the theses I've just briefly rehearsed here are going to repeat themselves, particularly in his great novel, *The Brothers Karamazov*—in the character of Ivan who is similarly concerned with the absurdity of the world, with the medieval problem of evil, with the fact that things don't always work out the way we want them to work out. Ivan goes crazy trying to deal with his problem. Sisyphus comes out, as Camus tells us, as a happy man.

This brings us back to Meursault in *The Stranger*. In what sense is he an absurd hero? The sense that he essentially puts himself into his life; is totally engaged in it. I think we could say that he is like the first solution to the Sisyphus problem, with the exception that with him there is no reflection, so there is no commitment; in a sense there is no throwing yourself into your life, there is just being there. In a sense, does he rebel? Certainly not at all in the first part of the novel, where he rather easily gives in to any request that is made of him (the path of least resistance). Nevertheless, if we look at the last part of the novel (the act before the chaplain) where he bursts into anger and screams at the chaplain in no uncertain terms that he doesn't really give a damn about his god, his afterlife, and all the rest, that is for Camus an act of serious rebellion; and at the same time, when he comes up with a philosophy which essentially maintains his innocence (now reflectively) in the face of the obvious fact of his legal and factual guilt, that too, I think, is a sort of rebellion. It is that rebellion, according to Sisyphus, that makes one the hero.

I think the problem is deeper than this, because when Meursault did his reflective stage in what passes for a philosophical soliloquy—talks about the meaning of life as being just the living of life itself, and it not mattering how one lives or the quality of life—there is a sense in which what he comes up with is something we find rather desperate. When someone talks about the passion for life, one could mean that this is a person who is enthusiastic about everything; or in Sisyphus's case, one thinks this is a person who has thrown themselves into their projects and work. At the same time, the idea of a passion for life could be a kind of desperate gesture—nothing left to live for except life itself.

The paradox goes deeper than this, and one thinks about both Meursault and Sisyphus in this regard. There is a sense in which when we ask about the meaning of life, what we want is a certain kind of answer. God has sometimes been thought to provide that. The future happiness of humanity has sometimes been thought to provide it. The truth of it is that either we find the meaning of life in our lives, or we are not going to find it at all. But, where do we find it? The message we get from *The Stranger*, and subsequently from *The Myth of Sisyphus*, is that insofar as you are wholly engaged in your life and you taste the experience that you have, that is the meaning. Once you elevate yourself to a philosophical level and start reflecting, and start asking yourself the questions, "What does it all amount to? What is its meaning?"—then suddenly you don't have an answer.

What Meursault does in *The Stranger* is he takes this reflective rebellion and he turns it into an acceptance of exactly what he lived before—the experience as he lived it and nothing more. It doesn't matter that it adds up to nothing. Sisyphus, on the other hand, as he reflects on the meaning of life, on the one hand throws himself into his work and that gives his life meaning. On the other hand he resents the gods who put him there. In a purely secular way, we might say, one resents one's place in life; one's role, lot, fortune. That is a very different sensibility. One of the things we are going to get from Nietzsche is that way of trying to give meaning to your life ultimately destroys itself.

What we get in Camus is very interesting perspective on our lives in which the idea is not to look at our lives objectively; look at our lives from a distance. When we do that—detach ourselves from our own experience and engagements—the result is something that is utterly unsatisfactory. Camus gives the example—a nice little metaphor—if you are looking at someone inside a soundproof phone booth yelling into the receiver, but you have no idea what the person is upset about or what the conversation is and you can't hear a word, there is something incredibly absurd about the whole scene. Kierkegaard talks about watching another couple make love. In the 19th century, making love refers to very simple kissing and caressing, not the full-blown acts that we talk about today. You watch a couple making love to each other, and there is a sense in which it looks ridiculous. It is only when you are the one that is engaged that it is meaningful. So too, Camus wants to say, it is only so far as we are fully engaged in our lives that life makes sense.

That raises an enormous question. What is the role of reason and reflection? How should we live if what we are supposed to do is somehow take philosophical charge of our lives? Can we be like Meursault and come to an understanding in which we simply throw ourselves back into our lives or resign ourselves to our fates? The attitude of most of the existentialists is: No, that is much too simple. Camus himself realizes that's much too simple. In the next two novels we talk about, we are going to see a very different set of problems present themselves.

Camus—*The Plague* and *The Fall*
Lecture 5

> The most fascinating character of the novel is a fellow named Tarrou. He is a combination of saintliness and cynicism, and I am tempted to say that he is by far the character in the novel who most closely represents Camus and Camus's own attitudes.

The Plague is Camus's most social-minded work, in which the plague is a metaphor for the absurd. The theme of the novel is impending but unpredictable death, both individual and collective. The plague is often seen as a metaphor for the Nazi occupation. The novel is set in Algeria, but Camus wrote it in southern France in the early years of the German occupation. As a metaphor for the Nazi occupation, the impersonality of the plague was the subject of considerable criticism. It is worth noting that Camus treats Nazism as a faceless evil, not as the result of the evil intentions of one man.

More important, *The Plague* is an exploration of how people together face the absurdity of a lethal threat. The plague cannot be cured or prevented. It cannot even be explained, although accounts proliferate along with the plague itself. Should one fight it, albeit without palpable success? Should one try to run and evade it? Should one take advantage of it? (Compare Sartre: "Each of us gets the war we deserve.")

Camus's characters represent these different ways of approaching both the absurdity of life and social solidarity. Among Camus's characters are a doctor, who would seem to be the hero of the novel, fighting the plague (the absurd), even with the knowledge that the plague cannot be beaten or prevented. There is also a very ordinary man, ironically named M. Grand, whom Camus curiously identifies as the hero, perhaps precisely because of his ordinariness. A young man, Rambeau, is separated from his wife by the quarantine. He spends his time trying to flee to join her.

An ironic and witty character, Tarrou, is torn between saintliness and cynicism. Tarrou is clearly closest to Camus in the novel, even if Rieux and Grand are identified as the heroes. Tarrou's irony (to be distinguished sharply from cynicism) establishes the philosophical poignancy of the novel and best illustrates Camus's conception of the absurd. A scoundrel, Cottard, profits from the plague. He is utterly amoral, the most human manifestation of evil in the novel. A priest, Father Paneloux, blames the plague on the sins of the people (and then dies of plague himself). We think immediately of the chaplain in *The Stranger*, trying to impose an otherworldly interpretation on a disaster that is straightforwardly secular. Camus harshly denounces the attempt to declare all men evil, bringing into relief his seemingly opposed thesis in *The Stranger* (and, later, in *The Fall*).

All in all, *The Plague* is a portrait of how we face death and the injustices of life.

All in all, *The Plague* is a portrait of how we face death and the injustices of life. The true evils in life are often faceless, and they are inevitable. In *The Plague*, the absurd confronts *all* of us, engendering a sense of solidarity. To deny these evils, or to attempt an escape from them, is what Camus (in *The Myth of Sisyphus*) condemns as "philosophical suicide." Camus disagreed with his Marxist contemporaries, who defended Stalinist cruelties.

In Camus's last novel, *The Fall*, he returns to the theme of reflection and lived experience, innocence and guilt. In a seedy bar in Amsterdam, we meet (Jean-Baptiste) Clamence, a once extremely successful, high-powered Parisian attorney. He reports to us, in considerable detail, his prowess before the bar, his good works, his charming and winning personality, his prowess with women. He makes it very clear to us that he has had an enviable life. In an important sense, Clamence's life is flawless and he has everything one could desire. At the same time, he describes to us his undoing—three seemingly trivial incidents that undermined him in the most profound way: a fight with a motorcyclist, a peal of laughter on a bridge, and his witnessing of an apparent suicide.

As elegant, articulate, and thoughtful as Meursault was thoughtless, Clamence leads us through a meandering but captivating monologue. Although there is a virtually silent interlocutor at the bar, it is evident that we, the readers, are the audience to whom Clamence addresses his "confession." If Meursault was "strange" because he thought, judged, and evaluated so little, Clamence is burdened by an apparent inability to stop thinking, judging, and evaluating. The target of his most bitter judgments is, it seems, himself. But, in fact, these judgments tend to ricochet back to the reader. As Clamence describes to us the hypocrisy and folly of his own successful life, we too are seduced into doubting ourselves and our own integrity. ■

Essential Reading

Camus, *The Plague*.

Supplementary Reading

Hallie, *Lest Innocent Blood Be Shed*, an account of the actual lives of the people of the region of France where Camus wrote *The Plague*. For parallel reading, see Hemingway, *For Whom the Bell Tolls*.

Introductory Questions to Consider

1. Does Rieux fit the image of the "absurd" hero? Consider your response in the light of *The Myth of Sisyphus*.

2. Do you think that the citizens of Oran are responsible for the plague as Paneloux suggests? How does Paneloux's own death affect your conclusion?

Advanced Questions to Consider

1. When Rieux says that he would rather be a man than a saint, Tarrou replies "Yes, we are looking for the same thing, but I am less ambitious." What do you think Tarrou means by this?

2. Contrast Grand with Meursault. Both seem to be perfectly "ordinary" heroes. But in what sense is either of them a hero at all?

Camus—*The Plague* and *The Fall*
Lecture 5—Transcript

Camus's most graphic illustration of his concept of the absurd is in his novel, *The Plague*. It was published just after the Second World War. He wrote it during the war. What he gives us is a picture of the social dimension of the absurd, as opposed to the strange isolation of someone like Meursault, as opposed to the mythological individuality of someone like Sisyphus.

On the face of it, it is a depiction of the Nazi occupation, characterized in terms of a mysterious disease that takes over a city. The Nazis were something of a plague to the French. Yet, the novel is set not in France, but in Algeria. The idea of the German occupation is something that should not be taken too seriously. It is too obvious an interpretation. Also, what it tends to capture here is the impersonality of it all. The book came under considerable criticism for making Nazism into a faceless evil, something for which no Hitler or no particular individuals were responsible. The idea is that when catastrophe happens, sometimes we have to all face it together and it doesn't matter what its precise cause; it doesn't matter whether someone is responsible. The real question—the existential question—is how we together will face it.

Now, the plague and the novel itself are actually borrowed from a novel by Daniel Defoe some years before. The plague is something which is utterly impersonal—has no face. It can't be cured. It can't be prevented. It is not clear how one catches it, and it is not clear how one can avoid it. There is a sense in which it is not even explained. It is diagnosed so that fairly early in the novel, the characters all realize that that is what it is.

The question about how one should live with it is the question that Camus wants to face. There are alternatives. One can fight the plague. What is most interesting about the fight is that it is futile—in any case, uncertain. Since we don't know how to stop it—how to prevent it—it is not clear what one does. You can perform all sorts of hygienic rituals, but as we know from our own smaller cases (when we are fighting the flu, for example) very often these things don't so much give us symptomatic relief—much less anything that could count as a cure—but they make us feel as if we are doing something to take care of ourselves. One can try to escape, but with the plague, what do you escape from? Where do you run to?

Or, you can take advantage of it. Sartre has a quotation often quoted out of context, but it tells a lot. He says, "Each of us gets the war we deserve." The idea is that there is a war on. You didn't choose it. In a sense, you can't do anything about it. What you can do—in fact what you have to do—is to choose how you are going to cope with it. What this novel is about is how different characters cope with the plague—cope with this collective absurdity—and consequently how they conceive of themselves and their lives in the face of it.

Let me go through the list of characters (not a complete list). There is quite an interesting spread. What Camus does with them, I think, is illustrative of the kind of reactions that he wants us to consider. First of all, the hero of the story (and its narrator as well, although we don't learn that until the very end) is a doctor, Rieux, who is in the midst of the plague and firmly committed—dedicated as a doctor—to doing everything he can to somehow fight it. It is not clear what he can do, and there is a sense in which he is the hero precisely in the sense that he throws himself into his work—he throws himself into the project of somehow coping with the plague even though it is highly unlikely he will have any real impact. It is highly unlikely he will invent a cure; nevertheless, he considers it his identity to throw himself into his medical practice.

There is a curious character in the novel who has the ironic name, Monsieur Grand. Monsieur Grand is anything but grand. He is the most ordinary character. He is a man—very simple, in a not very happy marriage—who is coping with his life as best he can. He has very little talent, but has nevertheless decided that he can be a writer. In a way, he is the sort of Sisyphus of the novel—even more than the doctor—because even in his attempt to write this novel he never gets beyond the first sentence, which he rewrites over and over and over again. He is so involved in the sentence, in the language, in the aspiration to do the novel that he never complains. He simply sees this as what he does. There is a sense in which, looking back to Sisyphus, Camus tells us in the novel that one might well consider Monsieur

Grand the hero. At the end of the novel he ends up fixing the sentence, he says, by taking out all the adjectives.

There is a character named Rambeau, who is a journalist. Rambeau is somebody who is really, literally caught. When he is doing a story in Oran—the city in which this takes place—suddenly the city is quarantined because of the plague. He has a wife to whom he is very attached who is elsewhere. Rambeau spends his entire time through the novel trying to escape—trying to get away—until finally Rieux convinces him, in particular, that that is not going to happen, so you had better spend you time doing what I am doing.

The most fascinating character of the novel is a fellow named Tarrou. He is a combination of saintliness and cynicism and I am tempted to say that he is by far the character in the novel who most closely represents Camus and Camus's own attitudes. I said that Tarrou is cynical, but that is not quite right. What he has is an enormous sense of irony. It is very interesting in Camus's works irony is not a feature much in evidence (unlike, for example, in Sartre who can often be ironic, and certainly unlike Nietzsche who makes irony his specialty, as does Kierkegaard). Tarrou's attitude toward the plague is that, yes, of course one must fight it, but one must fight it with a full consciousness of the fact that this is an absurd endeavor. There is nothing one can do of any significance, and yet nevertheless—much in line with Camus's philosophy—one must rebel against the absurd.

Finally, there is a character named Cottard. Cottard is the scoundrel of the novel. He is the one who wants to make use of the plague for his own enrichment. At the very beginning of the novel Cottard tries to hang himself, obviously unsuccessfully. Having recovered from what looks like a death and now facing the plague, which is possibly the death of everyone, Cottard is the one who is the true cynic and sees in the plague nothing but a chance to help himself.

There is also a priest, Father Paneloux, who quite predictably attributes the plague to God's vengeance, and points out that we are all sinners and now we are paying for it. He resembles no one so much as the chaplain in *The Stranger*, and in many ways it is pretty clear that Camus's response to him is very much like Meursault's response to the chaplain. The father denounces us all as guilty, and because we are guilty the plague is our punishment. Camus makes it very clear that this is an absolutely unacceptable interpretation, and with some irony he has the father himself die at the end of the novel, although not clearly of the plague itself. The picture that we are all in effect guilty—that we are all in effect facing divine retribution—is a thesis that Camus here denounces. One might ask the question how exactly this jives with the sense of original sin that one gets in some of his other novels—in particular, toward the end of *The Stranger*, and we will see in his next novel *The Fall*.

The question how we face death is an ancient question—one that the Greeks were obsessed with, and one we moderns tend to ignore or deny. We all know that we are going to die. This is a major theme in existentialism, but accepting the fact that you are going to die and what that means—accepting immortality—that is a very different matter. When we face death together, as in the plague situation, that is a very real question about who we are and how we think of ourselves. What should we do about the absurd? There is a picture here—an answer here—which we don't get in the earlier works we talked about, and that is that we have to face this together.

There is a very strong sensibility in Camus, even though it doesn't emerge in most of his novels and writings—a notion of solidarity; a notion of how we are all in this together. Although it doesn't come out as a theme in other works, in *The Plague* it makes it quite clear. If we are to understand the absurd and deal with the absurd in a straightforward and honest way, one of the things we have to recognize is that it is the absurd that faces all of us. In a later essay called "The Rebel," he says, "I rebel, therefore we exist." It is that sense of solidarity that he defends here. It is that sense which the doctor, Rieux, in particular best illustrates.

Evil is typically faceless. Even when it has a concrete face, such as, say, Hitler, there is a sense in which evil is inevitable. Catastrophe is going to strike all of us. We are all going to die and in the end perhaps humanity is going to be finished as well. The question is: How do we understand this? Do we understand this with a kind of despair? Do we understand this with cynicism and dismissal? Do we just deny it? Or rather, do we live on the basis of it?

Camus has a concept in *The Myth of Sisyphus* which applies very well here. He calls it "philosophical suicide." Philosophical suicide is the attempt to deny the absurd or escape from it. It can be done in a number of ways. Father Paneloux or the chaplain in *The Stranger* illustrates one of them. The appeal to God, to an afterlife, to a world beyond this one is a way of denying and diminishing the evils that happen to us here. If not saying, "They aren't real" (for example, death isn't real because there is another life after this); nevertheless it sort of shrinks them to insignificance. This life with all its sufferings is insignificant compared with the life of bliss which may follow. For Camus, that is philosophical suicide. It is not taking this life seriously. It is not living this life and all of its moments to the fullest.

There are other forms of philosophical suicide. For example, I mentioned that Camus has serious disagreements with some of his Marxist and Communist colleagues. One of them is the attempt to defend present cruelties, and even massacres such as were going on under Stalin, by the appeal to a future society—a Utopian society. (We should remind ourselves the word "Utopian" means, basically, "nowhere.") The idea is that to think of your life now and your behavior now simply in terms of some abstract future is a form of philosophical suicide too.

That *The Plague* is about facing our collective fate together and quite honestly, coming to the recognition that even if we can't change that fate, we can't just sit by and let it happen. Nor should we be as corrupt as the character Cottard turns out to be, and simply be a cynic and say, "I am in it for me, and the others don't matter."

In Camus's next novel, *The Fall*, we go back to a very individual character. Again, there is no sense of social solidarity. There is, as you will see, a kind of interaction of a perverse sort. It stars a character named Jean-Baptiste Clamence. The name is very strongly biblical. John the Baptist, to begin with, and the idea of clemency or mercy. We meet Clamence in a very seedy bar in Amsterdam. The geographical location here is quite significant. Amsterdam is one of the Low Countries. It is actually physically below sea level. Clamence, however, is French; he is Parisian. He lived in Paris, and in fact, he lived in a penthouse. So, there is a very strong picture of high and low here. The title of the novel, *The Fall*, already tells us pretty clearly that what this novel is about is a character who goes tumbling down. From his penthouse in Paris he ends up in this bar below sea level in Amsterdam.

One might note also that Amsterdam is a city with a very curious and picturesque geography. If you look at a tourist map of Amsterdam, what you see is a series of rings, which are the canals which expand outward. In the middle is the red-light district—the sailors' quarters where the seedy bar that Clamence likes to hang out is located. Thinking back in literature, it is pretty clear that what this could be made to represent are the circles of hell. It is the inner circle of hell which is reserved for the worst sinners. One might say that Clamence falls from the heavenly city Paris to something that is very closely akin to hell.

In Paris, Clamence was very much a success. In fact, I think it is quite important to see that Clamence, as he describes his life, is really kind of a near perfect human being. That is important, because it is very easy to look at him and look at what has happened to him and say, "Well, of course, because he did this or that wrong, or failed at this or that." We are very quick to do that. That has been true since back to Aristotle and his report of Greek tragedy—always trying to find the tragic flaw which makes the character in some sense responsible for his fate.

The way Clamence describes his life—and there is a trick there that I will have to talk about in a few minutes—the way Clamence describes his life it is clear that he was remarkably successful. He was a lawyer, and not just a lawyer; he was a defense attorney, and not just a defense attorney, but a defense attorney who devoted his career to the defense of what he describes as "widows and orphans"—in other words, the very poor, the oppressed, those who could not make a case for themselves, those who were falsely convicted, or, in any case, even if they were truly guilty of the crimes, they had no chance in the legal system. Yet, he was such a good lawyer he would often get them off and he would often make life easier for the people who were worse off.

So, despite all the lawyer jokes that we might tell today, as a lawyer Clamence had an enviable position—a noble position. He saw it back then as a truly noble profession. It is never clear where his money comes from; it certainly wasn't his clients. It is also clear that Clamence was quite wealthy. He drove a fancy sports car. He lived in a penthouse in the city. He lived, in general, quite well and quite elegantly. He was a hit with the women and makes it quite clear that his, shall we call it, social life was very full. In tune with the times his behavior might be construed as a bit sexist, but remember we are talking about the 1950s in Paris, and what he was describing then was pretty much par for the course.

The idea is—the important point is—that Clamence really had nothing wrong with him. He had a noble profession, great success, great social status. He lived exactly as he wanted to live in every conceivable sense. He was happy. But, he falls. To examine the nature of the fall is to understand something very important about human life. First of all, he explains to us what turned his life around—why he gave up his life and his career in Paris and ended up in Amsterdam as what he calls a "judge-penitent." Three trivial incidents—let me describe them.

The first: He got involved in a small traffic brawl—something along the lines of what we sometimes experience as a fender-bender—nothing serious. As so often, and given the gallant personality, this was a cause for some temper and a fight ensued between Clamence on one hand and the driver of a motorcycle who has somehow offended him. To put it simply, the motorcyclist gets in a sucker punch before Clamence is quite ready to fight. He is knocked down (certainly not out), at which point the cyclist gets on his bike and drives away. It seems to be a very small incident, indeed. Most of us, if we should be caught in such as event, would brush ourselves off, grumble a bit, go out for a beer, or go home and take a nap, and that would be the end of it. It wasn't for Clamence. He feels humiliated, and humiliated in a deep sense that I think most of us won't understand.

The second event: He is crossing one of the several bridges in Paris, when suddenly behind him he hears a peal of laughter. We have all had the experience of walking into a room and suddenly there is a burst of laughter and—it is almost an instinctual reaction—we look up and look around and try to see if people are laughing at us. It is a terrible thing to be laughed at. Most of the time, we look around, we realize: no, someone just told a joke or something funny has happened and no one even notices. Clamence looks around on the bridge—doesn't see anybody, so he has no reason to think that anyone is laughing at him. Nevertheless, the thought haunts him—the idea that he might be an object of ridicule.

The third event is a bit more serious, but again it doesn't add up to anything like a reason to turn your life around. He is crossing a bridge in Paris again, this time on a dark and cloudy night, and as he is crossing he dimly sees a woman standing off to the side of the bridge. After he passes, he hears a kind of shriek and then a splash, and comes to the conclusion that the woman has probably committed suicide. This is something that if it were to happen to us, I guess the immediate rational reaction—I would hope the automatic reaction—would be to see if you could do anything, but in any case, make a phone call. Clamence doesn't. He just walks off. As he puts it, there was sudden silence, and when he looked down, he saw nothing. He realized there was nothing he could do. So, he walked away. That final incident utterly undermines him, and we next meet him in Amsterdam.

In terms of the book itself, I should note that the language of the book is extremely eloquent. *The Stranger* is written in rather abrupt, matter-of-fact style, not only to fit the character of Meursault but also because Camus at that time was enamored, as were a great many French writers, with some of the Americans—people like Hemingway in particular, who had this short, straightforward style of writing. *The Fall* by contrast is a book that is written using the best and most complicated, most sophisticated twists in French grammar—eloquence. Clamence is a charmer—a very sophisticated, elitist charmer. In the book, he charms us. The truth of it is that whereas in *The Stranger*, written in the first person where we get to see through the character's mind to what he experiences, in *The Fall* what we find is we are at the other end of a conversation; you might say it is a novel written in the second person. There is another character in the bar where Clamence does most of his talking, but the truth is that character has even less to say than many of the interlocutors in Plato's dialogues—things like "Yes, Socrates," "Yes, Socrates," "You're right, Socrates." He doesn't even say that. The truth is that the person in the bar is utterly irrelevant, transparent—that what Clamence is doing is talking to us.

What he gives us is a kind of confession. Where Meursault thinks very little—reflects very little—Clamence can't stop thinking. It is in him, in particular, where one might say consciousness—reflection—becomes a "disease." He hardly tastes the delicious gin that he is drinking throughout the novel. He is hardly cognizant of the weather except in a purely descriptive sense. Everything is dwelling on his past and on the state of man. Everything is very philosophical. What he does, basically, is confess. In fact, the whole novel can be read as a "confession." A confession is something very interesting. Confession, of course, goes hand in hand with guilt. Guilt prompts confession. The question is, of what is Clamence guilty? As I said in those three trivial incidents, nothing. At most, in the third you might say it was some kind of good-Samaritan-like neglect. He should have made a phone call, and he didn't.

Nevertheless, the whole posture is one of the ultimate sinner. The idea that the novel is a confession—a confession to us—is really what the novel is about. What does he confess? Interestingly enough, what he does is tell us the story of his life. He doesn't just go back and say, "Here's a fact, and here's a fact, and here's a fact." What he tells us (and everything we get is through his current and ongoing description) is essentially the fraudulence of his prior life, the emptiness of the nobility of his profession, his hypocrisy in his supposed good works, and so on. He judges—and most importantly, he judges himself. One of the themes that is played with through the novel, beginning to end, is the biblical instruction: "Judge not, that you not be judged." The question of judgment plays a huge role in this novel, just as it played no role in *The Stranger*. Meursault never judges anything. He certainly never makes moral judgments. Clamence is making moral judgments all the time.

In particular, he makes judgments about himself. He confesses his hypocrisy, he confesses his two-faced nature, he confesses that he pretended to be innocent throughout his entire existence in Paris, but now he realizes he is guilty to the core. What is this all about? Well, I want to argue, basically, the idea is to ricochet to the reader and make these accusations he makes toward himself hit us. There is a sense in which Clamence is a seducer. He is charming; he is eloquent; he has a good story to tell. More than that, what he does is hold a mirror up to us. He says *ecce homo*, look at yourself. Who are you?

I don't want to say that the strategy of the book goes something like this: If this is a character whom we all find enviable, if this is a character of whom we don't find a fatal flaw or a fatal action, if this character who was quite literally on top of the world—who has all of the worldly goods that we would ever want, and additionally, has that kind of psychological sense of self-righteousness and innocence that most of us strive for—if this character can come to the conclusion that he is ultimately guilty, that he is a hypocrite; that, in fact, he is a fraud—then what are we to think of ourselves?

As I talk about *The Fall* in the next lecture what I would like to do is to try to make this strategy come to life and understand exactly what kind of philosophical tricks are behind it.

Camus—*The Fall*, Part II
Lecture 6

What Clamence does is talk to us. He convinces us of his own fraudulence and hypocrisy, and he forces us to examine ourselves—our lives and our actions—and ask whether we might be self-deceptively guilty of exactly the same kind of fraud and hypocrisy.

In *The Fall*, Camus displays reflection and guilt in extreme form. Clamence, the attorney, describes himself as a judge/penitent. He describes even his past accomplishments and virtues as hypocritical and manipulative. Clamence presents many of his past actions—including some of the most seemingly benevolent, altruistic actions—as motivated by vanity and selfishness. The real question is whether the misdescription and manipulation lie in his reports rather than in his past deeds themselves. The question of self-deception is unresolvable. Does Clamence really believe what he is saying to us? The pervasive question of the novel is why Clamence is telling us all this. It is not just that he is a compulsive talker. It is clear that he is trying to do something with us.

The question Camus poses remains: How does one reconcile reflection and experience?

With Clamence, consciousness seems to become a disease. In comparison with Meursault's happy innocence, Clamence, an extremely intelligent, successful, sophisticated cosmopolitan, wallows in misery and guilt. In comparison with Meursault's unreflectiveness, Clamence's pathological reflections throw one of the basic premises of philosophy ("the examined life") into question. The idea that consciousness can become a "disease" comes from both Kierkegaard and Dostoevsky's *Notes from Underground*. In one sense, Clamence is an extremely rational (articulate, strategic, manipulative) person. In another sense, he is clearly irrational. He gives up the good life, chooses misery over happiness, and undermines others out of what looks like sheer sadism of the "misery loves company" variety. The dominant aspect of Clamence's consciousness has been interpreted as pride,

The central question of Camus' philosophy was how to reconcile reflection and experience.

one of the seven deadly sins. The "fall," accordingly, is the fall of pride. Wounded pride becomes resentment, but resentment itself becomes the cause of self-justification. His arrogant pride at the end of the novel is no less outrageous than it was at the beginning.

Critics have claimed that Clamence never considers Christian redemption. But there are numerous allusions—from the book's title to the name Jean-Baptiste—that recall this tradition. The theme of judgment runs all the way through the novel. Clamence forces us to examine our lives. He doesn't judge us, but manipulates us into judging ourselves. Camus's notion of original sin has no religious overtones, however. Insofar as we are reflective, we will feel guilty.

Toward the end of his life, Camus intended to study Indian philosophy. Camus was killed in a car crash (the car was driven by his publisher). One can imagine the turns his thought might have taken and in what ways the path from *The Stranger* to *The Fall* might lead to Buddhism. The question Camus poses remains: How does one reconcile reflection and experience? ■

Camus, *The Fall*.

For parallel reading to *The Fall*, see Dostoevsky, *Crime and Punishment*.

1. What three discrete events led to Clamence's fall? Do you consider it plausible that these events should have had such an effect on Clamence, enough to make him throw off his entire enviable, successful life? Why do you think that they had such an effect?

2. Clamence calls himself a "judge-penitent." What does this mean? He says: "Don't wait for the Last Judgment. It takes place every day." Who is doing the judging? On what basis are we being judged?

1. Do you believe Clamence when he claims that the impetus behind the good deeds he performed in Paris was simply his own vanity? If not, why would he lie to us?

2. Contrast Doctor Rieux (in *The Plague*) with Meursault and Clamence. If Meursault's existence in the first part of *The Stranger* can be characterized as pure lived experience and Clamence's existence in Amsterdam as (more or less) pure reflection, how might Rieux be characterized? Does he surmount the limitations of the other two?

Camus—*The Fall*, Part II
Lecture 6—Transcript

Clamence calls himself a "judge-penitent." This is a very unusual coinage and it is worth understanding. First, notice the peculiar role of lawyers in the legal system. They are not on trial. They are not the accused but neither are they the judges, which gives rise to a huge number of arguments about to what extent they should act as advocates for their clients—to what extent they should have justice as an ultimate aim.

What is interesting for the purposes of our concern here is the sense in which lawyers are right in the middle of the judicial system, and yet they are not really part of it. They are not the accused. They are not the judges. They are innocent in a sense in that their responsibility—their guilt and innocence—is not in question, nor is it their duty to make judgments about guilt and innocence. To call yourself a judge-penitent is then to take your prior role as a lawyer and divide it and put it on each side of that polarity. On the one hand you become the judge. On the other hand you become the guilty—the accused. To put them together you judge yourself. You condemn yourself and you are the one that is trying to somehow find redemption. When Clamence talks to us—when he seduces us with his charm and his story—what he is trying to do is to get us to start doubting our own innocence—our own integrity. When he describes his past accomplishments, in one sense he is getting us rather successfully to envy him—to admire him. At the same time, as I said, he doesn't just describe these, but he describes them as hypocrisy and fraud so that we are tempted to view our own accomplishments as hypocrisy and fraud.

There is a philosophical trick here, and it is a very deep philosophical trick and one that goes back to Plato and many philosophers in between. It is something that is the basis of an argument that you have probably had with friends—possibly in college—and it comes back to the theme: Are people basically selfish? Is everything we do self-interested? If you remember how this argument usually goes, first, the hypothesis is: "Yes, that is the kind of creatures we are." The response is instantly, "Well, certainly not all of our actions. Some of what we do is selfish, but we can also act altruistically. We act generously. We act kindly. We care about other people." But, the reply to that is, "Why do you do that? Is it because it makes you feel good? In which case, isn't it selfish? Is it because you are afraid of the guilt feelings that will follow if you don't act in that way, in which case the avoidance of pain is a selfish motivation?"

If you think about it, everything that you do is aimed at some future advantage, if not present advantage. It is concerned with how you are going to feel—better or worse about yourself. It is concerned with how other people will think about you. That is all selfish. Giving to charity—in one sense that is altruistic, but of course, we all know people give large sums to charity and make sure their name is on the gift so it adds to their social prestige. Even if they give anonymously, one could argue, it is that sense of anonymity and the sense of what one has done and they don't know that still appeals to our selfishness. It is a trick in the sense that as Kant once said, "We are never in a position to know all the motives of our behavior." And to be sure, behind even the most generous or seemingly selfless action, there is a good chance that there might be some self-interested motivation.

At the same time, to assume that all of our acts are motivated by selfishness or self-interest seems to be most implausible. The trick, of course, is one can always find a way of turning what seems to be altruistic or noble into something that is vain and selfish. That is what Clamence does, for example. He talks about his exploits as a lawyer and how he would serve all these poor but deserving people, and he suggests that behind the nobility was a kind of almost incalculable self-righteousness. He enjoyed being innocent in the sense that he wasn't one of the accused. He enjoyed not being responsible for making the judgment; he only had to defend these people. In his life, he describes how even when he was being eloquent, generous, noble in the many senses in which he made it a point to be, it was very clear to him (or to him now) that what he was doing was acting out of a kind of sneaky self-interest—he was manipulating people. What he was doing, in effect, was something that was hateful—hypocritical.

He gives us an example. He helped a blind man across the street once, and when they got to the other side of the street he doffed his hat. He reflects on it and says, "What is the point of doffing your hat to a blind man?" Obvious answer: It is not for the sake of the blind man. It is for the sake of everyone else. It is showing off that you are such a good guy that you not only helped a blind man across the street but that here you are being deferential and respectful as well. I think this little incident gives us a clue about how this particular kind of argument works.

Here is an alternative description which I personally think is much more plausible. Here is a man who has been brought up in fairly high society. He was taught manners as a very young boy. When you are taught manners, it is certainly not the case that when you are mannerly you think to yourself, "This is an incident in which I should hold the door for someone," or "This is an incident in which I should ask a certain kind of question or perform a certain kind of gesture." I am sure that Mssr. Clamence had been doffing his hat to people for many years to the point where it was certainly a habit. So, in this instance, the person he is with happened to be blind but the doffing of the hat was a perfectly natural, automatic gesture.

What motives were behind it? I am not sure it makes a lot of sense to talk about motives behind habitual behavior to begin with, but insofar as we do want to talk about motivations, why would we ascribe selfishness as the primary motive in this case? It seems to me that it is simply a mis-description. So, too, I think when Clamence goes through his life and tells us what a hypocrite he was, how fraudulent he was, much of what I would describe is the same kind of mis-description. In fact, he behaved very much in character. His motivation was exactly as it seemed to be: to help this person, to do this deed, to be courteous and polite on this occasion. In his description to us, or his mis-description to us, he manipulates his memories (of course, we have no way of checking) such that what comes out is a life filled with fraud and deceit. Self-deception, here, plays a very clear role because we often deceive ourselves about our motives, and—I can speak for myself—I often do something which seems to be a very nice for someone else, and with reflection I realize that I really have a hidden agenda—hidden even from myself.

As Kant said, "We are never in a position to know all the motives that motivate us," and I think he is quite right, as well as all the philosophers since, when he says, "The truth is that why we act is often a mystery, but in many ways, it is the action itself that counts." The truth is that what

Clamence does throughout the first part of the book; that is, throughout the descriptions of his Parisian life—almost without exception, noble, unselfish, charming, sophisticated—all the things that, in fact, he tries to undercut in his description. Why would he do that?

Again, I think the strategy is that, on the one hand he seems to be putting himself down, but at the same time he is really undermining our conception of ourselves. We start thinking now, as I just did, about the generous acts that we perform that may have had a hidden motivation, or we start thinking about the selfless acts which were all about our self-esteem or perhaps about our reputation, which, of course, were all to our advantage. There is a sense in which thinking about the motivation of your action—in fact, thinking too much about what you have done—can become a real problem. I said before that *The Fall* is a good illustration of the kind of thesis we find in many of the existentialist writers, where consciousness, rather than being a blessing, becomes something of a "disease." When I said that Clamence can't stop thinking—reflecting—part of this is he can't leave well enough alone. He can't accept the way he lives as "That's just the way I have lived." He can't accept the way he is as "That's just the way I am." He is the very opposite here, in another way again, from Meursault, for whom accepting his life—accepting his fate—is just built into him. It is a matter of no thinking at all.

For Clamence it is a matter of thinking so much about who you are and what you've done and what it means and what it adds up to—leads to nothing less than a sense of misery and guilt. The question is: Why does he do this to himself? Again, we are tempted to go back to Aristotle and the conception of the tragic flaw. Because again, if we could see the ways in which Clamence was in some way off base, or a little bit crazy, or a sense in which he was a hypocrite in one way or another, then we could say, "Well, that is the way he is." But, since we don't get that, it is always, how much are we guilty of the same sorts of things that he claims?

It was said by Socrates many years ago that the unexamined life is not worth living. There is a point where you might want to ask, "Is the "examined life" worth living?" Is it true, as Socrates rather presumptuously claimed, that people who don't stop to think about virtue and who they are—who don't try to know themselves—live a distinctively inferior life? Looking at

Clamence, we ask the question, "Is it possible to know yourself too well?" Does the attempt to know yourself inevitably end in a kind of self-deception and a kind of self-putdown? It goes back to Kierkegaard, who also held such a view— the view that consciousness; thinking too much; reflection can be a disease. As I said earlier, it certainly goes back to Dostoevsky. Here I am thinking of his novelette called "Notes from Underground," in which a very perverse character, indeed, gives us this picture of himself as utterly paralyzed, incapable of acting, because he thinks things through so thoroughly.

I think Clamence fits into this picture too. In one sense, you might say he is extremely rational. In another, more obvious sense, he is completely irrational. He is rational in the sense that he thinks. He is articulate. He reasons. He thinks quite extensively in terms of means and ends and consequences. But, he is irrational in the sense that he quite systematically seems to make himself unhappy. It seems for most of us—without making the most sophisticated notions of rationality—the ultimate irrationality and the time when we are most likely to use that word is when we see somebody undermining themselves; when we see somebody who is essentially making themselves miserable. The emotions with which we make ourselves miserable to us are the most irrational of emotions; emotions with which we make ourselves happy are to us the most rational emotions, but let's throw that into question.

One of the ways in which we make ourselves feel good about ourselves is the emotion of anger. There is a sense in which getting angry is a way of putting yourself on top of things—of being extremely judgmental, accusatory. At the end of *The Stranger,* when Meursault bursts into anger with the visiting chaplain, he ends it all by saying, "With that burst of anger, I felt as if it had swept me clean. I was ready to start life over again." This is a very clear indication, I think, that anger has a very therapeutic side. Not that it can't go wrong, not that it can't get us into trouble, but anger—which is often called a "negative emotion"—here serves a very positive purpose. It makes us feel good about ourselves.

Or, to take a different kind of emotion, but one might notice is also on the official list of "seven deadly sins"—that is the emotion of pride. There is a sense in which Clamence is proud. This is a term that has many different meanings. In fact, one of the things that I would urge you to think about is how pride has been tumbled about in the philosophy of opinion over the last 2,000 years. Aristotle, for instance, in his list of virtues, would say that pride for a Greek is absolutely essential. I think today we would say it is really all about self-respect. If you don't respect yourself, you don't feel good about yourself. If you are not proud of your accomplishments, then there is something seriously wrong with you.

By the eighth century A.D., pride was considered not only one of the seven deadly sins—it was considered the worst of them. The idea was, to feel proud before God as opposed to humble is, in a way, the worst thing you can do. Today, pride has taken another tumble. You think of the groups that march under the banner of black pride, gay pride, and so on. Pride has once again become a very positive emotion. The pride that Clamence feels you might well be tempted to label as something like arrogance, or using an ancient Greek word, *hubris*. What we think of is the idea that what he is doing to us, and even to himself, while he is putting himself down, while he is making himself miserable, while he is trying to make us feel miserable too—what he is really doing is expressing an enormous arrogant pride.

His accusation against himself during his life in Paris is that it was all motivated by pride, here construed as a very special sense of self-interest— pride as self-respect, pride as self-esteem, pride as thinking well of yourself—and he accuses himself of being rather outrageous; outrageous in the fact that he never doubted his own innocence, his own importance on the judicial scene. He never doubted his own attractiveness before women. He never doubted his general sense of presence in society. Now, from his Amsterdam bar, he looks back at all this and sees what utter vanity it was. Wounded pride, even if the wound is self-inflicted, is a very dangerous thing. Wounded pride readily becomes resentment. Resentment very readily becomes indignation. Indignation very quickly becomes a kind of self-righteousness. What we find at the end of the novel is that Clamence, in fact, has become just as outrageously prideful as he was at the beginning.

Some of the Christian criticism of the novel points out that the one thing Clamence never considers is the Christian view—the possibility of redemption. It is more complicated than that, because this novel is chocked full of Christian symbolism, starting with its title, *The Fall*, which without any question alludes to the fall of Adam and Eve from Eden. Amsterdam is represented as a fairly clear depiction of hell. The bar that he hangs out at with all of its obvious sinners makes Clamence clearly in something like hell or purgatory. There is a sense in which his very name, John the Baptist (Jean-Baptiste), gives us a clue that this is something special that is going on that is not at all irrelevant to the Christian notion of guilt and redemption.

And, there are things all the way through the novel. For example, there is a stolen painting that is mentioned, which now is in Clamence's possession. (In fact, if you want to pick the one thing that he actually does wrong in the novel, it is what we would call "possession of stolen property.") The painting itself is one that, at the time, would have been very much in the news. It is a piece of the Ghent Altarpiece in Belgium, and it is the panel which is called "The Good Judges."

The theme of judgment goes all the way through the novel. On the one hand, the catch phrase might be: "Judge not, that you may not be judged." Of course, that has all kinds of variations, many of them kinds of wisecracks, but many of them very serious, indeed. One of the wisecracks is: "Judge them before they judge you." There is a sense in which one might see that Clamence, in his earlier life, despite his supposedly non-judgmental role as a lawyer, was very judgmental, and judgmental in such a way that other people didn't have a chance to judge him back. We all find that if you can judge somebody as being insignificant first, then what they say about you matters so much less.

More important, "Judge not, that you not be judged." That doesn't say anything about causing others to judge themselves. This is what goes on in the novel. What Clamence does is talk to us. He convinces us of his own fraudulence and hypocrisy, and he forces us to examine ourselves—our lives and our actions—and ask whether we might be self-deceptively guilty of exactly the same kind of fraud and hypocrisy. He doesn't judge us, but his confession is a way of manipulating us into judging ourselves and undermining ourselves. So, perhaps he doesn't judge us; nevertheless, it has the same effect. In fact, it has a more serious effect because we undermine ourselves so that, unlike Clamence himself, we no longer feel as if we know what to do.

The Christian symbolism here has another sense too. It goes back to our discussion of *The Stranger.* At the end of that novel, the idea of Meursault being put through the trial as a way of making him feel guilt; of making him come to the realization that insofar as he understands his life he must understand that he is guilty—I commented very briefly that this had something to do with the notion of original sin, even though Camus himself was an atheist. It has to do with original sin if you think again about how we all find ourselves, when we think about it, in a world in which we are actually pretty privileged—a world in which we are surrounded by suffering, by injustice.

To be aware of that is to make us feel we should do something about it. It is also to make us aware that there is so much suffering and injustice that we ourselves could not possibly do enough. There are a number of solutions to this. One is Mother Teresa's, which I think is always a very significant one. She said, in an interview before her death, "I never think except in terms of the one person I am dealing with at the time." When she was asked, "How do you cope with the millions and millions of suffering and dying people in India?"—that was her answer. One can also simply turn away to what I sometimes call the drop in the bucket syndrome. Why should I give to this charity? There are a million children starving in West Africa right now. What difference is my $5, $10, $100, even $1,000 going to do? Unless you can think of saving one child, or one family, that kind of despair is going to lead you to simply turn away.

What Camus means by "original sin," in fact, has no religious overtones. It has nothing to do with Adam and Eve. It has to do with the fact that insofar as we are reflective, we are aware of the evil—the inequities of the world—and we too are confused about what to do about it. If we are fully human, we will feel, in the appropriate sense, guilty. This is what Clamence, interestingly enough, doesn't allow himself to feel. Instead of this being a recipe or a recommendation for Christianity, I would say it is part of Camus's condemnation. What you get in Clamence is a kind of pride, which is very easily conflated with Christian self-righteousness. It is the idea that I have admitted to you, confessed, and made it clear that I do not think of myself as anything but dirt. It is the ultimate in humility. In that humility, there is a self-righteousness which in many ways is much more self-destructive. Clamence, while he does some lawyering—in a way some good deeds—while he is in Amsterdam, nevertheless in a way kind of writes off the universe in a way that Camus himself never did.

Since it is his last novel, *The Fall* is often thought to be a kind of self-portrait. The fact is that Camus died very suddenly and prematurely. He was killed in a car wreck in France. The car was driven by his publisher. He died almost instantly, but in any case, it is very clear that he didn't write *The Fall* with anything like the sense that it was his last work. What he did intend to do, according to a colleague of mine—an Indian novelist named Raja Rao who knew Camus quite well in Paris—he intended to go to India and study Indian philosophy. It is a very interesting kind of question. Since the dichotomy—the opposition that we have been worried about throughout these past five lectures—has been the opposition between lived experience and a sense of reflection, we have seen how, according to Camus, these things don't fit together easily at all. It is a very interesting set of speculations about what he would have picked up if he had undertaken the study of Buddhism that he intended to undertake; what he would have come away with if he had come up with a different view of what reflection consists of.

As I have been describing it, reflection is very much self-oriented. Reflection is very much in terms of thinking about your personal life and at the same time experience as your personal experience. One of the main features of Buddhism is the fact that this whole notion of individuation—your personal experience and reflection on your particular life—starts breaking down. The question—I always leave Camus with this the question: "How do you reconcile reflection and experience?" It seems to me that the dichotomy is much too harsh, as Camus himself certainly recognized. We have very few experiences that really do count as pure experience. There are very few bits of reflection which aren't reflections not only about, but reflections that are deeply in, our experience.

There is a sense in which there is a picture in Camus that comes out of the 18th century. It is something that dominated France for quite some time, but

I think more interestingly dominates America in a very powerful way. It is an image that comes from the Swiss philosopher, Jean-Jacques Rousseau. He is the one who talked about what is often described as "the noble savage." It is the idea that people are basically good inside, but society corrupts them. As they become more sophisticated, as they become more articulate, as they learn the language of good and evil, they become a different kind of being: a superficial, vain, merely social being. In Rousseau, the attempt is always to try to recapture that inner goodness. The real challenge is to try to capture it in society itself, and in politics, which is far beyond the scope of our study.

The image I want to highlight here is an image that looks something like this: In each of us there is an innocent, good-natured person, and that is corrupted by society in such a way that we become vain, overly eloquent, overly concerned with status. It is not hard to see in this simple description—the transition from Meursault in *The Stranger* to Clamence in *The Fall*—that in Meursault, we have a character who has so far not been corrupted by society, and when society gets its hooks on him in the trial, he ultimately refuses to take on the role; Clamence, on the other hand, is very clearly a character who buys into the picture of increased eloquence, sophistication, nobility all the way. As a result, he is utterly undone by it.

The question I want to leave is simply: What do we do with this kind of sensibility which divides the world so harshly into, on the one hand, experience; on the other, reflection? When we turn to Kierkegaard I hope to try to answer that question.

Søren Kierkegaard—"On Becoming a Christian"
Lecture 7

The question is: What is it to be a Christian? It is a very difficult question. On the one hand, [Kierkegaard] looked around, and he says that most of the people in his society simply assumed they were Christians because they were born of Christian parents and they were raised in a Christian society. ... He wants to say that is utterly insufficient.

S øren Kierkegaard (1813–1855) did not, in the usual sense, have a very happy or fulfilling life. He was crippled in both his appearance and in his emotional development. He was burdened by an oppressive sense of guilt and inadequacy. He spent virtually his entire life in Copenhagen while he despised bourgeois complacency and the whole of "the present age." As a young man, he carried on for a year in Berlin with his somewhat more hedonistic friend, Hans Christian Andersen. Hedonism was not for him, however. He experienced it as self-defeating, shameful, and humiliating. He rejected both the life of pleasure and the life of friendship. Pleasure ("the aesthetic") would remain a problem for him throughout his career. He rejected a promising career in the ministry and a potentially happy marriage to pursue his lonely and often controversial philosophical and religious mission.

The place of reason and the role of suffering and passion in life became some of Kierkegaard's primary concerns, in particular with regard to religion and religious belief. He described his own mission in philosophy as "to redefine what it means to be (or become) a Christian." He rejected the idea that simply being born a Christian is sufficient to be one. He also rejected the idea that simply growing up with certain beliefs was sufficient to make one a Christian. He insisted, much to the dismay of many of his Christian compatriots, that it is easier to be(come) a Christian if one is not already born one. Christianity is a commitment, not something to which one passively adheres.

Most so-called Christians, Kierkegaard says (the "mob" of what he disdainfully calls "Christendom") are not that at all. He accuses most Christians of blatant hypocrisy, empty belief conjoined with banal social membership. Most Christians display no passion for their faith at all. Most of Christianity is a mass or "herd" phenomenon. Christianity is not to be understood in terms of doctrines, rituals, or social belonging. Belief in doctrines is a part of Christianity, but not the essential part. Rituals are at most a minimal accouterment of Christianity. (This is obviously a reflection of Kierkegaard's Lutheranism and part of his rejection of Catholicism.) The fact that other Christians exist in the world is somewhat irrelevant. One is, ultimately, a Christian all by oneself.

Christianity is a paradox, but this paradox demands passionate faith. The paradox is one of belief, but its proper response is passion. In Kierkegaard's day, one of the reigning paradoxes was the idea that God could be both eternal and temporally present as a man. Today, a more pressing paradox for most Christians would be the so-called "problem of evil," the idea that an all-powerful, all-knowing, good and kind God would allow so much suffering in the world. For Kierkegaard, a leap of faith is necessary for a passionate religious belief.

> **In Kierkegaard's day, one of the reigning paradoxes was the idea that God could be both eternal and temporally present as a man.**

Kierkegaard's philosophical *bete noir* was G. W. F. Hegel. As a student, Kierkegaard studied with Friedrich Schelling in Berlin. Schelling denounced Hegel's philosophy as "negative." Schelling and Hegel had been college roommates and competitors. Hegel, who (along with Kant) dominated philosophical thought in Denmark, defended the idea of a supra-historical collective world-spirit (or *Geist*), leaving little room for the individual. Hegel's *Geist* was, according to the popular interpretation, identical with human consciousness and the world. Hegel thus denied the identity of God as entirely separate from his creation and from human beings. Hegel also defended the idea that *Geist* was rational and could be rationally comprehended by human beings. Kierkegaard, by contrast, offers the fear and trembling of a personal confrontation with God. He rejected both the collectivity of *Geist* and the idea that God could be rationally understood.

Hegel's relationship with Schelling was complicated. Schelling became famous very early, while Hegel was still struggling to find his way in philosophy. Later, Hegel became even more famous, Schelling's star faded, and Schelling was filled with jealousy and wounded pride. None of this was evident to Kierkegaard, but Schelling's prejudices fit in perfectly with his own predispositions. While Kierkegaard was studying in Berlin, two of his other classmates were the proto-Marxist Friedrich Engels and the anarchist Mikhael Bakunin. In Hegel, Kierkegaard found a paradigm of collective, rationalist thinking. In reaction, Kierkegaard became the champion of "the individual." ■

Essential Reading

Kierkegaard, *Journals*, (excerpted with other readings in Solomon, *Existentialism*, pp. 3–28).

Supplementary Reading

Gardiner, *Kierkegaard*; for a more literary perspective on Kierkegaard, see Mackey, *A Kind of Poet*.

Kierkegaard, *Fear and Trembling*. To appreciate Kierkegaard's polemic against Hegel, take a look at Hegel's *Introduction to The Philosophy of History*; for Kierkegaard's relation to Hegel, see also Thulstrup, *Kierkegaard's Relation in Hegel*, and Solomon, *Continental Philosophy Since 1750*, "Kierkegaard."

Introductory Questions to Consider

1. Kierkegaard claimed that "it is easier to become a Christian when I am not a Christian than to become a Christian when I am one." What did he mean by this?

2. Would Kierkegaard have approved of the attempts by philosophers and theologians to prove that God exists? Why not?

1. For Kierkegaard, God's existence is more palpable than anything else that he encounters in this world. Yet, in attempting to proselytize his reader, he deliberately refrains from insisting on the truth of God's existence. Why?

Søren Kierkegaard—"On Becoming a Christian"
Lecture 7—Transcript

I introduce the lectures with Camus because it seems to me that he sets the sensibility and raises many of the questions that we are going to be answering for the rest of the lectures. In a way, Camus is more a writer—more of a literary fellow—than he is a philosopher. His ideas are often thrown together in what, in the French, is quite simply an attempt—an assay. When we turn back to Kierkegaard back in the middle of the 19th century—the proper beginning of existentialism—we start getting into some really solid, and I would add difficult, philosophy.

Kierkegaard was an extremely intense individual, like most of the people we will talk about. He had a life that by any rights was not, in the usual sense, a happy one. He was crippled, both physically and emotionally. He was burdened by guilt. There was a story he told about his father, who at the tender age of something like 13, did something that these days 13-year-olds do as a matter of routine. He uttered a blasphemy; he cursed God. What Kierkegaard tells us is that for the rest of his life he was burdened by guilt, which he passed on, quite intact, to his young son.

Kierkegaard was Danish. He lived his entire life in Copenhagen. He really just spent one semester away, going to school in Berlin. Copenhagen was perhaps the most bourgeois of the cities of bourgeois Europe. In 1848, when much of Europe was bursting into revolution, Copenhagen has its version of revolution, which Kierkegaard lampoons as a bunch of people getting into their Sunday best and walking to the town hall. He was not sympathetic with his countrymen. He was not sympathetic with the climate—I mean the intellectual and culture climate of Denmark.

He was very disconcerted with what he called "the present age," which he called an age of reflection and repose—something that was absolutely lacking in passion. He comments that even a person who commits suicide does it out of over-reflection and doesn't do it because of despair. I mentioned that he spent one period abroad—slightly abroad anyway—in Berlin. His best friend, Hans Christian Andersen, a great writer, was with him. According to Kierkegaard's own account, it was a year of what we would probably not call, but he would, "libertine-age." He enjoyed himself or tried to enjoy himself thoroughly.

In truth, he found that pleasure didn't work. Hedonism, the life of pursuing pleasure, didn't work for him. In a way, he rejected pleasure. He rejected the life of friendship. He rejected the general life that most of us would aspire to or enjoy, because he (I think we can say) personally, psychologically was simply not suited to it. There is a comment in Nietzsche, which I have always found extremely revealing. Many people believe this, especially if they are not philosophers. What a philosopher tends to argue, however abstract or abstruse it might be, typically has to do with his or her personal problems. There is a sense in which philosophy is personality rendered explicit in some rather difficult words. Hegel, whom I will talk about in this lecture, also had the theory that this was true not just of individuals but it was true of entire ages—that philosophy really is nothing other than the mentality of the age rendered explicit.

With Kierkegaard, what we find is certainly an illustration of the first; he would not deny that for a second. Perhaps the most important word in his entire philosophical career is the word "subjectivity." Kierkegaard would argue, "Of course, my philosophy is subjective. Of course, it is an expression of my problems, my suffering, my interests. Whether or not it affects you, whether or not you accept it as true, really has to do with you, your life and your problems." In general, I think we can say that what begins as an unhappy year in his late teens culminates in a philosophical outlook which takes the whole question of happiness, of pleasure, of a life lived according to enjoyment and fulfillment—all this becomes a problem.

What Kierkegaard will refer to, using a very popular term at the time, is "the aesthetic." Subsequently, he rejected what promised to be a very successful career in the ministry where he was studying. He was also engaged to be married to a quite lovely young woman who later married another philosopher. He broke off the engagement, and his reason was that he couldn't serve a marriage, a ministry, in the way that he felt he would be obliged to serve and at the same time serve himself—this very, at this point still inchoate sense that he really wanted to be a religious man, but at this point wasn't quite sure what that was.

Part of his campaign was to understand Christianity. I think we should be careful here. Kierkegaard often talks more generally about the religious life, but what he almost always refers to is very specifically a Christian life, and more narrowly, something that has to do with Protestantism, Lutheranism—the sort of religion that he certainly learned in Denmark. What he said at several points in his career, most famously when he started his serious Christian writing in the late 1840s, was that his whole mission in life and philosophy was to redefine what it meant to be a Christian, or—slight variation—redefine what it meant to become a Christian.

There is a sense in which to be a Christian is itself a subjective projection. It is based on the fact that one suffers; is not happy. Some people have used this as an argument against Christianity, saying it is just a kind of psychotherapy. Kierkegaard would probably agree. That is no argument against it. Is that what it means to be a Christian? Is it just to apply therapy against oneself by believing in some doctrines which somehow rationalize or make you feel better about your problems? That is, for Kierkegaard, clearly not the case.

The question is: What is it to be a Christian? It is a very difficult question. On the one hand, he looked around, and he says that most of the people in his society simply assumed they were Christians because they were born of Christian parents and they were raised in a Christian society. They were taken to church once or twice a week. They learned certain prayers. They learned to assent to certain beliefs. Kierkegaard noted that to be born a Christian seems to give this presumption of being a Christian. He wants to say that is utterly insufficient.

It is also true, Kierkegaard noted, that people think they are Christians because they have a certain set of beliefs—or perhaps having beliefs is too strong. If you ask a good many Christians, "What exactly is it that you believe?" They would have a hard time answering. They would find the doctrines incomprehensible. Kierkegaard tells us that belief of assent to belief is not enough to be a Christian. You can imagine a philosopher, for example (and I have met quite a few myself), who can work very interestingly with various Christian doctrines; develop certain arguments about why these doctrines might not be true; but, nevertheless, they have not a bit of faith about them. For Kierkegaard, whatever else Christianity is going to be, it is about faith.

He says in one of his more dramatic statements that it is much easier to become a Christian if you aren't already one than if you were born one. As you will see, what he has in mind here is that Christianity is a kind of commitment. It is not something to be taken for granted. It is not something to be simply understood or comprehended. So, when he looks at people who consider themselves Christians just because they have been raised that way, or he looks at Christians who think of themselves as Christians just because they hold certain beliefs, he wants to say those people, in a sense, are hypocrites. What we really want to talk about is what it takes to *become* a Christian.

When he talks about Christians in general, he is often abusive. Let me be very clear here that when he does this he is perhaps being offensive, but he would say he is trying to be true to what he considers the true faith. It is not a question of attacking Christianity as we will see Nietzsche do. Rather, it is a question of what is it to be a true Christian, and that is the question that plagues him throughout his life. To the many people who consider themselves Christians, he charges that they are hypocrites—that their beliefs are empty. They think they understand what they can't possibly understand. What they consider their Christianity is really a kind of banal social membership. They belong to a church; they hang out together; but it doesn't have anything to do with Christianity.

What is Christianity about? I mentioned commitment, but perhaps the first thing to say is it is about passion. To be a Christian is to believe fervently in one's heart to the point where one experiences what Kierkegaard rather nicely calls "fear and trembling." It is an emotional relationship. It is not a set of beliefs, and it is not social membership. Most Christians, Kierkegaard tells us—it is really a "herd" phenomenon, a kind of cattle notion that he anticipates Nietzsche is using. People hang out together. They believe and assert what other people believe, and most importantly, they don't feel about it. He wants to say that Christianity is not about doctrines. It is only minimally about rituals. It is not about social belonging. In fact, it turns out that it is only a contingent matter that there are other Christians in the world. To be a Christian is something that one does all by oneself; he adds it is not as if it necessarily shows—you can't tell a true Christian by looking at him or her.

He talks very often about it being completely a matter of inwardness. It is an individual, passionate commitment which has or needs to have no external manifestations. As for the doctrines of Christianity, Kierkegaard points out rather dramatically that Christianity makes no sense. Christianity is a paradox. For example, in his day there were a great many theologians and philosophers who worried about the question of how God could be both eternal (which means outside of time) and present on Earth—in particular present on Earth at a particular time as Jesus. I find when I talk to people these days, even devout Christians, that doesn't strike them as such a problem.

Here is another one that we have already talked about in these lectures that goes back many centuries, and I think anyone would have to be quite insensitive not to take it very seriously. It, too, is a paradox. It is the idea of the "problem of evil." The problem of evil is the idea that God is, first of all, very good. He loves us. Second, God is all-powerful. Third, God is all-knowing. So, if there is evil, suffering, going on in the world, God certainly knows about it. God can certainly do something about it. Because he cares, he will do something about it. Yet, we look around, and we see that there is suffering and evil all around us. So the very difficult paradox that philosophers have struggled with now almost for two millennia is how is it possible to have such a God and at the same time to have evil and suffering on earth?

There have been many ingenious attempts to solve this problem. Nevertheless, it is one of those questions that a true believer really must get stuck on. The question is: How can you continue to believe in such a God in the face of what is the undeniable state of the world? That, for Kierkegaard, is a paradox. It is a paradox that any believer must face. It is something that all the explanations fail to explain. It is something that many people have tried to deny in various ways. Something awful happens; they say it is God's will. Philosophers defend this as the best of all possible worlds. Even if there is a lot of evil, you could not have a world with less evil and so on. The truth is, whatever your philosophical position, it gets stuck in your mind.

That is the idea for Kierkegaard. If Christianity said something that was commonsensical, if it said something we could all readily believe—take the example, for instance, two plus two equals four. I have never seen a student get passionate about two plus two equals four. It is simply true. On the other hand, if you tell somebody to believe two plus two equals five, and for some reason, you make it clear that this is something they really must believe—then you will see some very interesting behavior because it is not just going to be a matter of fiddling with mathematics. It is going to be a matter of trying to believe what is incomprehensible—what is impossible. That is not a terrific example. Certainly, the problem of evil—or in Kierkegaard's time, the problem of how God can be both eternal and timely—is much more rich in its connotations, and so on.

The idea is that Christianity invokes passion precisely because it is not something that can be simply accepted. You can't say to Christianity, "That makes sense." Quite the contrary, it requires what Kierkegaard coins as a "leap of faith." You can only understand so much, and in the realm of religion actually not all that much. At that point, you have to make a jump. You have to say, "I am going to believe this even if I can't understand it." So, there is a sense in which the paradox itself—the doctrines of Christianity—become in some sense secondary or merely a kind of trigger for the kind of passionate commitment that he talks about.

Kierkegaard has a target in many of his works. Certainly as a philosopher this target takes center stage. The target is a philosopher we have mentioned casually so far. He is the German philosopher Georg Wilhelm Friedrich Hegel, who was a philosopher in Berlin and died just 10 years before Kierkegaard made his own sojourn to Berlin and studied at the same university. At that time, Hegel was really *the figure* in philosophy. He was studied everywhere. He was interpreted very widely as a Christian, but a heterodox Christian—someone who defended Christianity, but in terms that orthodox Christians couldn't or shouldn't accept.

Consequently, when he was lectured about after his death in Berlin, there was a very strong tendency to give him a kind of dual attention—on the one hand acknowledging that he really was *the great philosopher* of the early 19th century; at the same time, the tendency was to lament the fact that his philosophy in some critical way left out the essence of Christianity. Or, in the words of a man named Schelling, who was at one point his roommate in college and later became his philosophical antagonist—Schelling was giving lectures in Berlin; Kierkegaard took those lectures—and Schelling made a big point of saying that Hegel's philosophy was negative. This has a number of interpretations, but let me try to explain it in the terms that Kierkegaard took away with him.

First, Hegel's philosophy, which is famously difficult and obscure, can be presented in two doctrines. The first doctrine is that there is not just a bunch of individual selves that populate the human world. There is ultimately a single self, something which Hegel called "spirit," or *Geist*, or "world spirit." The idea is that, first of all, people are all united in a very profound way. Individuality, in a sense, is an illusion. There were quite a few philosophers around in this period in Germany who were arguing similar theses. Hegel perhaps made it most concrete, and certainly became the most famous for defending it.

The idea is that the individual doesn't really count. I sometimes illustrate this by talking about Hegel's own life. He was alive and just beginning to teach when Napoleon invaded Germany (or what we now call Germany). That was back in the days when you could watch a battle from a safe hilltop retreat. Hegel, who was teaching in a town called Jena, watched Napoleon in battle in the rather famous Battle of Jena (Napoleon was at the height of his powers). One imagines watching a field of hundreds of thousands of young men in brightly colored uniforms attacking, retreating, killing each other. What you see from your safe distance is a mass of red coats moving one way, and a mass of green coats moving another way, and perhaps a mass of blue coats on a hill prepared to attack. You get the sense that the individual in such an encounter really amounts to very little—almost nothing.

Hegel's notion of the world spirit was in part an attempt to capture that sense that the forces of the world—and we are talking about the human forces of the world—were at this point so massive that individuals no longer counted. There was a more positive sense, too, which I think I should make clear. Kierkegaard didn't pay much attention to it; that is, that this idea of the world spirit was also one of the first philosophical attempts to be truly international—not just to say there are many cultures, and not just to talk about the possibility of world government, but rather to say that for all of our cultural and social differences we are ultimately all one humanity, in a quite literal way.

One of the first implications of this is that if there is such a world spirit and if we are all part of it, then talking about God as a separate spirit stops making sense. The world spirit is all encompassing, and all encompassing includes God. It was a thesis that had been argued some years before by the great Dutch philosopher Spinoza. But Spinoza at the time, it is worth noting, was pretty much banned in almost all of Europe, even in Holland, as an atheist. To say that God does not exist apart from his creation is a rejection of the traditional notion of God as an independent, all-powerful, all-knowing, just and benign entity. Hegel denied this, and it was only with a good amount of fancy dancing and some very obscure language that he managed to not be condemned in his life as, also, a kind of Spinoza. That first thesis, that there is a world spirit which encompasses us all (which includes God) is really the hallmark of Hegel's philosophy, and it is one of the things that is ferociously rejected by Kierkegaard.

It is rejected on at least two grounds. First, on religious grounds, Kierkegaard rejected Hegel's notion of spirit and its equation with God. Kierkegaard felt that you had to defend if you were to be a Christian at all, the idea of a God who confronts you, is separate from his creation—a God that is something other than simply the spirit of humanity. Kierkegaard gives us a picture of God as a personal encounter. This is something I think a great many people don't quite understand about him. It is not just that he insists that God is the orthodox God, the God of the Jewish people, the God of Christianity. Rather, it is the idea of a very personal God. It is the idea of confronting some really humongous being—someone who is so powerful, so great that you can't comprehend, but you can't step away. That is the origin of the fear and trembling that he talks about.

In order to have such a confrontation, you have to consider yourself separate from that God. You have to consider yourself face to face with that God—opposed to that God in a sense—and this is exactly what Hegel denies. Hegel's conception of God, also, is something that supposedly could be rationally comprehended. The idea of rational comprehension is something I have already pointed out that Kierkegaard rejects. The very idea, for example, of proving God's existence, which was a very popular activity among medieval theologians (and also among some modern philosophers), struck Kierkegaard as utter nonsense.

He gives an analogy. Suppose you went to see the emperor Napoleon (III, not the First) and said to him, "Sire, I am going to do something remarkable for you. I am going to prove that you exist." That would be ludicrous. If you say to God, in effect, as St. Anselm had some centuries before, "God, I am going to show rationally that you must exist," it is ludicrous. There is a sense in which to believe in God is to be face to face with this wonderful, overpowering being, and it doesn't work if what you are trying to understand is this as a principle; this as something which is rationally demonstrable.

Second, Kierkegaard rejected the collectivity of Hegel's notion of spirit. Throughout his life, Kierkegaard makes a great emphasis on philosophy as a way of understanding how you personally are to live. The idea that one can look at history as Hegel suggests, and come to understand the trajectory of world spirit as Hegel argues, gives no clue whatsoever to how one is to live one's life. In his journals, Kierkegaard writes as a young man, "What I seek is a truth for which I can live and die." He says, a bit more morbidly, on his tombstone he would like it to be inscribed, "The Individual." For Kierkegaard everything comes down to the individual. Where Hegel minimized the individual—rendered it insignificant in the scope of the wide forces of humanity and the world—Kierkegaard wants to refocus and say it is really the individual that is everything.

When he was in Berlin, Kierkegaard studied with Schelling. Let me fill that in a bit, because it is a fascinating story in itself. Schelling and Hegel had been roommates in college. Schelling got famous much before Hegel did, who was pretty much unknown for a good chunk of Schelling's career. Then, Hegel, through one really spectacular book, skyrocketed to fame and left Schelling in the dust. Schelling was extremely jealous, and when he gave the course in Berlin that Kierkegaard took, what he was doing, in many ways, was expressing his own envy and resentment.

Nevertheless, the idea that Hegel's philosophy was negative—the fact that it left out the critical core of Christianity—was obviously something that

Kierkegaard was very ready to pick up. I should add as a fascinating historical footnote that in the same class were two other visitors from abroad, Friedrich Engels (later to be known as one of the Marx brothers) and Mikhael Bakunin (who would become, perhaps still, one of the most elegant anarchists of all time). I sometimes imagine a dialogue in the lunchroom at the University of Berlin between Kierkegaard with his beginning super-religious sensibilities, Engels with his early socialism, Bakunin with his anarchist tendencies, and I wonder what they would have talked about.

It was Hegel who was the paradigm of this collectivist, rationalist notion of spirit, and consequently, in contemporary Christianity he stood for everything that Kierkegaard rejected. To be a Christian, for Kierkegaard, was through and through an individual decision. It was a commitment that you made and something that you passionately threw yourself into. To try to understand Christianity in any other way—to try to make it rational, to try to make it something that is collective, to try to make it something that is social, comfortable—is absolutely wrong.

Kierkegaard faces head on the idea that this is really just a rationalization of his own suffering. He was, as I said, an extremely unhappy individual. His response is interesting. He says in one of many, many aphorisms, that Christianity is not melancholy, but rather it is glad tidings for the melancholy. In other words, it is a kind of rationalization, but it is a rationalization that must be understood and appreciated in terms of individual choice and commitment.

This leads to a dichotomy that has become familiar to us through our discussion of Camus. On the one hand, there is what we might generally call objectivity—things that can be known, the world of science. In Kierkegaard's case, I think it is important to point out that he respected this world; never, in fact, argued against it. What he argued against was the intrusion of the scientific method, and so on, into the other realm—the realm of subjectivity, the realm of individual choice. When, for example, people argue in scientific terms that the miracles in the Bible literally might have happened, or when creationists argue that creationism is a scientific hypothesis, what they do is they confuse those two realms. What Kierkegaard is all about is adamantly wanting to keep them apart—wanting to keep religion on the side of subjectivity—and, as he says, "All power to the sciences, but that is not what I am doing."

Kierkegaard on Subjective Truth
Lecture 8

The subject of truth is a complicated notion, but the first thing to say about it is that it is a quite conscientious slap in the face of philosophers. For a philosopher, truth, whatever else it might be, is objective.

The central concept of Kierkegaard's philosophy is "subjective truth": making a commitment, making the leap of faith to believe. Kierkegaard allows that objectivity is fine in its place (e.g., in science). Kierkegaard is happy to say, "all power to the sciences, but... ." Questions concerning God and religion are not objective questions. Science attempts to undermine the miracle by making it plausible—e.g., the case of Moses crossing the Red Sea. Objectivity should not be allowed to invade the existential realm, the realm of personal meaning and significance. This is the realm of religion. It is also the realm of ethics, which Kierkegaard identifies with the philosophy of Kant. Kierkegaard puts great stress on what he calls "the ethically existing individual," the focus of his existentialism. To believe with Hegel that the world is ultimately rational does not give an answer to the question "How should I live?"

Subjectivity is, first of all, "inwardness and passion." It is a commitment, not a mere discovery or "correctness." Subjectivity is the realm where we find that very special sense of "existence" (from which "existentialism" will eventually get its name). It is living fully, which may not be outwardly evident. It is living inwardly, in the depth and richness of one's feelings. Passions, for Kierkegaard, are not mere feelings (sensations) but profound insights into the beings we really are. To say that a passion is subjective is to say (for one thing) that it can be known and appreciated only "from the inside," by the person whose passion it is. Personal choice is the key to subjectivity, "taking hold" of one's life. One does this by committing oneself passionately to what one chooses. Kierkegaard's own choice, which he advocates throughout his twenty-some volumes of writing, is Christianity, redefined in his own passionate way.

Christianity requires faith, which is not rational, but involves passion and commitment. The paradoxes of Christianity, quite the contrary of making faith less plausible, are required to provoke the passion that faith requires. Christianity—and existence more generally—involves "inwardness." Not only may it not be discernible "from the outside," but it may well seem meaningless to anyone else. You can love someone with all your heart without it being evident to anyone else. Kierkegaard gives the example of two people making love, a performance that would seem ludicrous to anyone other than the couple. Religious passion cannot, therefore, be collectivized into an organized religion.

Passions, for Kierkegaard, are not mere feelings (sensations) but profound insights into the beings we really are.

Collectivism is the very opposite of what a religious community might be (for example, a monastery where each individual keeps his faith to himself). Kierkegaard says he wants to break back into the monastery. Most of what he says could be translated to virtually any other religion. Because there is no "correct" form of subjectivity, it remains to a subjective author to seduce his readers, not to convince them rationally. Kierkegaard's books are an elaborate seduction. You can coax, not argue, someone into authentic existence. ∎

Essential Reading

Kierkegaard, *Concluding Unscientific Postscript,* (excerpted with other readings in Solomon, *Existentialism*, pp. 3–28).

Supplementary Reading

Gardiner, *Kierkegaard*; for a more literary perspective on Kierkegaard, see Mackey, *A Kind of Poet*.

Kierkegaard, *Concluding Unscientific Postscript*.

1. What is the relationship between "subjective truth" and "objective uncertainty"? Are they in conflict? Is the very notion of "subjective truth" self-contradictory? What is the relationship between "subjective truth" and that which we take to be objectively certain, such as science, particularly with regard to religion?

2. In what sense is believing in God necessarily irrational? Is this necessarily a bad thing?

1. Kierkegaard, like Camus, introduces a notion of "the absurd." For Kierkegaard, "the absurd is—that the eternal truth has come into being in time, that God has come into being, has been born, has grown up, and so forth..." For Camus, it is "the perpetual opposition between my conscious revolt and the darkness in which it struggles." How do you see their two very different perspectives on "the absurd," one having to do with the incomprehensibility of God, the other having to do with the impossibility of a rational life? How are they related?

Kierkegaard on Subjective Truth
Lecture 8—Transcript

In this lecture I would like to expand on the notion of subjective truth and the sense in which it [is in] the realm of religion, and I will show also ethics. I would also like to explain the very powerful term that Kierkegaard uses that becomes essentially the name of the movement we are talking about: "existence" and "existentialism."

Kierkegaard would not have understood existentialism. He certainly would have objected to his being a member of any movement whatsoever. Nevertheless, it is his very special notion of existence which is later picked up, in particular, by the philosopher Karl Jaspers and introduced by Sartre as the key to a movement, which includes Kierkegaard as its originator.

The subject of truth is a complicated notion, but the first thing to say about it is that it is a quite conscientious slap in the face of philosophers. For a philosopher, truth, whatever else it might be, is objective. In fact, objectivity and truth in many philosophies turn out to be pretty close to synonyms. To talk about subjectivity, on the other hand, for most philosophers is to talk about the merely personal, or the merely psychological. Going back to Plato, the distinction between knowledge and mere opinion—subjectivity—is often a putdown in philosophy as when we say, "That is your subjective opinion," or "That is just subjective." So, putting them together, "subjective truth" for most philosophers would be itself a kind of oxymoron—something that just doesn't make any sense.

To understand this in Kierkegaard, I think we should understand a number of things. First of all, you have to maintain the distinction between subjectivity and objectivity. If you are thinking of subjective truth as a funny kind of truth which is objective but not objective, then that, of course, does not make any sense. If you understand subjective truth is something that is unique to, as Kierkegaard puts it, "the realm of uncertainty"—instances where there is no way of getting an objective answer to the question you are asking—then the idea of a subjective truth at least doesn't run directly opposed to the notion of objective truth.

Secondly, I think more profoundly, there is a sense in which we can understand subjective truth not in terms of something which corresponds to reality or something that can be proven in a scientific way, but subjective truth rather refers to something that we might refer to as a commitment. J. L. Austin, the great Oxford philosopher in the middle of this century, talked about "performatives" as opposed to descriptive utterances, and talked about how language doesn't just describe the world. In other words, it is not just used for knowledge and objectivity, but language is also used to make commitments, to make promises—for example, to baptize, to do all sorts of actions. In other words, you use language not to say what is the case, but you use language to make something come into being. To say, "I promise," is to say, in effect, "It is now the case that I have an obligation to you." It is not a matter of describing something that has already taken place.

Think about subjective truth in this light. One might think about subjective truth as making a promise, making a commitment, and most central to Kierkegaard, the leap of faith itself—deciding to believe in something, participate in something, live your life in a certain kind of way. The passion that accompanies this is, in many ways, exactly what makes it subjective. It is not just a matter of making a decision—there are examples of ways in which scientists, for example, make decisions about which hypothesis to pursue—it is rather the passion with which this is pursued. That combination of passion and commitment is what I think most characterizes the idea of subjective truth.

Again, Kierkegaard is not against objectivity. He puts it in its place. As I said at the end of the last lecture, he is well to say, "All power to the sciences, but"—and what follows the "but" is Kierkegaard's own philosophy. In particular, God and religion are not objective. There are no proofs for God's existence. Such an attempt is, as I argued last lecture, really ludicrous. You cannot use the evidence of, say, miracles to prove God's existence, because as David Hume had argued some centuries before, basically the idea of a miracle already presupposes an exception to the laws of science. What Kierkegaard would certainly want to say is we are not talking about an exception to the laws of science; we are talking about a realm in which scientific explanation doesn't even get a foothold.

There has been an enormous move in the last few centuries (and one can look at this in grand historical terms). For many years, religion dominated science, and science always had to defend itself in the court of religion. Around the 17th century, those power relations got turned upside down, and by the 18th and 19th centuries, the period of Enlightenment and the period during which Kierkegaard is writing, religion had to defend itself in the court of science.

So what you got were arguments to show that what the Bible says might be true, scientifically. Here is a fast example. In Exodus, we read the story about Moses leading his people across the Red Sea, which miraculously parted at his command with the aid of God. That if anything in the Old Testament is a miracle—is certainly a miracle. But, meteorologists have used computer modeling to go back the appropriate amount of time—it is roughly 1000 B.C.—and what they have found is there was a set of conditions operative in the Middle East at that time such that the Red Sea may have been at very, very low tide—almost dry. It would have been easily possible for people, especially on foot, to cross. If you tried to follow them in heavy metal chariots you would very likely sink into the sand and drown in what water was there.

I don't know how plausible that is, but I want to point out what it does to the religious notion of "the miracle." It undermines it. By making it plausible, it no longer becomes a matter of faith. It becomes a matter of scientific evidence. This whole attempt at apologetics is something that Kierkegaard would utterly dismiss, because again, it mixes the subjective and the objective realms. Or, to take a more recent example which I alluded to at the end of the last lecture, to look at creation as something which must be in some way reconciled with scientific method—whether through the now standard idea of taking Genesis and interpreting the days in terms of eons, stretching the time so that evolution may have time to do its work within the context of Genesis; or creation science, which tries to use scientific methodology to prove something about the proof of Genesis. Again, it is a grand strategic mistake. Faith is faith. Science is science. The important thing is not to mix them.

Faith is the realm of personal meaning. It is the realm of subjectivity. I said before that it might be simply a matter of an uninteresting contingency whether there are any Christians in the world besides oneself, because the entire meaning of being a Christian is not social, not doctrinal, but personal. It has to do with the commitments you have made and where you put passion.

The idea of Christianity as Kierkegaard understands it is clearly in this realm. So, too, in a more problematic way is the realm of ethics. I'll talk about this at length in the next lecture but the realm of ethics is also a matter of commitment. This is something that philosophers have often tried to resist. There was a book about 20 years ago called *The Retreat to Commitment*, and there was an argument for objective or absolutist ethics. There are a great many attempts in philosophy, going all the way back to the Greeks, to defend what is right and what is correct in terms of some sort of natural facts—something that can be shown scientifically.

In Kierkegaard's own time, the philosophy of "utilitarianism" made it look as if all ethical decisions could be reduced to basically psychological decisions about what made people happy, what made them miserable, what helped them, harmed them, and so on. What Kierkegaard will want to say is that ethics, too, is in the realm of subjectivity, and while there might be in a very important sense rational rules about what it right and wrong (and he did believe in those), nevertheless, accepting the idea of being an ethical person or adopting the moral point of view—this too is going to be a subjective decision and it is not prone to scientific proof or evidence.

The notion of existence is very tightly connected with this notion of ethics, and Kierkegaard distinguishes in one of his most challenging and authoritative texts called *The Concluding Unscientific Postscript* (by the way a rock band that Woody Allen once formed had that name)—the idea of the ethically existing individual as opposed to the merely objective individual. One can make this distinction in a great many ways. Today, for example, we might distinguish between the person as a medical object and the person as a person with feelings and cares and values and emotions. In Kierkegaard's time, the important distinction was responsibility and making decisions and, of course, making commitments. The idea of existing, the notion of existence is absolutely essential to him. It has to do with "taking hold" of one's life; making decisions. It has to do with being passionate. It has to do with understanding the drama of life.

Kierkegaard distinguishes between really existing and what he calls merely "so-called existence." There is a sense in which everyone exists. In fact, this table, this coffee cup—they exist but not in a very interesting sense. I exist, I hope, in a very different way. It is not just because I am conscious, because consciousness can very easily be tranquilized into a kind of mere herd mentality. I exist because I am passionate, because I make decisions, because I in some sense have taken hold of my life. Kierkegaard makes the rather rude distinction between such people, among whom he certainly included himself, and the "herd," the "mob," the general run of what he called "Christendom"—people who did not make decisions, people who went along with the flow of the crowd, people who just did what they were supposed to do. There is a sense in which existence is a distinctively exciting notion, and that is going to be very important for everything we are going to do from now on.

Kierkegaard gives a little analogy. He says imagine a man who jumps on an untamed stallion and essentially just commits himself to hanging on, and trying to somehow not so much tame the stallion as just go with and stay with the stallion, however it should run, jump and so on—a very exciting prospect. Compare that to a fellow who falls asleep in a hay wagon. There is a sense in which one might talk about his riding (or actually Kierkegaard uses the word driving—this is before cars)—the idea is that there is a sense in which he, too, might be called a horseman, but he is asleep. He just goes where the horse wants to take him. There is no excitement, and if you want to talk about commitment at all, it is just minimal commitment to stay in the seat and not fall over while the horse is doing what it is doing. That is the way most people live, Kierkegaard says. Most people are asleep at the wheel. Most people do what the crowd has them do. But, they don't do what they are supposed to do. What they don't do is they don't take a risk. They don't take chances.

Again, that idea that I should find a truth for which I can live and die. It is finding that stallion, which for Kierkegaard was religion. Think of it in a different way—there is a sense in which the question, "How should I live?" has to be answered in terms of one's own propensities, and one's own psychological subjectivity. Talking about risk might sound a little grandiose for a man whose most dramatic gesture during his lifetime was breaking off his engagement, but as always with Kierkegaard, what we are talking about is "inwardness." What we are talking about is how a person lives emotionally and taking emotional risks.

He says over and over again that whether one really exists, whether one is really a true Christian is something that can't be—in a way, it doesn't matter—whether it is discernible "from the outside," what counts is inwardness. Kierkegaard takes the whole mark of subjectivity to be feelings. There is a complication here and something that we are going to have to deal with several times in these lectures; that is, on the one hand, talking about feelings, emotions, passions, which we typically think of in terms of their involuntariness—they're just happening to us—in general, we think of things that take over us. On the other hand, the key to subjectivity for Kierkegaard is commitment, where commitment is clearly and straightforwardly something we must do and take upon ourselves. So, to talk about passionate commitment might easily be construed by many philosophers as a kind of contradiction.

The idea of feeling very strongly about something inside and committing yourself to something absolutely on the inside, but not showing it—not showing good evidence in one's expressions and gestures and so on—but more importantly, from one's actions, is something that many philosophers would reject. They would say to be passionate is to take vigorous action. For Kierkegaard, the most powerful passions are precisely those that seem to involve no action as such at all. To resolve this particular paradox there are a number of steps one can take. The one I want to take, I think, is perhaps the most radical one, and I think it is pretty central to a great many of these philosophers.

I will say it rather bluntly to begin with. It is the idea that our passions, our emotions in general, not necessarily all feelings, are much more within the sense of our control and much more prone to our decisions than philosophers, psychologists, and common sense often make them out to be. When you fall in love, for example—and to begin, that phrase "falling in love" really sounds like something that happens to you like falling in a hole—when you fall in love, I would argue that a good part of that is making a sequence of very important decisions, starting with the decision to act on what you might interpret as the chemistry you have with someone else, to deciding whether or not to pursue a relationship from one date to another, deciding whether or not to kiss, deciding whether or not to say, "I love you." In general, I think one can say that while there certainly is a kind of involuntary aspect to passion, to emotion, there is a lot more by way of commitment and choice than philosophers, in general, have often suggested.

Kierkegaard, I think, can resolve this seeming contradiction between commitment on the one hand, and passion on the other, by accepting some such notion. When he talks about passionately throwing oneself into a way of life, when he talks about making a passionate leap of faith, part of what he is talking about is the idea of making commitments, such that one is choosing the passions and emotions that come along with them. Kierkegaard's own choice in terms of making a choice or commitment, taking charge of his life, was Christianity. Think about it. There is a sense in which no one can prove to you that Christianity is the truth about the world, or the true religion. What you have to do is yourself learn just enough about it and, more importantly, know enough about yourself to be able to make that choice. Once you make that choice, then you will find that the passions come along with it. The paradoxes of Christianity, for example, help provoke that passion. You decide to be a Christian, and you go to church or talk to people; or for Kierkegaard, really you can just sit at home and read the Bible very carefully and very sincerely.

Trying to cope with the various incomprehensibilities and paradoxes you meet there, that is what provokes the passion. Again, if it were simple common sense, you would read it and put it aside. What is most provocative about the Bible is not so much the miracles and it is not so much the narrative. Kierkegaard would say it is an overwhelming incomprehensibility, and at the same time, the overwhelming importance of what you are reading.

The idea is that first you commit yourself and the commitment might at first be simply a step. Once you have made that step, what you find is you encounter situations, or in the case of the Bible, you encounter passages that are going to provoke you and challenge you and that is going to require another step, another choice. What you will find is as you continue to make these steps, make these choices, to fight these obstacles, you are going to find that after a while you are deeply committed. The idea of a "leap of faith," while it is a wonderful phrase, in a way doesn't capture all of what Kierkegaard wants to get at here, because it might not be simply a jump/leap all at once. Many times—take falling in love, again, as an example—it is simply the step-by-step process. At the end of quite a number of steps, what you find is you have wholeheartedly committed yourself, even if at no point in the chain in decisions did you ever think that that is what you were doing. There is a sense in which making these decisions and having these passions may not be evident to anyone else. I have said that quite a few times. Let me make a little more plausible, that very notion.

If the emotion in question is perhaps rage, William James is certainly right when he tells us that it is impossible think of someone in a rage without at the same time imagining them prone to vigorous action. If the emotion in question is faith, what action is it that is relevant? There are some very unusual instances in which action may be obligatory, and I will talk about those in the next lecture. But, in general, the idea that in faith one is, as James would put it, "moved to vigorous action," doesn't make a lot of sense. The same might be said of love. The idea of love moving you to vigorous action (and let's leave aside some rather untoward suggestions)—you can love someone with all your heart, and this may never be discernible to them or to anyone else. This also emphasizes the importance of the personal nature of all these choices and passions.

There is an example in Camus that we mentioned just before we finished with him that comes from *Myth of Sisyphus*, where a man is talking in a phone booth and he is arguing or yelling or making gestures and he strikes us, as Camus puts it, as "absurd." Kierkegaard actually anticipates him with the same notion—the idea of people from the outside appearing absurd. He gives the example of making love, and again, let me say that making love here does not refer to having sex as it does today, but rather just to courting rituals of the sort that were very familiar up until the 1960s. Kierkegaard says you see another couple engaged in making love, and it is absurd. It is ridiculous. It doesn't mean anything. That is because you are not part of it. In religion, too, if what you do is basically take on a spectator's view—for example, you go to church and listen to the prayers and you see what is going on, you see that there is a God, and come to believe that the religion is a true one—there is a sense in which that is absurd. It doesn't mean anything in itself. The fact that you are acting along with other people and doing what you are supposed to, that is not what it is all about. Having faith is something very different.

The problem with organized religion is that what it does is it transfers what is a very personal experience to something which is, at its very heart, purely institutional. In this, one can see Kierkegaard's Protestantism reacting against Catholicism, something which was a very common move of the day. Also, he wants to move against Lutheranism itself, which, as far as he was concerned, had become much too herdlike, much too organized, and for all of its talk about the inner spirit and the emphasis on individual freedom, nevertheless, it is still too impersonal, much too social, for his taste.

At one point, he talks about the monastery. While one thinks about him in reaction against a certain aspect of Catholicism, in another sense, he wants to say there was something that Catholicism had right, which Lutheranism has abandoned. Martin Luther often gets credit for, as Kierkegaard puts it, "breaking us out of the monastery." What Kierkegaard says is he wants to break back in. There is a sense in which the monastic life—the life in which one is devoted wholly to God in which such questions about marriage and career as he faced don't arise—in a way, that is the ideal Christian life.

At the same time, he wants to say there is no "correct" form of Christianity, and because he so de-emphasized ritual and social institutions there is no true church, there is no correct way to behave, but it remains completely within. It is the religious person himself who must decide what kind of religion is suitable for him. I mentioned before that when Kierkegaard talks about religion and uses that general term, it almost always means Christianity, and Lutheranism in particular. I think it is very important to say that most everything that he says could be translated pretty easily into almost any other religion you like.

What is important is that it must not pertain to a kind of objectivity. It must have subjective forms. It must have some sense in which one must make a leap, or at least a series of choices to accept it. It can't simply be a tribal religion, in the sense of a religion which you belong to just because you are a member of the tribe. Nevertheless, I think of Buddhism as a fairly radical example. It seems to me that what Kierkegaard is saying about the religious life and religious choices can be very readily translated into something like a Buddhist ethic, as well. Going even further afield, in China, if you look at a religion like Daoism—not so much Confucianism, but Daoism certainly—one can make a fairly clear argument that committing yourself, and committing yourself possibly step-by-step through your choices, and passionately throwing yourself into the religion—this is the way it should go.

I have friends who have converted to Buddhism and to Daoism, and as I now retrace their steps in my mind, I can see that what they were doing was following a very Kierkegaardian recipe. They felt this enormous subjective hunger for something they usually call "spirituality." They didn't find it in their native religion. They had read some Buddhism, read some Daoism— were fascinated by it. That in itself was not a choice or a commitment, except in a very minor way. When they, for example, would go to join a monastery or when they would undertake a long series of ritual transformations, what they were doing was, in effect, making just that leap of faith that Kierkegaard talks about.

Under what circumstances should you make such a choice? As soon as I use the word "should," I have undermined my own point. Kierkegaard wants to say there is never a "should" about this, much less an objective thought. The idea is that people have needs. These needs vary. Kierkegaard doesn't speculate very much about where the needs come from, although in his case, I think we can fairly safely say it comes from his upbringing—from his rather neurotic father, from the sense of enormous guilt and this sense of inadequacy that he got as a young man. It has to do with his unhappiness and the idea that he was keen not on becoming a happy person (something he tried and decided was not for him), but rather his being so keen to find a truth for which you can live and die—his being so keen to find something that he could wholly devote himself to.

Suppose you are not like Kierkegaard. Most of us are not. What does he have to say to us? You could just read the whole thing as rather complicated autobiography, as rather fancy philosophical language, but I think that would be to misunderstand it thoroughly. Kierkegaard writes in a remarkably varied way. Some of his philosophy is almost a parody of the Hegelian form, with all of the Hegelian language and its obscurity. Much of its philosophy, especially the stuff he writes just for himself, is aphoristic. It is very simple. It is almost like little sayings and reminders about how one should live one's life.

The idea is that as we read this stuff and we become more and more moved as good readers always are by the emotions of the author, what we find is that we become seduced. That is language that Kierkegaard takes very seriously. You can't argue someone into religion. You can't argue someone into existence. What you can do is provide them with enough of the sensibility, so that what you do is get them of their own volition to come along with you. That is what seduction is all about. What Kierkegaard is doing to us is (as Clamence does to us in *The Fall*) he is seducing us into joining him in his way of thinking.

Kierkegaard's Existential Dialectic
Lecture 9

Every time you satisfy a desire, a new one takes its place. So, if the aim of the aesthetic life is satisfaction, there is a sense in which this is impossible. There is always frustration. There is always dissatisfaction.

In conscientious contradiction to Hegel's philosophy, Kierkegaard develops an "existential dialectic." Hegel developed a grand historical "dialectic," proving that history and humanity have an ultimate purpose, a pervasive rationality. Kierkegaard develops his "existential dialectic," a personal dialectic with no ultimate purpose, no rational direction. In Hegel, history develops through conflict, an idea later echoed in Marx. But Kierkegaard's dialectic is solely about the individual. We are faced with various choices, various "modes of existence" or "lifestyles." Although each mode of existence might dictate its own priorities or rationality, there is no reason or rational standard for choosing one rather than another. Kierkegaard distinguishes three such modes: the aesthetic, the ethical, and the religious.

The aesthetic mode of existence is the life of pleasure, of desire and satisfaction. Unlike many philosophers, Kierkegaard saw this mode—or its refusal—as a choice. The aesthetic mode might be exemplified in the life of Don Juan, the Spanish libertine. (Kierkegaard's favorite opera was Mozart's *Don Giovanni*.) Don Juan pursued his own pleasures, without consideration for others. He lived a life devoted to personal satisfaction. But the aesthetic life need not be so vulgar. Mozart himself could also be seen as living the aesthetic life. He lives in pursuit of the ideal satisfaction of beauty, to be found (or expressed) in the perfect piece of music. Nevertheless, the aesthetic life depends on personal satisfaction. The problem with the aesthetic life is its tendency to boredom. One becomes jaded with the very pleasures one pursues. Thus, one becomes insatiable, and the aesthetic life becomes self-defeating (Kierkegaard's own youthful experience). As in *Sisyphus*, the repetition is numbing. Goethe writes in *Faust*: "from desire I rush to satisfaction; from satisfaction I leap to desire." Thus, there is no aesthetic satisfaction.

The ethical mode of existence is the life of duty. The choice of being ethical is, for Kierkegaard, not itself a rational choice. Kierkegaard follows the moral philosophy of Immanuel Kant by insisting on the centrality of duty and moral principle. Kierkegaard also believes, like Kant, in the universality of reason, but with a subtle twist. Reason is universal in the realm of ethics, but not outside it. The ethical mode is defined by universal moral principles and consideration for the well-being of others. It is altruistic in the sense that it is other-directed rather than concerned with one's own satisfaction. The exemplar is Socrates, who died rather than compromise his virtue. To choose the ethical life is to choose to live rationally, but one does not rationally choose the ethical life. The ethical life has limits and frustrations, however, given the overwhelming number of injustices in the world. Thus, the urge to good also becomes self-defeating, as in compassion "burnout."

The aesthetic mode of existence is the life of pleasure, of desire and satisfaction.

The religious mode of existence has as its basis the belief in God. Kierkegaard seems to have paid little attention to religions other than Christianity. By Christianity, he means a somewhat constrained, "fundamentalist" version of Lutheranism. The religious life also includes aspects of the ethical life (Judeo-Christian morality), but conflict may exist between the ethical and the religious. This conflict is exemplified in the story of Abraham, which presents an intolerable dilemma to someone who both believes that God's word is ultimate and has a need to obey the moral rules. One of the most obvious moral rules, against killing your own children, is called into question by God's command. Kierkegaard describes the necessity for continued faith in such a dilemma as a "teleological suspension of the ethical." ∎

Essential Reading

Solomon, *Existentialism*, pp. 3–28.

One of Kierkegaard's most accessible books is *Either/Or*, 2 vols. The most systematic view of his religious conception of subjectivity is *Concluding Unscientific Postscript*. For the significance of Kierkegaard's thought in the broader context of Western thought, see MacInytre, *After Virtue*.

Introductory Questions to Consider

1. Kierkegaard discusses three "modes" or "styles" of existence—the aesthetic, the ethical, and the religious. Which are you? What does this mean? In what sense have you "chosen" this lifestyle? Does it make sense, according to Kierkegaard, to say that "some days I am x, other days I am y"?

2. According to Kierkegaard, is there a rational basis on which one can decide which of these three modes of existence to embrace, which one is right, which one is "right for you"?

Advanced Questions to Consider

1. For Kant, ethics begins with the autonomous, rational individual, who dispassionately determines what duty requires and acts accordingly. For Hegel, on the other hand, ethics begins with the community, which imbues its citizens with its ethical "substance"; the citizens in turn define themselves by the community's terms. Would Kierkegaard embrace either of these positions? If not, what would his criticism of each position be?

2. Kierkegaard asserts that "boredom is the root of all evil." Which mode of existence does he believe is most susceptible to it? Explain. Is Kierkegaard suggesting that certain modes of existence run up against their own internal contradictions? What would they be, in each case?

3. What does Kierkegaard mean by the "teleological suspension of the ethical"? Is he suggesting that the ethical and religious modes of existence necessarily come into conflict? Consider the foundation of ethics for those who look at the world from a highly religious perspective. Could Abraham have consistently rejected God's command in favor of his ethical precepts?

Kierkegaard's Existential Dialectic
Lecture 9—Transcript

Kierkegaard's rejection of Hegel might be viewed along two different dimensions. On the one hand, there is Kierkegaard's thorough rejection of Hegel's collective notion of the idea that the individual is unimportant. Second, Hegel's notion of spirit was distinctive in that it was firmly historical. One has said that Hegel invented history. This is an exaggeration. There is a sense in which there was history back among the Greeks, Herodotus and Thucydides. People have been writing history for thousands of years.

There is a sense in which Hegel developed an idea which only really became manifest in the 19th century. It was the idea that history has a purpose; history is the evolution of something. This manifested itself 50 years later in Darwin. In Hegel it pretty much was confined to the human, and the idea that the human spirit was something that evolved over huge amounts of time. Hegel went back to the ancient Greeks; he even went back to the Chinese and talked about how this human spirit developed over history in this kind of massive non-individualistic way. Kierkegaard rejects the second dimension too, and for many of the same reasons that he rejects the first. He rejects the emphasis on spirit, as opposed to the emphasis on the individual, because it leaves out what he and many people following him would say is most important; that is, that philosophy should tell you how to live your life. You personally. That means, ultimately, it comes down to the ethically existing individual.

Second, the idea of understanding this purpose of history—something which Hegel very dramatically developed—and the idea is that history has evolved to the point where we understand ourselves as universal spirit. That historical dimension is something that Kierkegaard also wanted to reject, because after all, wherever we are on the historical trajectory doesn't really help us make the kind of decisions we have to make. Hegel called this historical development, this "purposiveness" by the rather exciting Greek name "dialectic." One might say that Hegel's philosophy is, among other things, about the historical dialectic that shows us where we've come from, where we are going, and where we are. Kierkegaard, by contrast, also takes the notion of a dialectic but he makes it strictly personal. He calls it an "existential dialectic." The idea is that while there may well be the kind of interplay that Hegel talked about in great detail in history, there is also, and more importantly, a kind of interplay within each and every individual.

The notion of dialectic itself is fascinating. It gets traced back to the Greeks. It is a Greek word. Plato and Aristotle often talked about it. It is often said that the dialectic in one rather banal translation is simply a conversation. In its proceeding through history, through philosophy, the dialectic takes on a much more dramatic sensibility. It is not just a conversation, but a confrontation. In particular, Hegel's thesis was that history proceeds through one mode of conscious, one way of thinking, one way of living, in conflict with another until the conflict itself produces a kind of offspring—which may be a synthesis of the two antitheses, or it may be something else entirely. The idea is that history develops. It develops, in particular, through conflict. It is an idea which was picked up by Kierkegaard's exact contemporary Karl Marx, who turned Hegel's historical intellectual dialectic into something that was much more material and sociological.

In Kierkegaard, the idea of a dialectic has not to do with warring forces in history. It has to do not with warring ideas as such, but rather it has to do with what goes on in a subjective individual as he or she tries to make the decisions that are going to define his or her life. The personal dialectic is one that is existential in precisely the sense that it has to do with this notion of existence taking hold of one's life, making commitments, passionately throwing oneself into one way of life or another. Kierkegaard talks about modes of existence, or you might even say (he uses a term like this) there are lifestyles (that term is a little corrupted from California overuse). The idea is that there are different ways of living. In addition to making the particular decisions we make about what to do or how to act, we also make some very general, broad decisions about how we are to live.

Just to take a kind of homey example for us, deciding to join the marines would be choosing a lifestyle—choosing a mode of existence. There is a sense in which one simple decision can get you in. But no simple decision can get you out. There is a sense in which once you have entered into this lifestyle, you are truly committed, and once you have entered into the lifestyle, there are all sorts of structural and institutional reasons why you stay in that lifestyle.

Getting married—and let's think of it in a 19th century context rather than a 20th century context—is to choose a lifestyle. As you can guess from what little I have told you about Kierkegaard's autobiography, it is going to be the major example of his notion of a dialectic—whether or not to get married. It is not simply a choice of what do we do for the next few years, but really is a question of what sort of person do I want to become?

The important point here is that there is no rational standard for such choices. In other words, it is strictly in the realm of subjectivity, not objectivity. In Hegel, the dialectic was, in an important sense, objective. It was rational. So, by understanding this trajectory of history, one would understand not just the way things have been, but one would understand the way things in some sense have to go.

There is no such notion in Kierkegaard that choosing between lifestyles— choosing for example to be a religious person or an atheist, choosing whether to be an ethical person, or rather an immoralist—all this is a matter of choice. What he gives us, perhaps over simply, are three different modes of existence—three different lifestyles. The important point is again that there is no rational way of choosing among them. It is simply a matter of some objective choice.

The three styles are, very quickly: something he calls the aesthetic (As I indicated in the first lecture, the aesthetic to him refers primarily to the life of pleasure. It refers to the idea that one lives for satisfaction. I want to talk about that in some detail in a few minutes.); the second lifestyle is called the ethical (The ethical life is basically the life of—as you would guess—morality. It is doing your duty, fulfilling your obligations, keeping your promises, being a good person, caring about the welfare of others as well as yourself.); the third lifestyle, needless to say, is the religious life. Kierkegaard juxtaposes these against one another and says that it is a choice that we have to make.

With regard to the aesthetic, one might argue that this is not a choice. It is simply natural. There have certainly been a great many philosophers—the utilitarians, who are more or less Kierkegaard 's contemporaries, would be one example—who would say that pleasure is the natural end or purpose of human activity. On the other side, avoidance of pain (sort of negative pleasure) is the purpose, the aim of human activity. This is true not only of human beings; it is true of virtually all creatures, certainly of all creatures of any sophistication. Consequently, to talk about it as a choice really doesn't make any sense. It is just what people do. Lots of philosophers would say that it is simply a matter of logic—a kind of conceptual truth that people do what they want to do. People do what will give them satisfaction, or what they think will give them satisfaction. People do what will give them pleasure or help them to avoid pain. It is just natural; it is not a choice at all.

Thinking about Kierkegaard's life, we realize what it means to say that it is a choice. True, Kierkegaard discovered in his year of libertinism with his friend Hans Christian Andersen that the life of pleasure was not for him. That wasn't just a recognition. It was not just saying, "I am a person who is anhedonic. I am a person who doesn't enjoy enjoying himself." It is rather making a decision that you are going to live one kind of life rather than another. One can imagine Kierkegaard—and certainly one knows lots of people who are similarly anhedonic, who don't enjoy themselves very much resolving to learn to enjoy themselves—taking all sorts of great steps, often overstepping boundaries precisely in order to enjoy themselves when they do not now. Kierkegaard takes the opposite tack and says, "I am not enjoying myself. Maybe this is telling me something important about myself, and what I am supposed to do." So, he decides (and it is a decision) not to pursue pleasure.

The aesthetic life, in general, can be defined in terms of not so much the pursuit of pleasure and the avoidance of pain, even though that is a very important part of it. After all, the very word "aesthetic" comes from the word in Greek having to do with feeling. It also has to do with something broader, having to do with the notion of satisfaction. One might say that the aesthetic is a life devoted to personal satisfaction. It is not necessarily ethical, although I should add that it is not necessarily unethical. It is not necessarily unreligious either. It is a question of priorities. To choose the aesthetic life is to decide that your personal satisfaction is the most important thing for you.

Kierkegaard has an example—a rather controversial example—of the aesthetic life. One of his favorite operas was *Don Giovanni*, Mozart's great opera. I am often fascinated by the thought that before you had record players and CDs and cassettes and the Walkman and so on that people would hear their favorite piece of music perhaps a half dozen times in their lifetime. That is really kind of striking. Anyway, Kierkegaard saw *Don Giovanni* every chance he got. He loved the opera, and there is a sense in which the character of Don Juan plays a role throughout his philosophy. When he writes, for example, about seduction with reference; for example, to seducing his readers, when he writes about seduction in a rather straightforward sexual sense, it is Don Juan that he has in mind. If you think about, "Who was Don Juan?" the first answer is he was a man who pursued his own pleasures quite to the exclusion of any real consideration of other people. According to the libretto, it was a thousand and three in Spain alone. He couldn't have cared that much about any one of them. They were simply used. Thinking of the opera, you realize that not only is he callous about the women that he sleeps with, he is indifferent to human life. When he has to sacrifice the father of one of his conquests, he does so without even a pang of conscience.

As I said, it is not necessary to be immoral to be aesthetic. Nevertheless, as a question of priorities, it is a matter of, when the chips are down, choosing your own satisfaction over anything else. The aesthetic life is not necessarily quite so vulgar. As a contrast to Don Juan, let me take as an example Mozart himself. Mozart was also an aesthetic. Here we move from the early 19th century meaning of the word "aesthetic," having to do with feeling, to the later 19th century meaning of that same word, where it has to do with art and artistry.

Mozart was aesthetic in the latter sense, and if you accept the story in *Amadeus*—let's exclude Mozart's behavior under the piano and just talk about his behavior on top of the piano—basically, Mozart was someone who lived for satisfaction too. His satisfaction wasn't the conquest of women. His satisfaction was, in each case, the composition of a perfect piece of music. It may well have been that it also satisfied the standards of the time; that it was, in fact, in tune with the culture. The truth was that Mozart was satisfying himself. If he wrote an imperfect piece of music, he was the one who would toss it away. If he wrote a perfect piece of music, he was satisfied and often regardless of how it played for his audience. You might think of Mozart, too, as aesthetic in the sense that he lived for satisfaction.

The problem, Kierkegaard says, is that the aesthetic life, like any life, has its own liability. That liability is most obvious in the question of boredom. Don Juan is a good example. There is a sense in which one imagines what it would be like to have so many sexual partners, and there is a point where one wants to say, "How can he tell them apart? Isn't one just like the others?" Many writers on the Don Juan problem have come up with some rather extravagant metaphysical ways of expressing this. For example, the fact that Don Juan didn't love women—what he loved was *woman*.

All of this is a way of dancing around the real problem. The problem is when it's simply desire and satisfaction, there is a point where satisfaction becomes more and more difficult, becomes more and more all the same, where repeating something an indefinite number of times becomes inevitably tedious. Here we go back to Sisyphus, and Kierkegaard is very concerned with this question of repetition. He writes rather extensively about it and the ways in which one can prevent the repetition of the same from becoming totally boring, tedious. What he says is that essentially what Camus is later to say: one has to commit oneself—one passionately throws oneself into one's activities themselves. By so doing, one evades boredom, at least for a while. But, the truth is one can't do it.

Here Kierkegaard is presenting us with something that might sometimes be taken as a kind of objective psychological truth. But, I think that would be misreading him since he so strongly wants to emphasize the subjective side of this. Certainly, it was true of him, of most of the people he knew, and even without making it a point of scientific psychology, one can easily understand the logic of becoming jaded. One becomes tired of the pleasures that one has hitherto enjoyed. Or, to put it in a different way, one is never really satisfied. The great German poet Goethe in *Faust* writes, "from desire I rush to satisfaction; but from satisfaction, I leap to desire."

Every time you satisfy a desire, a new one takes its place. So, if the aim of the aesthetic life is satisfaction there is a sense in which this is impossible. There is always frustration. There is always dissatisfaction. In the end, there may well be only boredom—being jaded—at which point the one who has chosen the aesthetic life faces a crisis. The crisis is to continue in this self-defeating way, or to choose something else. Again, that all-important point: this is not a matter of logic, not a matter of rationality; it is simply a matter of trying to understand what one is feeling—what one feels that one needs out of life and making the appropriate choices. But one could, and one knows such people, stay in the aesthetic mode of existence even long after one is well past the possibility of satisfaction, even past the possibility of pleasure, where it is just a life of jaded cynicism and nothing else.

However, there is an alternative. The most immediate alternative is the ethical mode of existence, the ethical lifestyle. I said in the last lecture, perhaps a bit cryptically, that the ethical mode of existence is also on the side of subjectivity; it is an objective uncertainty. It is something that must be chosen and passionately committed to, and it is not simply something that can be proven by a philosophical analysis. Such proofs abound in philosophy. The most famous is by the great German philosopher Immanuel Kant. He tried to show that morality was nothing less than rationality itself. That still leaves an interesting question which Kant himself did not want to face. Why should I be rational? Why should I choose the ethical mode just because it is the rational mode? Couldn't I rather choose against rationality? Or could it be that the ethical mode is just, as one philosopher put it, a moral point of view? It is one point of view among many.

The idea that ethics is somehow objective, that there are truths about the world or truths about human nature that make it a compulsory choice, is something that Kierkegaard wants to reject, which is not to say that he rejects rationality in ethics. Rather, what he wants to say is that the choice of being ethical itself is not a rational choice. One can choose to be ethical or one can choose not to be ethical. Ethically, there is nothing much to say.

The ethical lifestyle can be rather simply defined in a number of ways. It can be defined as the life of duty, obligation. In one sense that takes us all the way back to ancient times—the idea in Aristotle for example, that one has to do what one is supposed to do. Or, Kant has a much more vigorous and rationalistic idea that what defines morality—what defines the ethical lifestyle—is defined by universal moral principles—principles of reason. Kierkegaard accepts this as his definition, and when he talks about morality, when he talks about ethics in the ethical style, what he is usually talking about is—directly or indirectly— ethics, morality as defined by Kant, categorical imperatives which tell us what our obligations, what our duties are—matters of reason, not matters of, for Kant, of subjectivity at all. But, very interestingly, they may be moral principles, which are universal by way of reason. But reason is here construed as internal to the ethical life. It is not something which transcends it in such a way that we can choose the ethical life as such, rationally. Rather, to choose the ethical life is to choose to be rational, which means to follow the moral principles as Kant set them out.

One might also say that the ethical life as opposed to the aesthetic life is other-directed in the sense that it is defined by concern for others. One example that Kierkegaard gives here is Socrates. Socrates is an interesting case here, too, because there is a sense in which Socrates, like Kant, was not particularly devoted to the idea of the well being of others so much as he was concerned with the kind of virtues (or in Kant, the kinds of moral principles) which are essential to morality or ethics itself. The idea is that to be a good person in Socrates's case is to be concerned with doing the right thing—with being virtuous above all else. Of course, the most dramatic single case in the history of philosophy—Socrates, when his virtue was challenged, when he was condemned to death by the Greek jury and essentially had a choice between violating his obligations or dying, what he chose was death—the idea of ethics here is something which is rational within, but not necessarily something which is rationally chosen.

Let's take an example—and the example is one that is absolutely essential to Kierkegaard's own life; consequently it plays a large role in his philosophy— suppose you are deciding whether or not to get married, and again I ask you to put yourself back into the middle of the 19th century instead of the much more casual notion of marriage we seem to have today. To decide whether or not to get married for Kierkegaard is to decide between two things. On the one hand, there is the aesthetic—the idea of trying to be happy, get pleasure out of life, be satisfied. On the other hand, there is the ethical where it has to do with obligation and duty.

One might draw this in a very different way. Kierkegaard, himself, tends to fudge this when he actually writes in detail about it. Suppose you saw the life of a male bachelor as the life of satisfaction, a life of aestheticism in the sense of just going after pleasure and satisfying your desires. By contrast, you saw marriage as a kind of realm of ethical duty. One talks rather horribly about the idea of conjugal duties—something that is done quite willingly as a bachelor seems to be a matter of obligation when you are married.

This distinction between the aesthetic and the ethical plays a rather large role in this instance. One might say that when one chooses whether or not to get married, what one is really choosing is a lifestyle—a mode of existence. To choose to be a bachelor is to remain more or less unconstrained, without obligation, free to do what one wants to do. To choose to get married is by contrast to choose a life of obligations and a sense in which there are all kinds of principles and rational ways of thinking about what one is obliged to do. Kierkegaard himself would say there is no rational way of making this choice. You have to look at yourself, you have to figure out what you want out of life, what kind of person you are, and then you have to make a leap. As we all know, getting married, no matter how passionate to begin with, is always a kind of leap of faith. One never knows exactly what is to follow, and one does it and takes one's chances.

Kierkegaard has a lot of powerful things to say about the ethical life, and, as I say, in a way he cheats a bit with the marriage question by in the end having a spokesperson he invents to talk in favor of marriage conclude with a discussion of marital bliss, which of course is basically an aesthetic notion to begin with. Here, what Kierkegaard is saying is you can have your cake and eat it too. You can get married, and if it is a happy marriage, you can be satisfied and get lots of pleasure and at the same time fulfill your duties. As I said, the important point is priorities. I guess the sort of sad question here is what are your obligations when you marriage goes sour? Certainly in the 19th century there was a very strong sensibility that you have obligations and your personal happiness and satisfaction is secondary.

The ethical life, too, has its liabilities. In this case, it is not going to be dissatisfaction. That is still an aesthetic notion, but it is still going to be a kind of frustration. We have all faced this. It is the idea that there are more wrongs in the world than can be righted, and we ourselves are very often helpless in the face of injustice.

There is a notion that has been circulating the last several years called compassion "burnout," and it applies to those of us who give rather heavily to charity. Basically, it has to do with receiving notice after notice. I find that I get maybe 500 solicitations a year, many of them from outfits which are essentially serving the same causes. For example, I am on about 10 different wildlife preservation lists. There is a point where you get tired. You get tired of making the decisions. It is not so much that you are unwilling to give, but just realizing you can't help everyone who needs help. One of the consequences in the larger society seems to be that, at least for a period, people were not giving any more because they were getting tired of the solicitations. They were getting tired of doing something, but not doing enough.

That is the problem with ethics. If you really devote yourself to the rational life of morality, if you devote yourself to the well being of your fellow human beings, you are always going to be frustrated by the fact that things don't usually work out right—precisely what Camus would later describe as the absurd.

There is another choice. Again, it is not a rational choice. It is a choice that one must make on the basis of one's own subjectivity. That is the religious way of life. What Kierkegaard has in mind here is Christianity; more particularly Lutheranism; more particularly his own personal interpretation of what that amounts to in terms of internal inwardness and subjectivity. There is a sense in which you might ask, "In what sense is this an exclusive choice? After all, isn't the whole Judeo-Christian tradition about ethics? Or, isn't the ethics just as important to it as the religious part?" There have been some recent philosophers, people who follow Kierkegaard, who have said, in effect, that we don't need the theology. You can be a good Christian if you just lead an ethical life. There is a question here in Kierkegaard. In what sense are the ethical and the religious to be opposed? He gives us a story.

The story is the story of Abraham. It involves what is probably the most horrible commandment in the Old Testament. It is when God tells Abraham that the son for whom he has longed for so long, and the son whom he has now brought up as a healthy young man, must be sacrificed as a proof of his faith. What was Abraham to do? On the one hand, there is no moral commandment more important than the commandment which says, in effect, you don't harm members of your family. At the same time, what could be more of a violation of a religious way of life than not obeying a direct order from God? Of course, God makes it come out okay. He stops the sacrifice before it takes place.

Kierkegaard says here is an instance in which the religious and the ethical go firmly against one another, and in the name of faith what Abraham has to do is what he calls "teleological suspension of the ethical." In other words, the religious has priority. The ethical does not. Abraham, like Kierkegaard, had made the leap of faith. So, too, Kierkegaard says, must we.

Friedrich Nietzsche on Nihilism and the Death of God
Lecture 10

Frederick Nietzsche, who died in the summer of 1900, might well be considered as the prophet of the 20th century. He anticipated much of what today is called "postmodernism," and a great many people have cited him as the end of the period of classical philosophy.

The watchword of Nietzsche's philosophy is "nihilism." This might be summarized, in his phrase, as "the highest values devaluing themselves." Among these values are truth, religion, and morality. Nietzsche himself, however, is no nihilist. His thesis is rather that the values we hold are themselves nihilistic, self-undermining. For Nietzsche, the ultimate value is life itself. The values he attacks are "anti-life" or "otherworldly." He rejects the preference for some other existence—whether it is heaven or the classless society—that is better than this one. His is a philosophy of aggressive acceptance of the world and ourselves.

Nietzsche's touchstone (as for so many German scholars in the nineteenth century) was the ancient Greeks. But the focus of Nietzsche's admiration was not the famous Greek philosophers Socrates, Plato, and Aristotle, whom Nietzsche saw as already "decadent." He admired instead the warriors of Homer's epics and the great Pre-Socratic tragedians. The philosopher he admired was Heraclitus with his "dark sayings." He says, "How they must have suffered to have become so beautiful." In Nietzsche's first book, *The Birth of Tragedy*, he suggested that "only as an aesthetic phenomenon can the world be justified." His moral philosophy is filled with warrior images and virtues.

In the realm of religion and morality, Nietzsche issues his harshest challenge. He repeats the (already classic) utterance "God is dead," an echo of Hegel and Martin Luther. This statement suggests not so much the truth of atheism as a diagnosis on the moral state of the modern world. Nietzsche offers us an alternative to Jesus in the form of the Persian prophet Zarathustra who, unlike Jesus, preaches "the this-worldly," not the "other-worldly." The statement also refers to a certain metaphysical picture of the world. It is a rejection of the "otherworldly." The "otherworldly" stance of religion can be traced back to Plato. This rage for unity manifests itself in monotheism but began with the Pre-Socratics. Nietzsche claims that reason itself can be an escape from life, again as in Plato: "Christianity is Platonism for the masses." Socrates endorsed "the tyranny of reason" and developed the vision of another, "truer" world of which this world is a mere shadow.

Nietzsche endorses a view that we might call "epistemological nihilism."

Nietzsche endorses a view that we might call "epistemological nihilism." He says, for example, "there is no truth" and our greatest "truths are only errors that we cannot give up." In many ways, he would seem to be a classical skeptic, except that he rejects the very ground and distinctions on which most skepticism is based. He rejects the distinction between the "true world" and the world of appearances as a form of the otherworldly. He defends "perspectivism," that is, the view that all our knowledge of the world (and of ourselves) is gleaned through one or another perspective, a particular point of view. Even science is just one of many points of view. There is no "objectivity" as such, no "facts," no unbiased point of view. Ideally, we should try to appreciate as many perspectives as possible. Using Kierkegaard's schema, Nietzsche adopts the aesthetic perspective. Nietzsche's view of truth is primarily pragmatic, anticipating later American philosophers. ∎

Essential Reading

Solomon, *Existentialism*, pp. 43–78. (For an overview, see *Continental Philosophy Since 1750*, "Nietzsche," pp. 111–126, or *From Rationalism to Existentialism*, pp. 105–139.)

Supplementary Reading

Nietzsche, *The Gay Science*, and *Twilight of the Idols* and *The Anti-Christ* (in *The Viking Portable Nietzsche*).

Two good short introductions are Stern, *Nietzsche*, in the Modern Masters series, and Tanner, *Nietzsche*, in the Past Masters series.

See also Kaufmann, *Nietzsche—Philosopher, Psychologist, Antichrist,* and Nehamas, *Life as Literature.*

Essays on Nietzsche's individual works can be found in Higgins and Solomon, eds., *Reading Nietzsche.*

Another general overview of Nietzsche's philosophy is *What Nietzsche Really Said*, by Solomon and Higgins. See also the Teaching Company lecture series *For the Love of Life: The Philosophy of Friedrich Nietzsche*, by Solomon and Higgins.

Introductory Questions to Consider

1. Was Nietzsche a nihilist? If not, why did he reject conventional morality and religion? What values did he believe in?

2. Nietzsche proclaims, "God is dead." What did he mean by this? Do you agree with his diagnosis?

3. Why does Nietzsche so virulently attack Socrates? Of what does he accuse him? Of what does he see him as a symptom? What do you take to be Nietzsche's overall attitude toward Socrates—contempt or, perhaps, envy?

Advanced Questions to Consider

1. Describe Nietzsche's brand of "epistemological nihilism." Does he believe that there is ultimately no truth of the matter and that we are simply the kind of creatures who need to believe that there is? Does he believe that there is a truth of the matter but that we simply cannot know it? Or does he believe that the whole question is simply beside the point and that we debase ourselves by searching for it?

2. In what ways is Zarathustra a Christ-like figure? How does he differ from Christ? What does it mean that he continually fails to get his message across? What do you personally make of him?

Friedrich Nietzsche on Nihilism and the Death of God
Lecture 10—Transcript

Frederick Nietzsche, who died in the summer of 1900, might well be considered as the prophet of the 20th century. He anticipated much of what today is called "postmodernism," and a great many people have cited him as the end of the period of classical philosophy.

Nevertheless, Nietzsche is misunderstood. The watchword of his philosophy in one sense is "nihilism." Nihilism is a fairly new word and concept in 19th century philosophy. It came from Russia where it essentially referred to the rebellion of the younger generation against their elders. Nihilism in Nietzsche is a very important concept. He sees it as, as he puts it, "a specter that is haunting Europe"—a phrase which we hear elsewhere as well. He defines nihilism in his notes as "the highest values devaluing themselves." The mistake that people make is they assume because Nietzsche talks about nihilism so much, because Nietzsche is so well known as an attack philosopher, a negative philosopher, that Nietzsche ends up defending nihilist thinking.

The truth is that Nietzsche really is against nihilism. He sees it as the great danger for modern culture. He is worried about the 20th century because he thinks that at that point nihilism could very well take over. Oddly enough, where he identifies the nihilist tendencies in society is precisely in those realms where many thinkers, including those today, would say that we find the bulwark against nihilism, mainly in religion and morality. It is not, Nietzsche says, as if religion and morality give us values, but quite the contrary. Religion and morality take our values away. To put it in a different way, the traditional values, the values of the Judeo-Christian tradition, are themselves nihilistic. How are we supposed to understand this?

Throughout Nietzsche's works, there is without a doubt the assertion of value. Nietzsche is defending values. He says we can't live without values and there is one value which has absolute status. That is the value of life itself. What he means by this is something that has to be interpreted in a number of different ways. It doesn't just mean survival is the only important thing. Quite to the contrary, there are many things more important than survival for the sake of life. What works as a theme throughout all of Nietzsche's works, and what explains his rather rabid attacks on Christianity and religion in general, is the attack on what he calls the "otherworldly"—the idea of some other existence which is better than this one.

Nietzsche's philosophy is very much a philosophy of aggressive acceptance—acceptance of this world, acceptance of yourself, of your faith. For example, the Christian notion of the otherworld, the heaven to which we can aspire, is to him a notion that utterly subtracts from the importance of this world and of this life. To take a different kind of theme, the socialists who were very active around Nietzsche's time, who promised a different kind of otherworld—this world in one sense, but a distant future in which things would be much better than they are now—that, too, is a kind of rejection of this existence and its attempt to escape life.

For Nietzsche, the ancient Greeks were a kind of a touchstone. As a student, Nietzsche showed great talent in the classics, and he ultimately did a degree and taught as a professor in the classics. He greatly admired the ancient Greeks. It is important to note that the Greeks that he so admired were not the ones that were the idols of most philosophers: Socrates, Plato and Aristotle. To the contrary, Nietzsche often attacked Socrates, and sometimes, rather viciously. What he admired were the philosophers who came before Socrates, the so-called "Pre-Socratics." In particular, he admired the philosopher Heraclitus, who, with his "dark sayings," gave a kind of inspiration to sages over the years.

He said of the Greeks in general, "How much they must have suffered to become so beautiful." Nietzsche's conception of the Greeks was that they did not have a notion of the afterlife. They really didn't have much of a notion of the future in the sense that we, since Hegel, have had notions of the future. Rather, they accepted life with all of its suffering in that what they became was a people who were immensely admirable. To talk about them as happy is, in a way, to miss the point. The notion of an aesthetic existence, the idea of there being a beautiful people, is for Nietzsche the highest praise. He goes back to the early tragedians, people like Sophocles. He goes back to Homer and Homer's two great epics, *The Odyssey* and *The Iliad*. He goes back to Heraclitus. From them all, he pulls an interpretation of early Greek life and thought which is very much at odds with Plato and Aristotle. He says in his first book, which is about the ancient world, called *The Birth of Tragedy*, he says "only as an aesthetic phenomenon is the world justified."

One can easily appreciate how this would run against many of the religious notions that were prevalent in his time, and also against many of the more ethereal philosophical notions such as the philosophy of Hegel, which were also very well known when Nietzsche was writing.

A couple words about Nietzsche himself: He was a man who came from a family of, interestingly enough, all Lutheran preachers. His father died when he was still a child, and he was raised by his mother and maiden aunts, and eventually by a sister, all of whom were rather devout Christians. He was surrounded by Christianity. He grew up in a small German town, and there is a sense in which the kind of bourgeois pomposity and righteousness of that kind of Christianity stuck in his craw.

He often talks in very belligerent, I would say, downright bloody, and often cruel images. He is again known as the great attacker and so on. But, the extent to which he says that his heroes are in some cases the most renowned warriors of ancient times, and other times some of the more infamous tyrants of modern times, gives Nietzsche a kind of picture which I think is very often misleading and distorting. He says, for example, perhaps his most famous line today, "That which does not kill me makes me stronger." The context in which he says that, in fact, what he is referring to is his own very frail health, and he is referring more importantly to the state of his ideas. It is often taken in a kind of "Conan the Barbarian" sense. In fact, I think that is quoted in the movie. Basically, the idea is that we have to separate Nietzsche's very enthusiastic, excited, sometimes overbearing prose—some of the most beautiful prose ever appearing in philosophy—from his philosophical ideas, which, in fact, are sometimes much more benign.

One of the most famous of Nietzsche's many outrageous statements is the claim that "God is dead." It is often lampooned and parodied. To put it in perspective we should understand, first of all, that Nietzsche didn't make that up. Hegel, who was known as a religious philosopher, had in fact said, "God is dead" in some of his early, not very respectful writings. Martin Luther had said, "God is dead" as a way of talking about the state in which Christianity had to be understood. To understand it simply as a religious statement or an atheistic statement is to misunderstand the profundity of what Nietzsche is getting at.

First of all, "God is dead" refers not to a theological proposition; rather to the moral state of the modern world. One looks at the world and what becomes evident (and here Nietzsche joins forces with Kierkegaard, in many ways his opposite)—one sees that much of what is called "Christianity" in these small towns, and so on, really is a kind of stale hypocrisy. It is force of habit. It is mere (to use a word that both Nietzsche and Kierkegaard love) "herd" behavior. It is going along with everyone else. In Kierkegaard's term, it absolutely lacks passion and commitment. In Nietzsche's terms, it really lacks any moral sanction. It doesn't do anything. People can consider themselves good Christians, and nevertheless go out, cheat and steal in business, and feel as if going to work an hour a week somehow makes it all better.

The truth of it is, "God is dead," in the sense that we don't believe in him anymore even if we claim to. Contrary to Kierkegaard's aspiration, which is to re-invent and re-invigorate Christianity in his own terms, Nietzsche would just as soon be done with it. "God is dead" then also becomes a kind of statement about the future of the modern world. In one of his best and most encompassing books, *The Gay Science*, he has a madman appear in the marketplace who announces not only "God is dead," but "We have killed him." Interestingly, the people who are there watch him with amusement, laugh at him, make fun of him and say, "Where is God? He got lost. What happened to him?" The point is that God is dead in our world; and nevertheless we are yet incapable of understanding what we have done.

In his most famous piece of fiction, a kind of very excessive quasi-biblical parody which is called *Thus Spoke Zarathustra*, Nietzsche reintroduces a character from the ancient world, the founder of the religion Zoroastrianism—also the character who in many ways was responsible for an important piece of the Judeo-Christian tradition, namely the division between good and evil, a dichotomy which Nietzsche is going to be very concerned with in his philosophy. Zarathustra essentially invented that along with the Manachians, and he essentially said that the world is a battle of two different sets of forces.

Put in a different way, it is a way of saying that morality really requires a metaphysical picture. It isn't just a matter of subjective feelings, culture, or opinion. The difference between good and evil is something that is true of the world. Zarathustra, in this long book, essentially urges us to get over that dichotomy which he himself once introduced. He also urges us to get rid of these ideals of the otherworldly. If Zarathustra has a philosophy, it is Nietzsche's philosophy. Namely, it is this world and this life only that really count.

The notion of "God is dead" has a much more general meaning, though. This is where it becomes particularly important philosophically. There is a sense in which the monotheism of Judeo-Christian tradition is of a piece with a kind of monastic obsession that the ancient Greeks share as well. The beginning of philosophy in the West, often attributed to the first philosophers in the seventh and sixth centuries B.C., is basically the search for the one basic element, or using Aristotle's term, the one basic "substance" which makes up everything. You find this metaphysical obsession not just in Greece, but also in a place where Greek philosophy may have come from—toward India and South Asia — where in the notion of Brahman, for example, and Hinduism, there is also this emphasis on the oneness of the world.

There is this rage for unity that we have, and that rage for unity manifests itself among other places in our belief in the monotheistic God. It is interesting to note that in the Old Testament, it is not as if there is only one God. The ancient Hebrews pictured their God as opposed to other gods. For example, in some of the most famous stories in the Old Testament, it becomes a kind of contest to see which god is bigger and tougher and stronger than any of the others. With the kind of monotheism that has certainly come to define the Judeo-Christian tradition since, what we find is not just the emphasis on one God, but a kind of emphasis on one world, which Nietzsche wants to overcome.

It is a metaphysical picture that has all kinds of manifestations. It is in science. After all, Einstein, this century, died looking for a unified theory. It has always been the aim of science to give us not just truths, or true theories, in this realm or that, but to give us ultimately that single picture which would tie it all together. This is tied to Nietzsche's concept of the otherworldly, and this explains, too, why Nietzsche is so concerned to reject the great philosophers of the ancient world: Plato, Socrates, and Aristotle—Socrates, in particular.

Nietzsche's relationship to Socrates is very complicated. Ultimately, Socrates is his hero and he envies him. Nevertheless, he bitterly attacks him all the way through. The reason is because it is really Socrates who invents the notion of the "otherworld." That may sound a little strange because you think of the Egyptians, and you think of the earlier Greeks with their concept of Hades, and so on. There is a sense in which it is really Socrates who gets the sense of the soul in another world. Still robust, Socrates fantasizes, for example, in one of his early dialogues that he could go on doing philosophy forever as a pure soul.

What Nietzsche wants to say is, it is Socrates, because of his own hatred of life (and he goes into that in some detail), who insists that we think about other possibilities—other worlds. Plato follows him and turns this into one of the more sophisticated metaphysics in our tradition. But the basic idea of the otherworldly which leads quite directly into the Christian notion of heaven and hell is something that Nietzsche says now has to be put aside. What we have to do is understand our world in a different way.

He accuses Socrates, among other things, of a kind of tyranny of reason, introducing another plot which is going to be very central to Nietzsche's philosophy. I mentioned with Kierkegaard in particular, that to understand his concept of existence, of subjective truth, what was important was to particularly understand the importance of the passions. It is really the passions that make life meaningful. It is the passions that define us as who we are. It is an interesting question with that as a backdrop to ask where the emphasis—one might say the obsession—with reason in philosophy comes from. Nietzsche thinks he has found the source. It is Socrates.

Socrates was very unhappy, according to Nietzsche, with his world. He was very unhappy with the political state of Athens, but perhaps more personally, Nietzsche says outrageously, he was unhappy with his looks. He says in one of his last books, quite bluntly, "Socrates was ugly." Ugliness among the Athenians was virtually a refutation. It is an outrageous claim—something I will talk about later—that very idea of an *ad hominem* argument in philosophy.

The idea is that Socrates was looking for an escape. Consequently, what he did was he constrained his passions. He constrained himself and instead took everything that he spoke as a matter of reason. It was all in defense of reason. Nietzsche thinks that although this sounds perfectly secular and so on—after all, the Enlightenment was a rejection of religion in the name of reason—nevertheless, Nietzsche comes to say that reason itself can be its own kind of escape from life; its own sense of the otherworldly. As he says in one of his pithier aphorisms, "Christianity really is just Platonism for the masses."

All of which leads to the question about which Nietzsche himself really believes and what he thinks is true. I said that he defends life as the ultimate value, but he is so thoroughly skeptical, so thoroughly challenging, so thoroughly concerned with nihilism as a problem that one might very well ask, What room is left for truth?" Especially once you reject the idea of monotheism and that image of the one reality behind all of the appearances. There is a real question whether we can ever get beyond the appearances—whether we can ever, in fact, get something that is true.

There is a sense in which Nietzsche adopts something which we might call—with some caution—"epistemological nihilism." To put it in a blunt phrase, it is the idea that "there is no truth." This could be taken as a kind of total skepticism of the sort that we have seen in other philosophers earlier in history, but that is not Nietzsche's intent. In fact, one way to put it rather banally is to say there is no truth, but there are lots of truths.

What we call truth—in particular, what we call that special notion of truth that philosophers are seeking and that religious thinkers find in God or in Brahman—are just our interpretations of the world. He says, for example, that there are no facts. There are only interpretations. He says that what we call truth are just those "errors that we cannot give up." With reference to someone like Kant, he wants to say that when Kant talks to someone about necessary truths, *a priori* truths, truths that are essential in the very structure of the human mind, Nietzsche wants to say, "No. These are simply schemata that we can't throw off."

You might think of him as a classical skeptic, and certainly, he does have something in common with say, David Hume or the ancient skeptic Pyrrho, but in a way, it is more radical. Hume, for example, makes a big deal out of the distinction between reality and appearance. His skepticism basically says that all we can ever know are the appearances—namely our experience. There is no way we can get behind the experiences to the world itself. In fact, perhaps there is no world in itself. It is not coincidental that one of Hume's empiricist colleagues, Bishop George Berkeley in Ireland, actually argued that we don't need the notion of a material world. It is enough to believe that God puts our ideas in our heads, and that would give us the coherence of the experience we have. We experience a world, but that does not mean that there really is a world.

Nietzsche, by contrast, rejects the very distinction between appearance and reality. He has much to say about the origins of that notion of reality, and he ties it back to monotheism and the insistence on one God. He says once we have learned to reject that notion of a "true world" behind this one, what we are left with is not nothing by any means. We reject the true world, and we reject the notion of appearance at the same time. After all, what sense does it make to talk about appearances if we are not talking about appearances of something?

Nietzsche's nihilism, here, is really rather benign. It has to do with the idea of rejecting what gives rise to skepticism and what gives rise to these illusions of the otherworldly, and so doing, plant our feet very firmly on the Earth and say this world and this life is what counts.

What takes the place of these ancient and modern theories? Two things. They are very closely tied together. The first is a view which has been called (although Nietzsche does not call it this) "perspectivism." It is the idea that we always see things from a perspective. We never see things from a God's-eye point of view. We never see things objectively. Objectivity is just a set of constructions that we put on our experience from our perspective. There can be very different perspectives using different kinds of constructions.

For instance, there is the idea that science gives us the truth. But, science just gives us one perspective, and it has one set of rather rigorous standards and techniques to ensure that we get "the truth" from that perspective, but whether or not science is the perspective we ought to take up—as we said in Kierkegaard's existential dialectic—that is not itself a scientific question. You can't just say to be scientific is to be rational, because even if you were to accept that equivalent, you would still ask the skeptical question, "Why should I be rational?"

Does that leave us with nothing? Not at all. Nietzsche, in fact, was quite fascinated with science, and he spent a good deal of time reading it and very often kept some of his theories in terms of it. He realizes that science itself is just a perspective. The virtue of science, which in his early work he greatly praises, is precisely the fact that it completely accepts this. Science does not deal in dogma. Science deals in hypotheses. Science deals in experimentalism. Science deals in evidence. Consequently, within science, what we see is that we are urged to take first this hypothesis or perspective, and then that hypothesis or perspective.

Nietzsche is perfectly happy to say that the more perspectives we adopt and the more evidence that we gain from different perspectives, the closer we are to having a good perception of whatever it is that we are studying. He still will not say that true thing because he thinks there is no true thing. It is always the thing as perceived from different perspectives. Nevertheless, the more perspectives, the better.

This means not just scientific perspectives. There are also ethical or moral perspectives, there are religious perspectives, and, of course, there are aesthetic perspectives. In Nietzsche, using Kierkegaard's way of breaking down the world into three different basic choices, I think we can say without any hesitation with Nietzsche it is always the aesthetic way of thinking of things and looking at things that wins. One can contrast the aesthetic perspective and the scientific perspective.

There is an image that I sometimes use. A friend of mine who is a poet and I were sitting in a café once and there was a flower on the table, essentially, as he would put it, "stretching its petals toward the sunlight." I thought, wonderful, but I was a biologist. I knew about turgor and all these other things that would explain why the flower was doing what it did. I thought, here is my scientific explanation and here is his poetic explanation. Which one is better? Obviously, it depends what we need them for. In the context of having a cup of coffee, I was perfectly happy to say the aesthetic was preferable. Nietzsche often plays off perspectives against each other. In particular, he is going to play off moral perspectives against aesthetic perspectives, against scientific perspectives and, most importantly, against each other.

What does this add up to? What essentially determines what perspective we adopt and what doesn't? Here the second influence comes in. One has to be very careful about describing this because Nietzsche himself describes it in such mixed ways. When Nietzsche was writing most of these works in the 1880s, he is coming only a few decades after one of the most powerful books published in the 19th century. That is Charles Darwin's *Origin of Species*. Nietzsche knew the argument of this book quite well. It didn't have the kind of acceptance in Germany that it had at this point already in France and England. Nevertheless, there are Darwinist tendencies which manifest themselves very powerfully in Nietzsche's philosophy. One can look at this kind of epistemological thesis from that perspective with great results.

Imagine a group of creatures who believe that the future will be unlike the past, which means in practical terms if something has happened it is highly unlikely that it will happen again. This is a question which many great philosophers of modern times have grappled with, because it really is right at the basis of science. If you don't believe the future will be like the past, if you don't believe the experiment you did yesterday is repeatable tomorrow, if you don't believe the hypothesis that you established last week is going to continue to be true of the world in the future, then it is hard to imagine how you could have any science at all. There is a sense in which this basic claim, "The future will be like the past," has been defended by philosophers, especially, again, by Kant as one of the basic, necessary beliefs which lies at the very foundation of all possible knowledge.

Nietzsche has a different view. Imagine this group that believes, contrary to that, that the future will not be like the past, and you imagine now two groups: the group that believes the future will be like the past, and the group that believes the future will not be like the past. You imagine lightening strikes a lone tree in a clearing. The group that believes the future will be unlike the past takes hiding under the tree to be the safest place to escape from lightening. It is not hard to imagine which group will survive and which will not.

In other words, the things that we believe—even those things that we believe at the very foundations of knowledge, even those things that we believe as a matter of utter necessity as proven by the philosophers—in effect, it is a matter of contingency. We are a certain kind of creature living in a certain kind of world, and as those creatures, we are going to believe some things because (to use a different kind of language) it is practical. It is pragmatic.

I would argue that Nietzsche's view of truth here is very much akin to the one that is defended about 50 years later by some of the American philosophers, John Dewey in particular—that what is true has to do with what works in a certain context, and that is about as much as you can say. The idea of *the* truth that lies behind it all is something on which we should remain respectfully silent.

Nietzsche, the "Immoralist"
Lecture 11

> Nietzsche certainly contributed heavily to the understanding of himself as destroyer, as an immoralist, as an antichrist. He claims himself to be an "immoralist," and I think this is perhaps, more than anything else, one of the reasons why he is so often attacked in philosophy and outside of philosophy as a danger. The truth is that Nietzsche was generous, kind, courteous, trustworthy, a good friend, and my guess is he probably never did an immoral thing in his life.

Nietzsche claims to be an "immoralist," at war with morality. In fact, he was generous, compassionate, and courteous, even if he does denounce such virtues in his flamboyant writings. Nietzsche did not attack morality as such. Rather, he attacks one particular sort of morality that he considers nihilistic. That morality is Judeo-Christian and the bourgeois morality defended by Immanuel Kant and suggested by the categorical imperative.

Universal principles, says Nietzsche, don't take into account the vast difference between individuals. Does love extended to everyone—per the New Testament—still deserve to be called *love*? Whether Christianity or utilitarianism, such universal principles have ignored an old philosophy with great credentials, one of virtue and character. Like Aristotle, Nietzsche argues that the focus of ethics is on individual character—"what kind of a person am I?"

In his book *Beyond Good and Evil*, Nietzsche suggests that there are basically two perspectives on morality, Master and Slave. These names indicate both the origins and the temperament of these two moral positions. Both master and slave morality refer to historical positions in the ancient world of Greece and Rome. Master morality originated with the "masters" of the ancient world, the powerful aristocracies that ruled even in the periods before Greek democracy flourished. Slave morality originated with the literal slaves and servants of the ancient world, the powerless, those who were deprived, by force or because of their own infirmities, of the good life enjoyed by the aristocracy. Nietzsche sees Aristotle as belonging to a decadent culture, after the "golden age" and the Homeric period of warrior virtues.

Master morality is by temperament aristocratic and independent. It takes as the prototype of "good" the masters' own virtues. It puts its emphasis on personal excellence (*areté*). Slave morality is, in contrast, a temperament that is servile, reactionary, and resentful. It rejects the virtues of the masters as "evil." It is primarily characterized by its motivation, which is defensive. It is also vengeful, bitter, and filled with self-loathing Slave morality considers "good" to be denial of desire, abstention, and self-denial in general. From this tradition, we learn that the good is self-denial. And we are left with two distinct moral types: one based on excellence; the other, on self-denial.

Universal principles, says Nietzsche, don't take into account the vast difference between individuals.

The modern age can be characterized as the result of two thousand years of slave morality, but the master mentality never disappears. Master morality is sublimated. It appears as "bad conscience." This is a war within between pride and humility. It is also a conflict between excellence and mediocrity. Masterly strength and virtue never truly disappear. The master morality may be driven underground or forced to sublimate itself into other outlets (e.g., the Popes in the medieval church).

Nietzsche envisions an evolutionary possibility that would be the ultimate expression of master morality as "spiritualized" by way of slave morality. This possibility is called the *Übermensch*, and it is, perhaps, Nietzsche's most famous (or notorious) creation. ■

Essential Reading

Solomon, *Existentialism*, pp. 43–78.

Nietzsche, *On the Genealogy of Morals*; *The Will to Power*; and *Thus Spoke Zarathustra* in Walter Kaufmann, ed., *The Viking Portable Nietzsche*.

An excellent view of Nietzsche's ethics is presented in Hunt, *Nietzsche and the Original of Virtue*.

For a postmodernist interpretation of master and slave morality and the will to power, see Deleuze, *Nietzsche and Philosophy*.

For an excellent analysis of *Thus Spoke Zarathustra*, see Higgins, *Nietzsche's Zarathustra*. See also Solomon and Higgins, *What Nietzsche Really Said*, Chapter 5, "Nietzsche's War on Morality."

Introductory Question to Consider

1. Nietzsche distinguishes between "good and bad" and "good and evil." How does he understand the difference between "bad" and "evil"? Does "good" mean the same thing in the two pairs of terms? If not, how does it differ in each?

Advanced Question to Consider

1. "That lambs dislike great birds of prey does not seem strange; only it gives no ground for reproaching these birds of prey for bearing off little lambs. And if the lambs say among themselves: 'these birds of prey are evil; and whoever is least like a bird of prey, but rather its opposite, a lamb—would he not be good?' there is no reason to find fault with this institution of an ideal, except perhaps that the bird of prey might view it a little ironically and say: 'we don't dislike them at all, these good little lambs; we even love them: nothing is more tasty than a tender lamb'" (Nietzsche, *On the Genealogy of Morals*, Book I, Para. 13). What is Nietzsche's point here? What is he saying about master and slave morality?

Nietzsche, the "Immoralist"
Lecture 11—Transcript

Nietzsche certainly contributed heavily to the understanding of himself as destroyer, as an immoralist, as an antichrist. He claims himself to be an "immoralist," and I think this is perhaps, more than anything else, one of the reasons why he is so often attacked in philosophy and outside of philosophy as a danger. The truth is that Nietzsche was generous, kind, courteous, trustworthy, a good friend, and my guess is he probably never did an immoral thing in his life.

One is tempted to ask, "Was he so out of sync with himself that the philosophy, on the one hand, praises and defends immorality, while he himself was a perfectly moral, good citizen?" I think the answer is no. That is not what is going on here. It is not a matter of the philosopher out of sync with his philosophy. Nietzsche, more than anyone, insisted that the philosopher should be an example of his philosophy. Then we have to understand what he means by "immorality." It is not what you would immediately think it to be. I think a good interpretation of this aspect of Nietzsche is to say that what he attacks, first of all, is a particular kind of morality, not morality across the board, and certainly not ethics and values as such. He attacks Judeo-Christian morality, and even that—I think we should be very careful of—not all aspects. What he dislikes about Judeo-Christian morality is, first of all, its emphasis on the otherworldly and its detraction from our enjoyment of—our attention to—this life.

More deeply, there are a number of notions in Judeo-Christian morality which lend themselves to cruelty and hypocrisy. It is these that Nietzsche wants to call into question. In particular, there is an interpretation of Judeo-Christian morality which emerges in the beginning of the 19th century (the end of the 18th), defended by Immanuel Kant and some of his followers. It takes the Judeo-Christian morality to be essentially a kind of rational morality. It is defined most of all by what Kant calls the categorical imperative—the notion of a general, universal, rational principle which is binding on all rational creatures—in other words, on all human beings.

What is wrong with such a morality? Just to start, one can ask whether universal principles in any form, whether defended by reason or not, do in fact apply equally to all human beings. One can go cross-cultural and very quickly ask whether, for example, a native of Samoa or India or South Africa or Finland really should be subject to the same kinds of moral strictures that a citizen in bourgeois Germany would be bound by. One can ask more insightfully whether principles do apply to everyone equally, or rather, whether it might be that every universal principle—which is applied without attention to the particularities of the individual—might very well be disadvantageous or hurtful, as opposed to beneficial and good, for everyone involved. Take something I have to do quite often—grading a class of students. There is a sense in which whatever grading procedure I adopt, what I am doing is going to be more to the advantage of some students (I hope those who work hard), than to others. One problem with Judeo-Christian morality and this idea of universal rational principles is that while it pretends to be taking everyone equally under its umbrella, in fact, what it does is to the advantage of some and the disadvantage of others. We will see that this is going to be an absolutely central thesis of Nietzsche's attack on morality.

To put it in a different way, one can think of the Judeo-Christian tradition—now moving to the New Testament—in terms of loving thy neighbor and a certain kind of respect. Here, too, there is a very real question about whether love so spread out—whether love extended to everyone including strangers and enemies really deserves to be called "love" at all. Or whether respect, something we can certainly understand with people whom we are admiring of, can be stretched so thin as to respect every human being and still have the concept mean anything.

Here is the interpretation I would want to give. First, when Nietzsche says that he is an immoralist, he rejects the rather particular notion of morality which appears first in the Old Testament as the Ten Commandments, and is updated and defended by Kant as a sequence of rational principles. That notion of morality as it appears in the New Testament in which love and respect are stretched so thin that they no longer have anything like the power that they are supposed to have—here too, there is a more philosophical interpretation. One might look at it in this way. What Nietzsche is doing is he is rejecting not even so much a kind of morality as opposed to a certain way of looking at morality. Again, let me go back to Kant. The idea is that if morals are defined by rationality, then by its very definition, it must be universal, applicable to all human beings, and quite independent of feelings, culture, individual considerations, and, Kant would even say, of consequences.

On the other hand, one might take the philosophy of utilitarianism, which was also very powerful in the 19th century. John Stuart Mill was roughly a contemporary of Nietzsche. Take that philosophy—the greatest good for the greatest number—that one always ought to act in such a way as to maximize benefits and minimize harms. Think of that as a way of characterizing ethics or morality. One comes up with the rather obvious conclusion—Mill himself worried at great length about it—whether, in fact, such universal principles and the general notion of pleasure or happiness and the supposed commensurability of different kinds of pleasures and preferences and interests can be used as an adequate notion of morality as such.

What Nietzsche wants to say against both—the kind of philosophy we get in the Old and New Testaments and defended by Kant, and the kind of philosophy we find in people like John Stuart Mill and the utilitarians— is that as much as these might seem to be different, in fact, they are all of a piece. What they do is they tend to focus, in particular, on particular actions—the idea of whether an action for the utilitarians has good or bad consequences, whether an action in Kant is motivated by the right kinds of intentions or what he calls "a good will," whether an action is motivated as in the New Testament by love, or whether an action is motivated as in the Old Testament by the fear of God and a universal commandment.

What he wants to say is there is an alternative to thinking about things in this way. There is an alternative focus which has been ignored, and it is a very old philosophy—one that has very strong credentials, but has almost disappeared from modern thinking. The way I would put it is that it is a philosophy of virtue—a philosophy of character. One thinks, for example, about the ethics elaborated by Aristotle. It is defined not by rules, not by the right thing to do—certainly not by love, fear of God. Rather, it is all defined in terms of and motivated by a person having good character—a person having the right kinds of virtues.

One of the interesting features of having the right kinds of virtues is it escapes from the kind of dilemma which has come down to us as the essence of Christian modern ethics. That is the kind of split between pleasure on the one hand and duty on the other. Or to put it in a different way, the split between how one conceives of oneself as a righteous person, and how one conceives of oneself in terms of self-interest. Or very simply, the kind of split we find in such modern writers as Ayn Rand, between selfishness on the one hand and altruism on the other.

What Nietzsche wants to say is this is a false dichotomy. If you look at this idea of virtue as it is defended by Aristotle—and Nietzsche and Aristotle are very close on many of these points—what comes off is not that one makes a choice between one's righteousness or duty and one's own advantage or pleasure. Quite to the contrary, Aristotle tells us that one enjoys being virtuous for its own sake. This is not quite to say that virtue is its own reward. That is a kind of cheap followup that suggests that if you do the right thing you will be rewarded. That is exactly what Nietzsche and Aristotle want to get rid of. Rather, the idea is that you are so identified with your virtues you think of yourself as an honest person, a person who doesn't lie, a person who is trustworthy, a person who is a friend. Consequently, that is what motivates you, because not to act in your own character—to act out of character, to act against character—is so debilitating, so offensive that it is not something you would ever think about doing.

When you think about people who are very trustworthy and honest and you ask them, "Why don't you lie?" They might give you a Kantian answer: "Lying is wrong; it is a universal rational principle," or they might give you an answer of the sort that Mill would give: "Lying hurts people's feelings; it makes you untrustworthy in the future." A virtuous person, someone like Aristotle or Nietzsche, would rather say, "I don't lie because I am not a liar. That is really the end of the matter."

To put it very succinctly, Nietzsche says he is an immoralist, suggesting that he defends all kinds of really bad actions. In fact, he doesn't defend virtually any bad actions; what he says instead is that we have to look at morality in a different way. In particular, I would put Nietzsche side by side with Aristotle, and I would add side by side with the earlier Greeks' notion of ethics, and say what Nietzsche has in mind is a way of thinking about ethics that puts all its focus on the notion of individual character. What kind of a person are you? I put that in the second person. For Nietzsche, it should, as in Kierkegaard, almost always be put in the first person. What kind of person am I?

One of the things that Nietzsche defends throughout his philosophy, although I would add not always consistently, and certainly not consistently as a person, is the idea that we spend much too much energy judging other people. This itself is a sign of a certain kind of nihilism, a certain kind of decadence, a certain kind of immorality. For Nietzsche, the idea of judging other people is already something gone wrong. The person you judge is yourself, and you judge yourself in terms of whether or not you are, and have lived up to, the character that you can be and want to be.

In terms of this idea of looking at morality in a different way, Nietzsche gives one of his most dramatic accounts in this case of the history (he would say the "genealogy") of morality. It goes back to the notion of perspectivism that I discussed in the last lecture—the idea that one always sees a phenomenon, a thing, sees the world from one perspective or another. I mentioned that there are aesthetic perspectives, scientific perspectives, religious perspectives, moral perspectives. Nietzsche plays these off against each other.

One thing to say is that Nietzsche, playing off the perspective of the aesthetic view and the perspective of the ethical view, almost always comes down on the side of the aesthetic view. Just as he said the ancient Greeks were so beautiful because they accepted their position and lot in life and made something of it, one might say that Nietzsche in the realm of morality finds virtuous people beautiful, not so much good or even morally good (a term which he uses very reservedly); rather, the idea is that we see them as beautiful. In ethics, as in aesthetics, the idea is to be beautiful. In line with his perspectivism, Nietzsche also suggests that there are perspectives within the realm of ethics—within the realm of morality. This is not something we normally think of. I used the phrase in the last lecture, "the moral point of view," suggesting that there is just one—that there is a way to view the world morally; the very word morality suggests that it is in some sense one thing—one set of principles.

Take the Ten Commandments—or Kant, when he is talking about morality, talks about the categorical imperative. Notice he talks about *the* categorical imperative as if there is just one of them. Even when Kant goes on to give an elaboration of different (as he puts it) formulations of the categorical imperative, the idea is that still morality is something singular and unified. Nietzsche, by contrast, distinguishes between what he calls "Master morality" and what he calls "Slave morality."

His history, or genealogy, tries to trace back these different notions and the concepts of good and evil, and good and bad (which as you will see are quite different) through history with an attempt to understand how we came to use these terms in the ways that we now do. On the one hand, it is straightforwardly historical investigation. What he is trying to do is find the sources of our moral prejudices. At the same time, it is genealogy (rather, I think we would say "etymology") in the sense that he is really interested in the language, and how the language emerges, and what terms are related to what terms through history, and how we come up again with the understanding of morality that we now have as a singular, unified set of principles.

Let's begin by talking about master morality. Master morality is easy enough to find in the ancient world. One finds it most notably in ancient Greece and, of course, in Greece's subsequent culture, Rome. One finds it throughout the Middle East and throughout the Mediterranean in ancient times, and one thinks of virtually all the great societies of the ancient world—in Samaria, in Assyria, in Babylon and, of course, in Israel, because we should not forget that Israel was at one point a great state in the Middle East. (We will go back and talk about that in a number of different ways.) Most notably, of course, Nietzsche is concerned with the Greeks, whom he adored.

When he talks about the Greeks—again, while I think Aristotle is an example of what he is talking about, a much better example in his own mind would be the Greeks of Homer's epics—here, as often, Nietzsche talks in a rather severe warrior mentality; often exaggerates the case. In fact, the book in which he most thoroughly discusses this, called *The Genealogy of Morals*, he subtitles *"A Polemic."* We should make no mistake that Nietzsche is trying to shock us. In particular, he is trying to shock us into seeing morality in a different way.

What is master morality? When you think about the masters of ancient Greece, of course, we are taking about a very small class of aristocrats and rulers and they are supported by an enormous number (perhaps in the millions) of slaves, captives, and other people—craftsmen, soldiers—who are not aristocrats. The structure of society in the ancient world is for the most part a triangle, with a very small number of very privileged, powerful people at the top, and an enormous number of people who are not so well off at the bottom—many of whom, most of whom, are slaves, whose lives consist of essentially supporting and making possible the life of the Greek aristocrat.

Aristotle, for example, had no tolerance for the work. He never worked, I think, a day in his life. He acted as a tutor—but he didn't think of philosophizing and teaching as work—for Alexander the Great. When he goes to talk about commercial society and talking about merchants; when he talks about the peasantry, the kind of work that people do with their hands, you can sort of feel the disdain. It is the presence of such people, however, that make his life as a philosopher full time possible. It is those people who make possible the pursuit of the kind of excellence that the masters generally admired. That is where the focus of master morality lies—precisely in that notion of excellence.

Aristotle uses a word which can be translated either as virtue or as excellence. One might think those are two completely different notions. The idea of virtue is a moral notion, whereas the idea of excellence is a practical credential. You can be excellent at archery or excellent at hut building. That has nothing to do with morality. If we are talking about virtue, isn't that honesty and trustworthiness and things that really fit into a very special conception—a moral conception—of ourselves? Precisely what is important here is the fact that these two things are not opposed.

What we are doing when we pursue morality—broadly construed (master morality)—what we are pursuing is our own excellence. Virtues are excellences. When Aristotle goes on to list the virtues, we might be surprised to find not only just such things as honesty and trustworthiness, but also something like wittiness, being a good friend—in short, being congenial, being a sort of person who gets along with others. The idea is that in pursuit of being a really good person, a beautiful person, everything gets taken into account. There is no reason to privilege some particular virtues or traits over others, not in general. It really takes the whole package—what Aristotle refers to as the unity of the virtues: the idea that a really good admirable person is going to have not just one virtue, but all of them in proper proportion.

Nietzsche, as I said, rejects Aristotle, at least in this sense. He sees Aristotle and his two illustrious predecessors, Socrates and Plato, as already belonging to a period in Greece which is, in his words, decadent. It is already on the downward slide. Some of this reflects Nietzsche's rather anti-democratic thinking. In fact, this is a period of Greek democracy and, interestingly enough, Socrates here is on Nietzsche's side. Socrates also was an opponent of widespread democracy. The idea was that Greece in its glory was the period before. Consequently, the conception of the virtues, and the conception of excellence that Nietzsche really admires, can be found much more in Homer and the early tragedians than it can be found in Aristotle and his contemporaries.

The idea here is unmistakable. It is on the one hand a celebration of warrior virtues—as always with Nietzsche, it is warrior virtues understood metaphorically. So, Nietzsche often talks about his own writing and the courage it takes to write, to express your opinion, the courage it takes to examine and to overcome yourself, in very warrior-like terms. Notice none of this has anything to do with killing people. Nietzsche's own very short stint in the military was, for the most part, in a non-military role. The truth is that what it amounts to is a kind of celebration of a certain kind of pursuit of excellence—which Nietzsche wants to claim has much disappeared from the moral scene—and that is illustrated by the fact that we tend to distinguish on the one hand the moral virtues and on the other hand what we simply call "excellence" or some kind of accomplishment.

Let's turn to slave morality, because that is where the heart of the argument lies. To be very blunt about it, what Nietzsche calls slave morality is what we simply call "morality." That morality has, in effect, eclipsed master morality, and the big question for Nietzsche is, how has that happened? Slave morality gets traced, as does master morality, back to the ancient world. In searching for the source of slave morality, Nietzsche points out that the people who originated this morality were literally slaves. He is thinking, for example, about the ancient Hebrews. Here it is important not to think of the ancient state of Israel, which as I said was one of the great states of the ancient world; rather, the Hebrews in the time of exile and their enslavement in Egypt. One can imagine one brilliant Hebrew slave thinking to himself, "Why do we always have to be the inferiors in this social arrangement?" Or, in terms of its logic, slave morality is, as Nietzsche puts it, a "reactive morality." It is an attempt to reject, to turn upside down, the excellence morality pursued by the masters.

It takes the following form: for example, the masters think that wealth is a wonderful thing; then in the New Testament we read, "It is easier for a camel to get through the eye of a needle than it is for a rich man to get into the kingdom of heaven." Suddenly wealth, rather than being a virtue and a benefit, is a real liability. One looks at the masters with very often their superlative educations, and although this is a later phrase, one comes away with the idea that "ignorance is better." Ignorance is even bliss. One sees the warriors of the aristocratic class with all their power and fighting ability, but the New Testament tells us, "The meek shall inherit the Earth." What is going on here?

One can put it in a very systematic way. Whereas master morality pursues excellence—in a way pursues one's own conception of what it is to be a great person, what it is to be admirable — it is not so much comparative as it is, "Here is what I can be." In slave morality, to the contrary, it is reactive. The slaves see the masters, and they envy them. They feel inferior to them and, consequently, they come to resent them. Insofar as resentment is a very clever emotion, what the slaves at some brilliant point in history learned to do is to turn the masters' values upside down. So, what the masters would call good, the slaves now refer to as "evil." Wealth, power, education, even freedom is something which is no longer viewed as particularly desirable, but rather something to be avoided.

On the other side of it, the masters make a distinction between good and bad. Bad means failure. It means pathetic. On the one hand, if a master fails to achieve what he sets out to achieve, that is bad. He looks down (the metaphor is significant), at all these people who are not even in a position to try to achieve the things the master aspires to, and he sees them as bad, meaning pathetic. It is interesting to note that Aristotle does not even allow for the possibility of slaves and other non-aristocrats to be happy. They might be good slaves, or they might even be in some sense good people. Nevertheless, they can't achieve the kind of happiness, fulfillment, excellence that that masters insist upon.

On the other side, if the slaves emphasize evil as the primary category, they have a notion of good, which is in many ways dependent on the notion of evil. If what is evil is what the masters consider good, and if these are things to be avoided because they make you in some sense a worse person, then to be good is, in fact, to have less of these things—or best, none of these things. The ultimate result of this is a kind of self-denial. At its extreme, what we get is the phenomenon of asceticism, which Nietzsche talks about at some length—people who utterly deny themselves.

I think we underestimate to what extent this is so part of our ethic. I am not talking about extreme Christian or other religious sects that, for example, refuse to eat anything just above subsistence. Rather, I am thinking for example of many of us who go on diets, have various kinds of food restrictions and so on beyond the point of medical health, or in some cases (for example, vegetarians) moral righteousness to the point of quite conscientious self-denial. The truth is that from this tradition what we learn is that the good is self-denial; that denying oneself is quite apart from its medical or even ethical benefits, a good thing in itself.

Now we have two warring conceptions of morality. On the one hand, we have master morality, with its emphasis on excellence. We have slave morality, with its emphasis on self-denial. What happens? A theology makes the difference. The masters are convinced by roughly the third century of the new millennium that being a slave, being self-denying, is ultimately much more beneficial in terms of one's prospects for heaven and so on. Curiously, after 2,000 years of slave morality, master morality has not been erased. It has only been sublimated.

Nietzsche points out the phenomenon of what he calls "bad conscience"—which is in naturally strong and powerful people—this kind of war within themselves as they try to restrict their desire and restrict their sense of what they themselves can be. What you get is a curious battle of pride and humility, of excellence and mediocrity. One thinks, for example of the medieval popes—enormously powerful men who at the same time were obviously obliged to the Christian sensibility and Judeo-Christian morality (slave morality) in such a way that they could not, on the one hand, simply admit, as an ancient Greek would have done, that he or she was better than anyone else or better than those around him. Rather, there is a kind of humility here which is forced, artificial—and yet the notion of master morality continues, with 2,000 years of slave morality that has given us the self-discipline that comes from self-denial, which is going to allow for the spiritualization of morality.

What Nietzsche is really after (quite the contrary of an immoral, anti-Christian position) is really a new conception of spirituality—something that has not the liabilities and disadvantages and hypocrisies of the old tradition, but something very new. Something which we will see later manifested in what he calls the *Übermensch*.

Nietzsche on Freedom, Fate, and Responsibility
Lecture 12

What we do, because we are the kind of creatures we are, is we act. Because we are the kind of introspective creatures we are, we try to think we must have caused that action through some more or less deliberate mental activity. Nietzsche wants to say most of our lives are not so reflective—not so deliberative. Nietzsche is one of these philosophers who says that consciousness is something that is vastly overrated.

One of the most fascinating and perplexing aspects of Nietzsche's philosophy is his seemingly contradictory defense of fate on the one hand and existential self-realization on the other. In Nietzsche's example of the lambs and birds of prey, he suggests that our characters are inborn. We are born with certain talents. We must "realize ourselves." We are not without limitations. Nietzsche repeats Pindar's admonition to "become who you are."

> **Eternal recurrence— the idea of reliving one's life over and over again—can be read, in part, as an affirmation of fate.**

Nietzsche follows Schopenhauer in his heavy use of the word "Will," but he rejects much of what Schopenhauer has to say about it. He rejects Schopenhauer's pessimistic depiction of life as amounting to nothing. He also rejects Schopenhauer's metaphysical understanding of the Will as a "thing in itself." Nevertheless, he agrees with Schopenhauer's rejection of free will. Free will depends on an "imaginary" notion of the self or subject, as advocated by Kant. Free will confuses causes and effects. For Nietzsche, consciousness is overrated: We are biological creatures whose every action can (in principle) be explained naturalistically. All actions can, therefore, be explained (but not justified) by motives and intentions.

Nietzsche follows the ancient Greeks in his belief in fate. For the Greek tragedians, fate was an undeniable aspect of human life. The notion of fate does not have to be understood as a crude and mysterious force. Heraclitus says, "fate is character," and this is a view that Nietzsche would wholly endorse—that we can become what we were born to be. Nevertheless, Nietzsche insists that we can and should "give style to our character"—in other words, our character is to some extent our own doing.

Eternal recurrence—the idea of reliving one's life over and over again—can be read, in part, as an affirmation of fate. The idea of eternal repetition does not cause, but reiterates, the idea of an inevitable outcome. Eternal recurrence is, above all, an affirmation of who one is, one's character, and therefore one's destiny. Nietzsche praises *amor fati*—the love of fate—as the most positive outlook on life. The love of fate does not preclude taking responsibility for "becoming who you are." Fate is not blind resignation, but it is the acceptance of who you are and what you have to do with your life. Nietzsche, unlike Kierkegaard and Sartre, has an ambivalent attitude toward the notion of responsibility. ■

Essential Reading

Solomon, *Existentialism*, pp. 43–78.

Supplementary Reading

Nietzsche, *Twilight of the Idols* in Walter Kaufmann, ed., *The Portable Nietzsche*.

Introductory Questions to Consider

1. Does it make sense to deny that we have "free will"? What does this mean? Does it mean that our choices are mere illusions?

2. What does it mean to believe in fate? How is fate different from luck? From chance? What kind of "necessity" is it that makes fated events come about?

1. Can you have a concept of responsibility without the presumption of freedom? Would it make sense to hold people responsible if fate determines what they do?

2. Does it make sense to say that the self is the cause of our actions? That we bring about our actions by intending them? Or is Nietzsche right that we find ourselves acting, then read back into the action the notion of prior intention?

Nietzsche on Freedom, Fate, and Responsibility
Lecture 12—Transcript

That notion of the *Übermensch*, and with it the notions of master and slave, raises one of the most perplexing questions about Nietzsche's philosophy and his overall worldview. It has to do with the notion of freedom, which in my first lecture I described as basic to existentialism; and with it the notion of responsibility, also the essence of the "no excuses" approach. But Nietzsche's views on these matters are quite complex, and in particular, his notion of "master and slave morality" makes a suggestion that really freedom and responsibility might be beside the point.

Let me explain. There is a sense in which Nietzsche suggests one is born as a slave—not necessarily a slave in the political social sense, of course. One is born with servile attitudes. One is born as weak. One is born with a relatively low capacity for self-discipline. On the other hand, one might be born a powerful person with great self-discipline, with an important sense of oneself and one's possibilities. You don't have to look at too many babies to realize that certain kinds of inborn dispositions are there right from the start, if you look at, for example, your fellow who is growing up. (I went to a high school reunion several years ago. One of the interesting things is they are the same people they used to be—they are just grown up, as they seem to have become. They were just more of the same, in some ways, literally.)

The idea is that we are born with a certain personality, with a certain "proto-character." Consequently, there is not a whole lot that we can do in terms of changing ourselves, making the kinds of choices that Kierkegaard talks about, exercising the kind of freedom that will become so essential to Sartre's notion of existentialism. To make this point in his discussion of master/slave morality, Nietzsche makes up an analogy. It is an analogy between birds of prey and lambs.

He says that the lambs, the vulnerable, resent and come to hate the birds of prey. In the kind of upside down turning of values that goes on in slave morality, one can imagine the lambs saying, "Why can't the birds of prey be more like us? Why can't they be gentle and not feed on little lambs?" The point that Nietzsche wants to make with this very biological example is that

159

there is the sense in which one is by nature a bird of prey, or one is by nature a sheep, first a lamb. If that is so, then we have to ask, what kind of control do we have over our lives? How much are we, in a sense, the victims of fate and the contingencies of our birth, health, how our mother takes care of herself, and in our childhood how we are taken care of?

There is a notion of fate that plays a very central role in Nietzsche's philosophy. One can say first of all that this is something which, given his admiration of the early Greeks, is going to be very important to him. He talks about the love of fate and takes it as itself a great virtue, but at the same time, when I include Nietzsche in a series of lectures about the existentialists and, in a way, include him as an existentialist, what I have in mind is that he does have a keen sense of those notions which are so central to existentialism— the notion of freedom and responsibility.

One can't overdo it. There is a sense in which the debate between Hegel and Kierkegaard might be viewed in a practical and personal way as the view of to what extent we are molded, shaped, determined by the larger forces of society and the larger forces of history—what Hegel refers to as "spirit," or "the world spirit," or *Geist*. On the other hand, there is Kierkegaard who says, "Whatever the world does with us, however it shapes us, the world produced me, Kierkegaard, as a rather neurotic, upset young gentleman." What I do with that is in some sense up to me. I think that is the way we should understand Nietzsche, too. On the one hand, we are all born with certain inborn talents, abilities, capacities, dispositions, personalities. At the same time, the idea does not suggest, "Accept what we are." It is also to make something of ourselves. What we can make of ourselves is also to a large part determined by our times, our upbringing, and so on.

The key word here—a very modern word, and unfortunately now very much abused—is the notion of "self-realization." It can be traced back to Aristotle. Aristotle talks at great length actually about how a young man must be raised in the right way, taught the rules of his culture, made to exercise the kind of judgment that will allow him to be independent, autonomous, and excellent as an adult. After this period of education and externally imposed discipline, there is a point at which a person has to realize him or herself and take the talents, the abilities, and turn them into something. With Nietzsche, too, we might find that we do have certain talents, dispositions; but nevertheless, there is a sense in which we are then responsible for them. A talent isn't self-realizing. A talent is something that must be realized. If, as a young child, you find or your parents find you have exceptional ability in music, it is not as if, left to yourself and your own devices, that is necessarily going to manifest itself as musical genius. Musical genius, even if it turns out to be something which is inherited or genetic, is something which must be worked upon, cultivated—and that is one's responsibility.

The key to Nietzsche's philosophy comes once again from the Greeks, in this case the Greek playwright and poet, Pindar. It is a phrase that goes, "Become who you are." It is an interesting phrase. Very often parents will say to their adolescent children, supposedly in order to help them, "Just be yourself, dear." I think the proper response of the adolescent is, "What is that supposed to mean? How is that supposed to help? Who else could I be?" Thinking about it, you realize you could be, or at least try to be, lots of different selves. Just within you, in terms of your inborn talents and abilities, you could push yourself in a number of different directions. One of the hardest decisions that my best students have to make, many of whom are multi-talented in many different disciplines often very far apart, is they realize they have to choose. They have to pursue one set of talents at the expense of another. Here what we find is that Nietzsche runs, again, against Aristotle in a very critical way—even though, I think, the general framework is the same.

Aristotle talks about the unity of the virtues. Nietzsche talks about their disunity. In *Zarathustra,* he discusses how the virtues are at war with one another. Any student who has just wrestled through the problem about: "Should I do this? Go into business for which I obviously have great talent, or should I go into music for which I have great talent, or any number of other things which are similarly diverse?" It is very easy to realize that the kind of choice you make is something which really does determine what/who you are going to be. It is not simply a tautology that you should be yourself. You have to choose, in a way, what you will become.

I think in Nietzsche what you get is a juxtaposition of these two different attitudes, so we get both this sense of fate and the lot you are born with. At the same time, there is a very powerful sense of self-realization. I think one of the reasons why students are so turned on by Nietzsche generation after generation is because they see, even if they don't really understand the text, that the basic message is one of self-actualization—turning yourself into something. While it is true that a lot of student Nietzsche response has to do with just drinking too much and perhaps using some rather foul language, I think what people see when they read him is that he is really urging them to make something of themselves. That is the key notion.

This idea of "free choice" has been stretched beyond the bounds of plausibility in philosophy. Philosophers for a long time, certainly through the 18th and 19th century, were found of talking about "the will," a notion that goes back at least to medieval times. It means something very valuable in lots of philosophies. The essence of it is that kind of push that we give to ourselves when we decide to do something. We talk about "will power," where will power is measured by the amount of resistance we can overcome. It is will power not to eat that piece of chocolate cake which looks more delicious to you than anything you have ever seen. If you have enough will power, what you do is push yourself to, in this case, refuse. The will power of an athlete in the midst of a competition—to push him or herself to excesses which they have never realized before.

That notion of the inner push raises all sorts of interesting philosophical questions, mainly whether it makes sense to talk about such a thing. The most immediate context for Nietzsche's use of the word "will"—and as we will see he uses it quite often—is his mentor, Schopenhauer. I want to talk about Schopenhauer for a minute because of the philosophical influences on Nietzsche; even including the ancient Greeks, I think his is the most powerful.

Arthur Schopenhauer is known as perhaps the crankiest pessimist in the history of philosophy. He, teaching in the early part of the 19th century, rather unsuccessfully as a teacher, taught that essentially reality—the world as it is in itself—is really something that we can, contra-Kant, experience. It is not a reality behind the appearances. In one sense, we experience the will in ourselves. It is will that is reality—the reality in itself.

Notice here that I am using the notion of will in a very odd sense, in one way because reality—throughout the whole of Western tradition, as I argued—has this kind of obsession with singularity, with monism. When Schopenhauer talks about the "will," he is not talking about our individual wills, something each of us has. He is talking about *the will*, the reality, which underlies all of us and manifests itself simply in each of us. It is not in any sense our own. Quite the contrary. Whereas other philosophers, notably Kant, had talked about the rational will, the will which is bound by the rules of reason, Schopenhauer makes it very clear that the will has basically its own ideas. The will is not something which is bound by rationality. It is not, as Hegel would suggest, something with an ultimate purpose—that human history, and human life in general, and life in general—in fact, it is just a manifestation of the irrational will.

This is perhaps most obvious in us in a way that we can easily understand in, for example, our sexuality. You don't have to be an adolescent anymore to remember (or perhaps a very short memory) how irrational sexual desire can make you—going against all social prohibitions, going against moral standards, really in a sense—out of your mind. There is a sense in which Schopenhauer tells us this is the will manifesting itself in us. To think of it as something that we have individually is really to miss the point. While we think about sex as an activity which each of us indulges in for ourselves, our own pleasure, the truth is that sex has a purpose that has nothing to do with our enjoyment or pleasure. The purpose of the will is to continue the species. The purpose of continuing the species? Simply to continue life. The purpose of continuing life? To tell you the truth, there is no purpose. Schopenhauer gives us this really depressing picture of the life of all creatures, including human beings. He takes one of those mayflies that appear, essentially all at once, on a day in spring. There is this feverish mating and all of the bugs drop dead, first having given birth to a new generation who will repeat the same ritual next year, and the process will repeat itself over and over again. What does it amount to? Nothing.

Here we can see the influence of Schopenhauer, among other people, on Camus and his notion of Sisyphean futility. There is a sense in which, for Schopenhauer, the will is something that really is the essential us, but it is not at all individual. It gives rise to his pessimism. After all, if we are not masters of our own fate, if we essentially are thrown about by these forces within us, what is the point of life? Schopenhauer's philosophy is there really isn't one, and the best that a philosopher can do is to try to give us an escape. Schopenhauer suggests, among other things, Buddhism and aesthetic appreciation as at least temporary ways of getting us out of ourselves—ways of rejecting the will and not being the slave of its forces.

Nietzsche was very impressed by Schopenhauer when he picked up a book of Schopenhauer's called *The Will*—that the world is will in representation—when he was a student. He utterly rejected Schopenhauer's pessimism. Furthermore, as we saw in the first lecture, he also rejected the idea of the will as the thing in itself because, in Nietzsche's words, "There is no thing in itself." Once we get rid of the thing in itself, we get rid of the idea of mere appearance, too. This has more dramatic manifestations, because it is the idea of the will, in one sense or another, that makes possible the notion of "free will." Nietzsche and Schopenhauer reject the notion of individual free will—Schopenhauer because the will is not in any sense each of ours, but something that is much larger and thus acting through us; Nietzsche for a much more sophisticated and subtle reason. The notion of free will depends on what he would consider an imaginary or an illusory sense of self. If you think, for example, of Kant, who defended such a notion of free will, it is the idea that we must presuppose that for the purposes of morality, for the purposes of action, that we are not bound by any deterministic principles. Even the laws of nature, in an important sense, are suspended in this conception of ourselves. Kant rather dramatically and confusingly says that the self as the self of action, the self of morality, must be conceived of as outside the world of crosses.

What Nietzsche wants to say is that there can be no such notion of self. The self is always embedded, contextualized. The self is always indistinguishable, in a sense, from the person—the person with his body, the culture, the world, biology, all sorts of natural forces and contingencies. To pretend that in any sense we can pull away and look at the self as something detached and act as if we are entirely autonomous, is illusory. It is imaginary. It just makes no philosophical sense.

On the one hand, Nietzsche wants to reject free will because the self on which the notion of free will depends is an impossible notion of the self. Let's say not right away that Nietzsche doesn't reject the notion of the self. Obviously, "Become who you are" presupposes a very dynamic notion of selfhood. But it is not the sort of detached and philosophical self that is talked about, in particular by Kant, and a great many other philosophers. The other thing to say here is that talk about free will confuses, Nietzsche says, causes and effects. We talk about our behavior as if, first of all, there is some sort of act of will. That is the cause. Then, as an effect, there is an action. This is a very common picture. It makes good common sense, and many of the philosophers in the last several hundred years have used it as a paradigm of causality. It is how we understand the very notion of causality. We can cause our bodies ourselves to do things.

Nietzsche gives us a very different picture. What is this act of will? What is the willing that philosophers refer to? There may be actions, (certainly you can think of some) in which you make a special effort—in which there actually is some mental commotion that precedes the course of action. Most of the time, we just act. We just do things. When we act and we do things, because we have among our other metaphysical prejudices this idea that every effect must have a cause, we think that because we act, there must be some preceding cause. Where would that cause be? It must be in the mind. At this point, we start talking, perhaps rather perplexedly, of unconscious causes or something very much like that. What Nietzsche suggests is that, in a sense, there is just action.

What we do, because we are the kind of creatures we are, is we act. Because we are the kind of introspective creatures we are, we try to think we must have caused that action through some more or less deliberate mental activity. Nietzsche wants to say most of our lives are not so reflective—not so deliberative. Nietzsche is one of these philosophers who says that consciousness is something that is vastly overrated. He doesn't, as Kierkegaard and Dostoevsky do, treat it as a disease. Nevertheless, he sees that most of our behavior is not conscious, not reflective, not deliberative; we just do it. We do it because of the kind of creatures we are.

First of all, we are biological creatures. Here, that sort of image of the lambs and the birds of prey comes back into focus. There is a sense in which what we do we do as a matter of necessity. To explain our actions is, first of all, to explain motives, but more importantly, it is to explain it in terms of our habits, our characters, the kinds of creatures we are. The age-old philosophical routine of trying to justify actions is something Nietzsche simply puts aside.

We have spent too much time judging, he says, and we have spent too much time justifying. There is a sense in which we do what we do because of what we are. Insofar as we do have control over our actions, it is by way of cultivating a new set of automatic actions, which is what we call our "character."

When Nietzsche talks about fate, one can think of this in terms of the ancient Greeks as a rather crude notion. For example, in Sophocles' great play *Oedipus the King* (*Oedipus the Tyrant*) we have a very clear picture of fate as some sort of mysterious invisible hand which is actually reaching down and intruding on human behavior. Oedipus is told his fate is to marry his mother and kill his father. He takes every possible step to try to avoid this situation, but it comes through anyway. One wants to say fate is like this invisible hand that makes things happen quite to the contrary of our desires and intentions.

One can find such a notion of fate in the Greek tragedians. I think it is a mistake to see it as this mysterious force. Rather, looking back to Heraclitus, Nietzsche's favorite Greek philosopher, one might say fate really is character. When we talk about fate, what we are often thinking of is not something mysterious and outside of us, but rather just the person we have become—to a large extent, the person we were born to be. Nietzsche says in one of his wonderful little bits of advice in *Gay Science*, "Give style to your character. It is a great art." What he has in mind is that it is true we are born with a certain character, a certain personality, but what is within our resources is to shape it, cultivate it, according to our fashion. This does not mean that we have free will in the objectionable sense. What it means is that part of our character itself may be to make choices, and to have the strength to carry them through. All this comes back to a notion of fate, which is in many ways much more primal. It doesn't have to do with being born as a particular person with particular character and so on, as much as it has to do with being born—being alive.

There is a sense of existence we talked about in Kierkegaard, in which what is important is to be passionately aware of yourself and your possibilities and to pick yourself up through your choices to determine who you are going to be. Nietzsche doesn't have that notion of choice. He certainly doesn't have that notion of freedom as we have seen. Nevertheless, that notion of being passionate about one's life—about a very special notion of existence which is not just going along with the crowd, which is not just existing, but something very special and characterized by passion—is something central to his philosophy too.

He has an idea (he sometimes calls it his greatest idea, but Nietzsche says that about several of his ideas)—it appears in some of his early work, but reoccurs in *Zarathustra*, in *Gay Science* and in some of his late works as well. It has the idea of "eternal return," or "eternal recurrence." On the one hand, it harks back to ancient times. The very early Greeks had a mythology in which time was circular and repeated itself, rather than time as in Christian mythology in which time is a single dimension that goes from the beginning to eternity. One also finds this notion of eternal recurrence in the mythology of the ancient Hindus who believed that time was like a wheel; with their doctrine of reincarnation believed that things happened over and over again.

Nietzsche toys with the possibility of a scientific proof of this dramatic image, but only gives it up—never publishes it. What is much more important is to understand it as a kind of test—a test of one's own attitude toward life; a test of one's own ability to really live one's life without the kind of illusions and evasions that really give rise to this notion of the "otherworldly" that he is so bitterly against. The way the test goes is something like this: Imagine if you had to live your life, exactly as you have lived it, not just once, but over and over again. The repetition gives your life a certain kind of weight—gives each moment a certain kind of weight. It is this notion of weightiness and lightness that Milan Kundera in his great novel, *The Unbearable Lightness of Being*, toys with at the beginning of the book. If something happens just once, we can say, "That is done with. It is over." If something is going to repeat itself an infinite number of times, one is much less willing to say, "Okay, let's do that again."

The test is: How much do you love your life? How much are you consumed with regret? It is very important to be able to say, thinking this, as Nietzsche puts it, terrible thought, that one would grasp at this possibility of repeating one's life over and over again with enormous enthusiasm. It is a sign of something pathetic if your response is, "No. I'd rather not do it at all." One thinks of Camus's character Meursault, who, when he is in his argument with the chaplain conceives of the afterlife as nothing other than the repetition of this life, and who thinks of any moment of life as one which one could dwell on infinitely.

One thinks for example of Kierkegaard's discussion of repetition, which we didn't really discuss, but has as its outcome trying to turn repetition into a kind of meaning. There is a sense in Nietzsche in which all of the questions converge on the question of whether you really accept life itself, and that means your life. We all wish that in some sense things were different. We all wish that we had a different body, voice, culture. We imagine being born in a different time in a different century. We imagine being richer than we are, healthier than we are. Nietzsche himself was a very sickly, even pathetic human being who fought with sleeplessness, horrible headaches, and various illnesses all of his life, and died very young. Nevertheless, it is clear that what Nietzsche would like to have replied to this thought of eternal recurrence is, "How godly, how divine. That is what I want to do. To live my life exactly as it is an infinite number of times."

One can take this in a number of different ways. I think I have highlighted what is for Nietzsche the most important one. It also goes back to this question about fate and free will, and the question about how one becomes who one is, because in a sense what this test does is it asks, "How satisfied are you with yourself?" It doesn't have to be totally fatalistic. On the one hand, Nietzsche celebrates what he calls *amor fati*—the love of life, the love of just being who you are, of having a life. At the same time, it is clear that eternal recurrence has a different implication. Eternal recurrence can be seeing what your life is like, seeing what you really don't like because you are not willing to repeat it, and then changing yourself, cultivating yourself, and becoming not who you simply are, but who you would be. There are all sorts of limits to this, depending on who we are and how we find ourselves and where we fit into our society. But fate here is not blind resignation to what will happen. It is rather acceptance of our limitations, and it is rather trying to make something of ourselves in accordance with who we already could be.

Unlike Kierkegaard and Sartre, Nietzsche is quite ambivalent about the notion of responsibility. Nevertheless, I think we would make a huge mistake if we dismiss the notions of responsibility and responsibility to realize our talents from his philosophy because, after all, that is what it is all about.

Nietzsche—The *Übermensch* and the Will to Power
Lecture 13

In this, the last lecture on Nietzsche, I'd like to talk about two of his most famous and most notorious notions—the notion of the *Übermensch*, the superman or overman, and his idea about the "will to power."

The *Übermensch* is Nietzsche's best-known invention, in part because of George Bernard Shaw's lampoon of the notion in his play, *Man and Superman*. In fact, the notion only appears in one of Nietzsche's books, *Thus Spoke Zarathustra*, and then only at the beginning. Nietzsche does speak with some frequency of "higher men," clearly within the realm of the human, however. The *Übermensch* is portrayed by Zarathustra as a "possibility" for the future, something to which humanity can aspire. Nietzsche is clearly in Darwin's thrall in many ways. Nonetheless, he doubted Darwin's supposed premise that the best survive. But Zarathustra simultaneously introduces the more likely evolutionary possibility of "the last man," the self-contented, self-satisfied utilitarian modern man. "We have invented happiness," says the last man ["and he blinks"]. Zarathustra intends to horrify his audience with this vision, as he would inspire them with his vision of the *Übermensch*.

The *Übermensch* can be conceived in terms of ancient master morality, "spiritualized" by two thousand years of humility, ready to reassert itself in more refined form. The *Übermensch* is free of resentment and wholly independent of the "herd." Although the *Übermensch* is conceived of as an evolutionary possibility, Nietzsche does not pursue Darwin and clearly fears that any such "improvement" of humanity is highly implausible. Nevertheless, Nietzsche clearly distinguishes between those who aspire and are "higher" and those who merely react and resent and are, thereby, "lower." The poet Goethe is Nietzsche's most frequent example of such a higher man, clearly suggesting that the realm that concerns Nietzsche is not so much biological evolution as human spirituality and creativity. What distinguishes the higher from the lower, at least in some of Nietzsche's pronouncements, is a difference in the "will to power."

"The Will to Power" is a phrase that Nietzsche employs throughout his philosophy. "The Will to Power" is to some extent borrowed from Schopenhauer's "Will" and should be taken with a grain of salt, because Nietzsche rejects Schopenhauer's metaphysics. By "power" Nietzsche does not mean military power or power over others, but power of creativity and imagination. Power is best conceived as self-mastery, inner strength. Schopenhauer took the Will to be a metaphysical force, "the thing-in-itself." Nietzsche rejects all such metaphysics and the very idea of "the thing-in-itself."

For Nietzsche, the will to power provides a serious theory of motivation. Human behavior (animal behavior, too) is motivated by the desire for power. Nietzsche is often ambiguous about whether power itself is desired or the feeling of power. (These are not the same.) Nietzsche makes bold universalist claims, but the idea of power as goal and motivation is best considered as a limited empirical hypothesis, not a theory of human nature as such. The desire for power (self-mastery, self-expression) is directly opposed to the pervasive hedonic theory—that people (and animals) act to pursue pleasure and avoid pain. The utilitarians, for example, use the pleasure principle as a central tenet. But Nietzsche sees power as a profound version of what we would limply call "self-esteem." Thus, such passions as love and pity often have ulterior and sometimes dubious motives.

"The Will to Power" is to some extent borrowed from Schopenhauer's "Will" and should be taken with a grain of salt, because Nietzsche rejects Schopenhauer's metaphysics.

The will to power might also be taken to be a celebration of the passionate life. The history of philosophy is filled with praise for tranquility and peace of mind. This is the height of slave morality, the idea of cutting attachments and losses. But Nietzsche presents us with an alternative ideal, the idea that passionate attachments (whether to ideals or art or people) are what life is all about. The metaphor of energy pervades Nietzsche's works. Energy (as opposed to matter) was the central term in nineteenth-century physics. The dynamics of energy provide Nietzsche with a model for human behavior that does not conform to the traditional notions of inertia and momentum in human behavior. Excitement and adventure become the keys to a good human life, not (as in many philosophers) resignation and contemplation.

Passion represents energy in human life and experience. In this, Nietzsche again resembles no one so much as Kierkegaard. Not every passion is desirable. Some passions are "life-stultifying" and stupid, such as resentment. They "drag us down." Others are highly refined and cultivated. These are the "grand passions" that make life worthwhile. For Nietzsche, as for many other philosophers of the century, "nothing great is ever done without passion" (the phrase is from Hegel). Nietzsche ultimately rejects the dichotomy between reason and passion. The passions themselves have "their own quanta of reason." They are themselves forms of insight.

Nietzsche's philosophy is a philosophy of passion and energy. The ultimate passion is the love of life, but not simply life as life. It is the love of your life and what you have done and are doing with it. The test of this love of life is what Nietzsche calls "the thought of eternal recurrence." Simply stated, how do you feel about living your life, exactly as is, once again? Philosophy, contra Schopenhauer, is an affirmation of life. Eternal recurrence also provides an existential test, an ongoing means of scrutinizing how one is living and what one is doing with his or her life. ■

Essential Reading

Solomon, *Existentialism*, pp. 43–78.

Supplementary Reading

For a postmodernist interpretation of master and slave morality and the will to power, see Deleuze, *Nietzsche and Philosophy*; for an excellent analysis of *Thus Spoke Zarathustra*, see Higgins, *Nietzsche's Zarathustra*.

Nietzsche, *The Will to Power*, and *Thus Spoke Zarathustra* in Walter Kaufmann, ed., *The Viking Portable Nietzsche*.

1. What is the will to power? To what extent do you think this phrase unavoidably refers to power over other people? In what sense does it refer to self-discipline and self-mastery?

2. Zarathustra announces the coming of the "*Übermensch*." Who is he? Although Nietzsche says very little about him, what sense do you make of him? What do you make of the possibility that he is "super human"? Is Nietzsche making an evolutionary prediction? (He is writing only a few decades after Darwin.) Explain.

1. Eternal recurrence has been described as a "metaphysical doctrine": Time is not linear but loops around such that what is happening now has happened an infinite number of times in the past and will happen an infinite number of times in the future in exactly the same way. Eternal recurrence can also be interpreted as a "psychological doctrine" (a metaphorical tool for enabling us to determine how we should will) and an "ontological doctrine" (only active, master-like willing will return; reactive, slave-like willing will not). Which of these views—if any—do you embrace? Why?

Nietzsche—The *Übermensch* and the Will to Power
Lecture 13—Transcript

In this, the last lecture on Nietzsche, I'd like to talk about two of his most famous and most notorious notions—the notion of the *Übermensch,* the superman or overman, and his idea about the "will to power."

The *Übermensch*, I am convinced, is famous largely because of a play that George Bernard Shaw wrote parodying the notion, called *Man and Superman.* It was a comedy and it was very successful. The fact is that that *Übermensch* really just appears in one book of Nietzsche—by no means in the whole book. That is at the beginning of *Thus Spoke Zarathustra.* Nevertheless, Nietzsche speaks of "higher men" all the way through his work. The distinction between "higher" and "lower" is something which is absolutely central to his thought. Zarathustra talks about the possibility of the *Übermensch.* He often talks as if the *Übermensch* is an evolutionary step. He says at one point, following Darwin, man is a bridge between the ape and the *Übermensch.*

There are many ways of understanding this, but I think for our purposes now we should mention that Nietzsche's relationship to Darwin is very complicated. He was clearly under Darwin's thrall in many ways. I pointed out a few lectures ago that in his epistemology and his views of truth, he had a view which was very much a kind of pragmatized form of Darwinist evolutionary theory.

Nevertheless, with regard to Darwin as a whole, I think he took him to be much too much in the tradition of looking at man as the highest accomplishment of evolution—probably not true of Darwin. He also saw Darwin as taking the thesis that survival of the fittest meant that the best survive. What Nietzsche is very concerned about is the idea that if you look at evolution, it is not necessarily the best that survive at all. There was a theory that was circulating a few years ago, courtesy of the novels of Tom Robbins, that said basically that the final stage in evolution, the last two creatures to fight it out, will be the cockroach and the gonorrhea bacillus. The idea is that basically evolution gives no guarantees of giving us the better. I think we should look at Nietzsche's and *Zarathustra*'s promise of the *Übermensch* as a mere possibility—something to aspire for; something to dream about.

As evidence for this, in the same speech where he talks about the *Übermensch* trying to turn on the townspeople and get them excited about this possibility of overcoming themselves and becoming more than they are, he introduces another character called "the last man," where the idea is to get people truly disgusted with themselves and to see that this is another possibility for evolution—another way that we might turn out. In fact, it is a way that is very close to the way we are. The last man is the ultimate bourgeois consumer—the ultimate couch potato. He/she is a person who has no aspirations—is merely content, comfortable, satisfied.

As Nietzsche puts it sarcastically, the last man says, "We have invented happiness," and blinks. The blink is on the one hand a sign of idiocy; on the other a sign of just not wanting to see what life is really like. So, there are two possibilities: the *Übermensch*, which clearly Nietzsche portrays as an ideal; and "the last man," which is a kind of counter-ideal—in fact, precisely the ideal that would be defended by a great many utilitarians as the best that we could possibly have.

To understand the *Übermensch*, I think we should go back to the discussion of master morality and slave morality. When Nietzsche talks about master and slave morality, what he distinguishes there is strength and weakness. The difference is primarily one of power and also of independence. The master assumes his power. He assumes his abilities, and he aspires to excellence. He also does this in an important sense alone—not that he doesn't have friends and allies, but there is a sense in which the values, the talents, the ideals that he pursues are very much his own. Slave morality by contrast is a morality of the weak. The slave is very concerned with what other people think. The slave is very concerned about not being different. The slave is very concerned, and primarily concerned, with defense—with protecting himself from those who are stronger.

The picture of slave morality that Nietzsche gives us, which he sometimes also calls "herd" morality, is of lots of weak people (most of us, in fact) herding together for self-protection. What characterizes us as slaves is weakness. Weakness is not necessarily physically—not necessarily just in terms of our status in society—but Nietzsche makes it very clear that there is a sense in which weakness of spirit, soul, will is what it is really all about. The relationship between the master and the slave, consequently, looks something like this: The master is independent and powerful. The slave is relatively powerless and consequently resentful. As we saw, slave morality is basically a reaction against master morality.

One way to understand the *Übermensch* is to understand the *Übermensch* as a version of master morality. As I ended one of the previous lectures, you might say that the *Übermensch* is master morality spiritualized by 2,000 years of slave morality and its self-discipline. To characterize the *Übermensch* in this sense, we might say, first of all, in contrast with slave morality, the *Übermensch* is free of resentment. Some of my colleagues would even define the *Übermensch* as a character who is so free of regret and resentment that he can fully and enthusiastically endorse that thought experiment we call "eternal recurrence." Would you like your life lived over, and over, and over again exactly the same? The *Übermensch* is someone who can say, with no hesitation whatsoever, "Yes, gladly I would accept this."

The idea of the *Übermensch* as a step in evolution raises a number of problems for Nietzsche because, first of all, as I said, it is by no means guaranteed that this is what we are going to become. Secondly, it has been possible for him in some of the things he says for us to become really anything. This goes back to the kind of biological determinism I talked about in the previous lecture. There is a sense in which we are born as the creatures we are. We are born with our boundaries—limits—and the consequence is, what we become is just ourselves. When it comes to aspiring to be the *Übermensch*, one might say that for Nietzsche this is absolutely implausible. One can't become something so much more than one is. The *Übermensch* really is just a way of our looking at ourselves, and seeing that we are really not so hot as we often think we are.

He often makes enormous fun of those who would call for the improvement of man. Here he is talking not just about Christians and the kind of transformation that Christianity is supposed to bring about, but also he is talking about the social movements of his day and Socialism in particular.

We can think to our own century and all the horrors that have been imposed upon people by societies that have tried to change them from selfish egoistic capitalist to something more socialistic, more egalitarian, and so on.

One thinks, for example, of the Khmer Rouge in Cambodia, and one is horrified. Nietzsche would say, of course: You can't change people in that sense. People are as they are, and what we have to do is work within the realm of what we are. So, it is implausible to say that we can aspire to be and work toward being an *Übermensch*. Nevertheless, he continuously distinguishes in his philosophy between those who are higher and those who are lower. "Higher" and "lower" here typically referred to the "will to power"—something I wanted to talk about in some detail in a moment.

Before we think that power, here, refers just to a kind of aristocratic status and just to a kind of military prowess—which in the ancient world that Nietzsche admired certainly would be the case—I think it is important to point out that the person who emerges as the higher example of human being in Nietzsche's works more often than any other is the German poet Goethe. "Goethe was," he says, "someone who exercised all of his talents, who created himself as a unified human being on the basis of them."

Goethe also fit the role as somebody who, in Nietzsche's terms, "experimented with his life." At various times in his life he was a civil servant, he was a lawyer, he was a poet and he was a playwright. Within the scope of his writing, he tried many different styles, and, of course, his works are voluminous. He was a passionate man and had a rather intricate social life. In other words, he was just the sort of person who explored the limits— who exercised his talents to the maximum that Nietzsche really admires.

When we talk about the *Übermensch*, when we talk about higher and lower, when we talk about the will to power, I think it is very important to keep in mind that what Nietzsche is ultimately concerned with is creativity; with a kind of spiritual life, and not simply with a world of power as that phrase might seem. The notion of the will to power itself is problematic. It is a phrase Nietzsche discovered early on, and he really fell in love with it. We all know how this can work. You fall in love with a phrase and you keep using it but its meaning keeps changing and it often carries with it connotations that you would really just as soon do away with.

To be very particular about this, the notion of the will to power is really borrowed, in a way, from Schopenhauer, Nietzsche's mentor. Nietzsche rejects Schopenhauer, and he rejects him rather fairly as a pessimist, and he rejects his metaphysics. In particular, the will to power is derived from Schopenhauer's notion of "the will," where the will refers to the thing in itself, reality in itself, what is behind all the appearances of the world. As we saw, Nietzsche rejects that very distinction between appearance and reality. The idea of a core reality, a reality behind the scenes, is something that he utterly rejected. The notion of will in Schopenhauer is one of the first things to go in his rejection of Schopenhauer. I would argue that perhaps the will to power should go with it, but it doesn't.

Second, the notion of power itself: Power itself is not military power. The word Nietzsche uses here is the word *macht,* not *reich.* Power is very often the power of thought, the power of the imagination, and the power of creativity. There is a sense in which what we are talking about is not so much power over other people as self-mastery. Nietzsche, despite his attack on asceticism and slave morality, makes self-mastery one of the centerpieces of his entire philosophy. It applies to the masters also, but there is a sense in which here it is much less desperate—the idea that masters also master themselves in their pursuit of excellence. There is a sense in which the discipline of slave morality, which really has allowed us to deny ourselves and, in a way, shape ourselves in ways which we can aspire to—here too, we see that tension in Nietzsche between the extent to which we are self-realizing and we are capable of self-mastery, and the extent to which, in some sense, we are the product and the victim of the way we are brought up, our genes, and so on.

Schopenhauer took the will to be metaphysical. Nietzsche rejects metaphysics and rejects that notion of the will to power. A better interpretation (although Nietzsche occasionally falls into the idea of talking about the will to power as the basis of everything) and one that fits his theory, I think, in a more sympathetic way, is that the will to power really is a kind of slogan covering a theory of motivation. Here, too, Nietzsche gets ambiguous. There is a sense in which he sometimes thinks about this theory as universal and covering everything. He sometimes talks about the animal kingdom, as well as all human behavior, as motivated by the will to power. When he is in his more modest moods, and I think his more reasonable moods, he talks about the will to power as a more particular motivation—one that motivates a great many human behaviors and leaves aside for a moment the animal kingdom.

Basically, the idea is that what motivates us is a drive to feel powerful. There is an ambiguity here, too, because Nietzsche sometimes talks about the will to *having* power, and sometimes he talks about the importance of the *feeling* of power. While we can see how these two might fit together, they are certainly very different. One can be very powerful without knowing it. One can have the feeling of great power, and the feeling might be an illusion. The idea is that what we act for, for the most part, is power.

How should we understand this? I think the first way to do it is to oppose it to its most obvious motivational rival; that is, hedonism, the idea that people act for the sake of pleasure or for the avoidance of pain. In the utilitarians, who are more or less his exact contemporaries, this theory—that we act for pleasure and to avoid pain—is absolutely the centerpiece of their philosophy—its first premise, if you like. The idea is that you can understand human behavior by understanding what people enjoy, what they don't enjoy, what gives them pain. Then you can look at their behavior as a kind of means/ends strategy to achieving the most pleasure and avoiding pain. Nietzsche wants to say, "nonsense."

Look at how people behave. To be sure, sometimes they act for pleasure, and sometimes they act in a delayed way for gratification at the end of some means and causal continuum. The truth is most people don't act for pleasure; they act for all sorts of reasons. The ones that Nietzsche wants to highlight are those which he would call "power." When I think about how to understand power here, I think maybe the best way to take it is something very close to what we call "self-esteem." That is a very limp notion, perhaps because it has been around California too long.

The basic idea is that self-esteem is not just feeling good about yourself, but it is being energized by your own ideas, and energized by your own desires, and energized by your own talents. Self-esteem isn't just a kind of superficial feeling about yourself, and it certainly isn't about standing in front of the mirror in the morning and doing some affirmations. Self-esteem can be taken as a kind of very deep notion, in which what you do is think of yourself as confident, and you think of yourself as capable, and you think of yourself in terms of your ideal. What Nietzsche says is if you watch human behavior, what you will see is that a great deal of our behavior can be much better characterized as the will to power in this sense, rather than as the pursuit of pleasure/avoidance of pain.

Take the idea of the ancient martyrs, early Christians who allowed themselves to be persecuted in the name of their faith. You have to really stretch to come up with any theory that says this is for the sake of pleasure and the avoidance of pain. One can bring in the theological picture and say that they are willing to take an awful lot of pain in the short term for an infinite amount of bliss in the long term, but that is not very convincing. Even if they believe that, there is a sense in which what motivated them is much more powerful than the promise of eternal pleasure in the future. What motivated them was, first of all, the sense that they were right and righteous—the sense that they were standing for a cause that was much more important than their mere individual lives could possibly represent.

Think of the way our students behave. I often ask them, "Why are you taking this class?" Of course, they flatter me and say, "It's because we enjoy it." I say, "No. I am glad that is true, but why are you taking this class?" Inevitably, if we trace the chain of reasons, it has something to do with how they think about themselves; what their ultimate aspirations are. While there is a kind of lip story about "this will make me happy at the end of it," it is very clear that what motivates them is something much more powerful, and that is their notion of themselves.

The idea is that the will to power is a theory. It is a theory about what moves us. It often, in Nietzsche's language, takes us into some of the really gory details of human self-deception and hypocrisy. Talking about Christianity, for example, he says that a great deal of what Christian psychology talks about—for example, loving thy neighbor and having compassion and pity for those worse off than yourself—really is a kind of hidden screen for motivation that is much more vicious.

What is often called "love" is a kind of contempt. Love in the more romantic sense, which we celebrate as the most selfless of all emotions, Nietzsche wants to say is not selfless at all. When you come right down to it, what we call romantic love is really possession—power straight and simple. Pity, an emotion which is much praised through history, particularly in the Christian tradition, he wants to say we think of in terms of simply feeling sorry for someone who is worse off. When you think about pity, what you come to understand very quickly is it is the kind of smugness of superiority; it is feeling higher, more powerful, more fortunate than this other person. One might also note that pity can give one a certain sense of pleasure. "Better him than me." Even the sense of pleasure (note that it follows from the sense of power and superiority), is not itself the goal.

There is a picture that Nietzsche has which he pursues in many details. I would argue that the real interest is in the details and the kind of psychological analysis he gives us. The idea is that the will to power is a theory of human behavior which, whether or not it covers all cases, covers more than enough cases to make it a very plausible and very often dominant theory about what makes us tick. One can think of the will to power in another way. I think this is something that also permeates Nietzsche's philosophy, and it does not have to do with motivation at all, and it is certainly not metaphysics. It is the will to power as a kind of celebration, in particular, of what I call "the passionate life."

If you think back over the history of philosophy, both East and West, what you find is an overwhelming amount of emphasis on freedom from the emotions. The idea is that emotions enslave us. Rather, it is a life of reason, a life of contemplation, and philosophers since ancient times have often talked about peace of mind and tranquility and what at one point was called *apathea*. This is sort of translated in our current term as apathy, which does not mean not caring, but it does mean being free from the enslavement of passion.

For Nietzsche, as for Kierkegaard, there is a very powerful view to the contrary. Namely, it is, "What makes life meaningful is passion." A life without passion would be essentially meaningless. Some of the ancient stoics used to say we should live our lives without attachments. The idea was to make us invulnerable to fortune and fate. The less you are attached to, whether it is people you love or things that you own or positions that you hold, the less that anyone can take away from you. Ultimately, you can reduce yourself to the point where all you can lose is your life, but having removed other attachments, even that is no big loss.

This is the height of what Nietzsche calls slave morality. It is not an accident that at least some of the ancient stoics were slaves. (I should add that one of them, at least, was a Roman emperor.) The idea is this whole thought about cutting attachments—cutting your losses—is exactly the kind of defensiveness that characterized slave morality. By contrast, what Nietzsche wants to say is that attachments are what life is all about. Attachments to people? Perhaps. Nietzsche himself was not big on relationships. Attachments to ideals, attachments to aspirations, attachments to works (works of art, your own creativity), are absolutely essential. So, against the general trend in philosophy to praise a kind of meekness—a kind of withdrawal, a kind of emotional absence—Nietzsche wants to say life is passion.

One of the things we might note is that throughout Nietzsche's works there is a metaphor of energy that permeates much of his works. One should say that in terms of the history of science, the notion of energy was a kind of new arrival. There was some semblance of the concepts of energy in earlier centuries, but it is only really in the 19th century that the notion of energy comes to hold a central place in physics. Before that, people talked about matter in motion, and inertia and momentum, and so on.

The idea of energy as something which was distinctive in its own right was something that was fairly new. As I mentioned in the first lecture, Nietzsche was by no means opposed to science. He looked at science as the source of some great ideas. This notion of energy was what he wanted to pick up as a kind of metaphor for human life too. What the human soul or human psyche operates with is energy. It is not far to see that Freud picks up the same metaphor, and makes it quite literally the centerpiece of his early psychodynamics.

Thinking of energy now not as a physical notion, but as something very much a key to human life, one thinks of a life of excitement and adventure. One thinks of, especially, the kinds of adventures that give rise to the "grand passions." Nietzsche, here, wants to say, along with Kierkegaard, that it is the passionate life, and passionate commitment, and passionately throwing yourself into what you do that makes life worthwhile.

Let's be very careful here. Not every passion is desirable. When Nietzsche defends the passionate life, he is not saying any passion at all is okay. Some passions are what he calls "life-stultifying." One can take as a primary example the passion of resentment. Resentment is the passion that defines slave morality and the life of slaves. Resentment is a passion which is, on the one hand, rather brilliant. It can even be creative. The very notion of resentment suggests someone who is very low in self-esteem, someone who is putting themselves down, someone who is unwilling to be constructively creative because their life is tied up in this kind of simmering derivation of someone whom they hold responsible for their problems.

What Nietzsche is concerned with are the grand passions. The philosopher Hegel, whom Nietzsche often puts down, said "Nothing great is ever done without passion." (It is often ignored the fact that Kant said something very similar earlier.) For Nietzsche, this becomes the very centerpiece of his philosophy—not a side slogan. Love, for instance, is absolutely essential. It is not necessarily romantic love—which Nietzsche was inexperienced at, didn't do very well with, and he did not think was very important; rather, it is the kind of love that he had for the ancient Greeks, the kind of love that he had for the future of perhaps not mankind, but for the possibilities of evolution, the *Übermensch*. It was certainly the passion he had, and he shows, in his own work. No one writes more passionately than Nietzsche. No one uses more exclamation points. There is a sense in which what Nietzsche takes life to be is manifested in his work.

He also says that there is really no distinction, no dichotomy, as philosophers have often argued, between reason and passion. This goes back all the way to Plato at least. Plato, Nietzsche says, turned his reason into a tyrant precisely to keep his passions under control. Passion is often conceived of in an animalistic, bestial way, as if they are foreign forces trying to take over. Freud notably referred to the passions in general as the "It"—the "Id." There is a sense in which, as Nietzsche points out, every passion has its own quantum of reason. Passions are not simply irrational forces from our animal nature.

Rather, passions are themselves forms of insight—ways of understanding the world, ways of orienting or gearing ourselves to our lives. This, ultimately, is what is important for Nietzsche. As opposed to life's stultifying passions like resentment, he praises the life-enhancing passions, like love. Ultimately, it is the love of life itself which is his highest ideal.

Life affirmation—and that means not appealing to another world, a Christian heaven or a future state of affairs in society, but simply accepting your life as your life and loving it—is the highest virtue. This is where eternal recurrence fits into his philosophy. It is the test. How do you feel about your life? Are you capable of affirming your life in such a way that you would repeat it exactly as it is an infinite number of times? The opposition here is his teacher Schopenhauer, who said looking at life—much less thinking about it as repeating an endless number of times—what you come up with is the conclusion that it amounts to nothing.

In Nietzsche's existential test, what we come to see is the possibility of a very different picture. We can look at our lives, and look at the sorts of things that he has been talking about, even our own limitations, and say, "Yes. This is what I want, even infinite times more."

Three Grand Inquisitors—Dostoevsky, Kafka, Hesse
Lecture 14

In this lecture I'd like to discuss three literary figures who fit quite well into the sensibilities that we have been discussing. They are the Russian author Dostoevsky, the Czech author Kafka, and the Swiss author Hermann Hesse.

Fyodor Dostoevsky (1821–1881) was Nietzsche's contemporary, had a Kierkegaardian religious sensibility, and anticipated some of the central themes in Heidegger's philosophy. In his *Notes from Underground*, Dostoevsky introduces us to a character who is obsessed with free will, his "most advantageous advantage," and is utterly spiteful, indecisive, and ineffective as a result. His reaction to his own liver disease is to let it get worse. The central theme is freedom or free will. Dostoevsky attacks the Enlightenment notion that freedom and happiness go hand in hand. Being spiteful isn't a personality disorder but a philosophical position, a manifestation of free will. In his novel *The Idiot*, by contrast, Dostoevsky introduces us to a character who is "perfectly good," who is motivated only by the purest moral sentiments, and who becomes a disaster for all around him. This is, in one sense, a defense of Kant's position that intention is what matters.

In his *Brothers Karamazov*, Dostoevsky introduces the problem of nihilism by way of brother Ivan, anticipating Nietzsche a few years later. Ivan, educated in the West, has imbibed much of Enlightenment philosophy. Between his sensual older brother, Dmitri, and his younger brother, Aloysha, we see the spectrum of European philosophy. Dostoevsky poses a number of dilemmas about human life that are intended to place the movement of nihilism in higher relief. In *The Brothers Karamazov*, he also introduces "the Grand Inquisitor," the head of the Christian church who, when faced with Christ's second coming, insists on executing him once again. In *Crime and Punishment*, Dostoevsky pursues the idea that "if there is no God, then everything is permitted."

Franz Kafka (1883–1924) was a Jewish writer living in pre-communist Czechoslovakia (Bohemia). His writings exemplify "the Absurd." They also raise the question of self-identity in a brilliantly original way. Gregor Samsa becomes a giant insect in "Metamorphosis." The story emphasizes a Cartesian separation of mind and body. Our self-identity is construed by our role in society. Kafka's images of guilt and innocence in *The Trial* powerfully influence Albert Camus in *The Stranger*. For Kafka, human beings are guilty by virtue of their very existence. This theme is common to many of our writers—consciousness, instead of being a blessing, may be a disease. With consciousness, comes despair.

> **Kafka's images of guilt and innocence in *The Trial* powerfully influence Albert Camus in *The Stranger*.**

Hermann Hesse (1877–1862) was a German-Swiss writer who bridged the abyss between European and Eastern (Indian) thought, particularly Buddhism. In *Siddhartha*, Hesse retells the story of the Buddha and his enlightenment in very human terms. Hesse was also an admirer and advocate of Nietzsche. In *Demian*, he presents a quasi-occult image of the exceptional person, a child who prefigures the *Übermensch* in being "beyond good and evil." In *Steppenwolf*, he gives us a superior adult, who thinks of himself as half man and half wolf. Consequently, he is miserably unhappy, trapped in a Nietzschean image of himself. Like Kafka, Hesse challenges Nietzsche's aggressiveness and optimism. Ultimately, Hesse claims that one has many selves. Like Kafka, Hesse radically challenges our ordinary concept of self. In *Steppenwolf*, he offers us the Eastern image of a "no self" self, the self as an onion—not a peach—with many layers but no essential core. With Hesse, one starts with Nietzsche but attains a certain passion that even Nietzsche didn't understand. ■

Essential Reading

Solomon, *Existentialism*, pp. 33-42 (Dostoevsky); 166-168 (Kafka); pp. 79–92 (Hesse).

Dostoevsky, *Notes from Underground* and *The Grand Inquisitor*, trans. by Ralph E. Matlaw, and *The Brothers Karamazov*, trans. by Constance Garnett.

Hesse, *Demian*, trans. by Michael Roloff and Michael Lebeck, and *Steppenwolf*, trans. by Basil Creighton.

Kafka, *Metamorphosis and Other Stories*, and *The Trial*, trans. by Breon Mitchell.

Introductory Questions to Consider

1. Do you believe that "if there is no God, everything is permitted"? What does this mean?

2. To what extent to you think that "Kafkaesque" descriptions of the world are true and warranted? Is life ultimately supposed to make sense?

Advanced Questions to Consider

1. Can you describe the Buddhist "no self" in terms that are congenial to Western philosophy, existentialism in particular?

2. Kafka's character Joseph K. is arrested for no reason, put on trial, and ultimately condemned to death. In what sense are we all "guilty" in some such sense?

Three Grand Inquisitors—Dostoevsky, Kafka, Hesse
Lecture 14—Transcript

In this lecture I'd like to discuss three literary figures who fit quite well into the sensibilities that we have been discussing. They are the Russian author Dostoevsky, the Czech author Kafka, and the Swiss author Hermann Hesse.

Dostoevsky shares with Kierkegaard a very powerful religious sensibility. At the same time, he shares with Kierkegaard the view that being a Christian is by no means easy and not necessarily a happy state of affairs. Rather, being a Christian—having faith—requires going through the dark night of the soul and being steeped in doubt. He also shares a number of themes with Nietzsche. As you will see, some of the harder aspects of Nietzsche's philosophy come out in some of Dostoevsky's most brutal novels. They did not know each other, although Nietzsche was vaguely familiar with Dostoevsky's work toward the end of his life. We will see, too, that Dostoevsky anticipates some central themes in Heidegger's philosophy.

I'd like to talk about a couple of Dostoevsky's works, most importantly, perhaps, *The Brothers Karamazov*. Let me start by talking about a novelette that he wrote called *Notes from Underground*. In that novelette, he introduces us with a really unlikable character who describes himself in the first paragraph as a mean man, a spiteful man. Indeed, spite and resentment characterize almost everything that he does. We are told right away that he is suffering from a disease of the liver, and to the suggestion that he ought to see a doctor, his response is: "Let it get worse."

One can interpret the novel in various different ways. A central theme is the theme of freedom and what other philosophers would call free will. He is attacking the Enlightenment and with it the idea that people can improve themselves—a thesis that goes back to Nietzsche. He is attacking the idea that people can have free choice in such a way that it leads to happiness. This is an assumption that we often make. Certainly, in this country especially, the idea is that freedom and happiness go hand in hand, and "un-freedom" and unhappiness go hand in hand. What Dostoevsky shows us here is that the two are opposed. Happiness is often precisely the absence of freedom.

In his *Notes,* as in his other novels, Dostoevsky launches a vigorous attack on the whole Enlightenment. The Enlightenment among other things portrayed the idea of rationality and freedom in such a way that we could figure it all out; we could construct for ourselves the perfect society in which we would all be happy. It was represented, perhaps, by some of the festivals and some of the enterprises of the time in which philosophers, even in Russia, were starting to talk about the promises of the future and how everything could be put right. What gets left out, according to this character, is our personal freedom. He says with reference to the whole Enlightenment mode of thought and the whole idea of reason: "Two plus two equals four," as if that is what it is all about. His idea is that what is most important to us, what he calls our "most advantageous advantage," is our own free will.

Insofar as we fit in with the rational schema—insofar as we go along with the plans that this Enlightenment society gives to us to make us happy—what we lose, no matter how happy we become, is our freedom. So, being spiteful is not just a personality disorder for this character. Being spiteful is a philosophical principle. Insofar as one is spiteful, what one does is exercise one's freedom, even in the face of one's own personal advantage. The idea is that freedom is supposed to be a means—freedom is a means to happiness by choosing what is to our own benefit. What the Dostoevsky character tells us is, it is the very opposite. Freedom is a good in its own right. It is the most important benefit that we have. To sacrifice it, by way of joining the others and seeing ourselves in terms of this grand plan for the good society is to essentially render ourselves inhuman.

Needless to say, this view renders the underground man all but impotent. When he has to make a simple decision he finds himself incapable of doing it because insofar as freedom is something that can be predicted, that means it is not freedom at all. If you tell me that what I ought to choose is this, which will make me happier, then according to the underground man what I ought to choose is precisely the opposite. One can argue this in a number of different ways, so we are not surprised when throughout the novelette the character himself ends up being not only very unhappy and spiteful, but ends up doing nothing.

A very different picture is drawn for us in one of Dostoevsky's longer and more brilliant novels called *The Idiot*. The idiot in this case is a character who is rather highborn. His name is Prince Myshkin. The Prince has all the traits of, as Dostoevsky himself tells us, the "perfectly good" man. Again, what he is attacking is a certain kind of Enlightenment and philosophical picture; that is, if you have a person who is perfect or even very good, this will contribute to the well being of society. It was an assumption Aristotle made 2,500 years ago. It is built into the idea of Christianity, that Jesus is a figure to be emulated. It is because of Jesus, and Jesus as a moral example, that we all know what society should look like. It is key to the Enlightenment that what we try to do is develop character and develop rules such that we all get along together.

What is fascinating about *The Idiot* is that by doing good, he makes everyone's life terrible. He is surrounded by suicides, broken marriages; people are in many different ways rendered unhappy. The truth is we don't know what to do with goodness. The idea is that the consequences of goodness are not always good themselves. One can think of this as a kind of defense of Immanuel Kant's philosophy where he says it is really the intent that counts and not the consequences. This goes all the way back through the Judeo-Christian tradition. There it is intention of good will that is at stake, not necessarily what follows from our actions, which is often not up to us. Taken as such, it is a rather extreme example of how we can still say that Prince Myshkin is a perfectly good man, even if what he causes in his life is utter disaster.

The Brothers Karamazov is, I think, Dostoevsky's crowning achievement. In it he discusses, among other things, the whole question of nihilism, a concept that is very central to Nietzsche. As with Nietzsche, we should not think of Dostoevsky in any way as favoring it, but as being rabidly against it. "Nihilism" is a Russian term. It came from some earlier Russian authors. Dostoevsky was fully aware, as Nietzsche was aware, that it was a force that was really overtaking Europe. Like Kierkegaard, Dostoevsky didn't see the answer to nihilism as simply a renewed celebration of life. Quite to the contrary, he saw it as a return to traditional Christianity, even through Christianity as a very difficult pursuit, indeed.

The Brothers Karamazov concerns a family, the Karamazov family. The father, Fyodor, is a dirty old man. He drinks too much. He chases women. He has no religious sensibilities. He is basically a pig. He gives this, among other things, to his oldest son, Dmitri, who also has his father's sensuality, but just a bit more conscience. The second son, who is really the focus of the book, is the brother Ivan. Ivan has been well educated in the West, and he has adopted pretty thoroughly the Enlightenment philosophy, which Dostoevsky sees here as largely atheistic, overly rationalistic, and, consequently, as nihilistic as well. Ivan's thought experiments really dominate a good part of the novel.

The youngest son, Aloysha, is a sort of practicing novice saint. At the very beginning of the book, he witnesses the death of his elder, his mentor, and is shocked to find out that when the elder saint dies, his body is corrupted like any other body. Aloysha has his own struggles with doubt through the novel, many of them fed by brother Ivan. Between the three brothers one sees the whole spectrum of sensuality on the one side to a kind of spirituality on the other, with Ivan caught in-between with Enlightenment thinking.

There are two episodes in the book that I want to pay particular attention to. In a way, they are sort of off the center stream of the story because they are both stories that Ivan tells to Aloysha, partly in order to express his own doubts about Christianity, but also to spare Aloysha's doubts as well. The first is a section called "Rebellion," in which Ivan presents what we have already been introduced to as the problem of evil. That is the idea that how can a perfectly good, all-powerful, all-knowing God allow so much suffering to take place on the Earth.

In Ivan's telling of it, we don't focus on the larger statistics, the sorts of overall calamities that some of the earlier philosophers have dwelled upon. Instead, he takes a rather horrible example of one Russian nobleman, who dealt with a child who had essentially killed one of his dogs, and had the dogs set loose on the child. The dogs ripped him apart. The story is told in such bloody detail that anyone who reads it—Aloysha who hears it—is shocked and repulsed. Then Ivan ends up by saying, "How can we believe in a God who can justify any such event?" Basically, he says: If believing and accepting such an event—such cruelty—is the price of believing in God, then personally, I don't want to pay the ticket.

The second example is perhaps the most famous single section of the book. It has to do with an even deeper doubt than the problem of evil. The idea is that Jesus essentially is our Savior not just in the sense that we are in some sense relieved of our sins. He gives us a kind of freedom. "The truth shall make you free." That idea that freedom is essential to Christianity is something that Dostoevsky wants to throw seriously into question. One way to read this is to look at it as a kind of internecine squabble between the two primary sects of Christianity—Catholicism on the one hand, Protestantism on the other. I think that is looking at it in much too narrow a fashion. It is really a dilemma of human life written large that is being covered here, and it really has nothing necessarily to do with Christianity and Christianity's sects particularly.

The story, very briefly, is that the second coming actually happens. Jesus comes back to Earth, and he happens to come back right in the middle of the Spanish Inquisition. The "Grand Inquisitor" who was in charge of all this is stunned by Jesus's reappearance. In a long dialogue with the Savior, he comes up with the idea that Jesus really has to go. What Christianity has done over the past almost 2,000 years (1,400 years) is it has succeeded in making people happy. They are happy at the hopes that it raises. They are happy at the idea of being saved. They are happy at the very idea of being in the shadow of Jesus who has not yet appeared. With Jesus's appearance, people now have to face reality.

Christianity is not about freedom. It is not about happiness, or at least it can't be about both of those. Given the choice between freedom and happiness, people will always choose happiness; rather, the Grand Inquisitor chooses it for them. At the end of the story, Jesus is re-crucified, and what we find is that the easy interpretation of Christianity—the idea that freedom, happiness, and faith can all fit together in a happy package—is just not the case.

The same kind of gruesome picture is depicted for us in Dostoevsky's novel *Crime and Punishment.* The story is really very simple. A man commits a gruesome crime, essentially under the spell of nihilism. There are no values.

There is nothing that is worth obeying. Although the crime itself is rather petty (also rather brutal), the character throughout the course of the novel finds himself haunted by a kind of deep guilt.

The story itself is the story of how this guilt manifests itself. It goes back to a line (perhaps the most famous single line of *The Brothers Karamazov)* where Ivan, as he is going insane toward the end of the novel, concludes that "If there is no God, everything is permitted." This is a slogan that is often used to interpret Nietzsche's philosophy. I hope I have said enough about Nietzsche's philosophy to show that Nietzsche intended nothing of the sort. Rather, in Ivan, what we get is picture of nihilism at its absolute worst—the idea that it is a world that entirely depended upon God for its values and for the authority for us to obey those values, and without God we are left with simply nothing.

Franz Kafka wrote primarily in this century. He was a Czech philosopher and author. Anyone who knows any of Kafka's short stories can very quickly identify him as one of the primary authors of what Camus would later call "the absurd." The concept appears in Kierkegaard almost a century before. The idea of the absurd is taken to spectacular heights in Kafka's works. I want to talk about two of them here, both of which we have mentioned before.

First of all, there is his short story, perhaps his best single work, called *Metamorphosis*. That is the one where Gregor Samsa wakes up in the morning and finds himself turned into a giant insect that is pictured as a cockroach—a particularly disgusting insect. Samsa is a clerk—a perfectly ordinary person. He lives in a family—a perfectly ordinary family. He is a good family member. He is a good worker. When he wakes up in this rather striking state, his first thought and the thought that pursues him throughout the first part of the text, is simply the thought: "How am I going to get to work today?" It shows, in a sense, a very deep question about self-identity, because there is a sense in which we think of ourselves, body and soul, as inherently fused in a certain way—especially, we think of ourselves as dependent on who we are in terms of what we look like and what our abilities are.

What this story does is, it emphasized a very Cartesian way of thinking about mind and body. In this story, the body is thoroughly changed in a way that most of us can't really imagine at all, but the mind remains exactly as it is. What happens throughout the story is that Samsa has to cope with the idea, first of all, of how he is going to get out of bed, then, how he might get to work—then the main part of the story is that he has to work with his horrible effect on his family. One can imagine waking up in the morning and finding one's sibling or son turned into an insect. It is a story with an unhappy ending. How else could it end? One could interpret it as a kind of rehearsal of Kafka's own very difficult time with his family, and in particular with his father.

I think there is a more important theme here; that is, how our self-identity is construed and in what sense it is construed first of all by our body (that is not the important issue) as much as how our self-identity is construed by a role in society and how other people treat us. So, when he finds himself incapable of doing the job with which he identifies himself, when he finds himself horrifying his family who come to despise him and hate him, that raises for Samsa a very real problem. We will see it repeated when we talk about Heidegger and then Sartre.

The other novel I want to talk about by Kafka is his novel called *The Trial.* I emphasized in my discussion of Camus and *The Stranger* that Kafka provided a sort of model for the trial that Camus stages for us, for Meursault. The idea that pervades here in virtually all of Kafka's works is the idea that we are all essentially guilty. It does not have to do with any particular crime. There may be no crime at all. There is a sense in which just being human— just being conscious—makes us guilty. We will see this theme repeated in Kafka, who is going to say in his own language that human beings are essentially guilty just by virtue of their existence. What we find here, too, in *The Trial,* is the idea that that guilt pervades everything we do just by virtue of the fact that we are conscious.

Here we can see a theme that is common to Kierkegaard, to Dostoevsky, and now to Kafka. It is namely the idea that consciousness, contrary to being a blessing to us, can also be a disease. It allows us to see our life in a way that animals, for example, never see their lives. It allows us to be aware of good and evil in a way that animals never see values. It allows us to see ourselves as essentially inadequate creatures. We don't simply accept ourselves unthinkingly as we are. We are always self-conscious, and with that self-consciousness comes not only guilt but a kind of despair.

All of Kafka's novels and short stories give us different ways of viewing and manifesting that despair. When we describe something as Kafkaesque, what we clearly have in mind is something that is not only absurd, but something that is very upsetting to our very notion of ourselves as human beings and our concept of life as it should be—in some sense rational, orderly, predictable. That is exactly what it is not in both *Metamorphosis* and *The Trial*.

Hermann Hesse was a Swiss writer. He was very well educated. We are now talking about a writer who worked in the mid-20th century, so he was already aware of Heidegger's philosophy, so I don't want to say that he influenced Heidegger so much as the other way around. The main philosophical influences on him were two. The one of most importance to us here is Frederick Nietzsche, because Nietzsche was someone Hesse read, and I think we can properly call him a follower. At the same time, he was influenced very powerfully by Buddhism. Buddhism really doesn't play much of a role in Western thought, and that is something that is really curious in itself. It has been known in outline by Westerners for a very long time. The first philosopher to really talk about Buddhism and bring it into the core of his philosophy was Arthur Schopenhauer in the 19th century.

Hesse is one of the few writers who also tries to bridge European and Indian thought. He actually writes one full novel called *Siddhartha*, the Buddha's given name. What he does there is brings Buddha into a kind of Western picture or a picture that Westerners can easily understand. In terms of his admiration of Nietzsche, which is what I want to talk about, he takes on a number of different themes. I want to talk about two of his works in which these themes become prominent. The first is a picture of a young man, a schoolboy, named Demian. These days Demian often represents a kind of satanic figure. The idea is that he may even be the son of the devil.

I am thinking of a recent television episode. Basically, Demian is really just a well-adjusted young man, so well adjusted that he is independent in a way that children are not supposed to be independent. He has what Hesse refers to as the mark of Cain. Let's not talk about devilishness here so much as we should talk about something very different—a kind of independence, a kind of refusal to go along. Demian's influence in his fellow classmates and friends is something which, far from being demonic, is always just the kind of puzzle, just the kind of challenge, that philosophers in this tradition always like to talk about.

More important, perhaps, is Hesse's depiction of a much older man. In fact, he is at the rather precise age of 55. This is the novel *Steppenwolf*, in which the central metaphor is this character Harry Haller, who is half man and half wolf. It is important because it is a metaphor that was used by Goethe several generations earlier. Goethe talks about man as half human—rational, sensitive, cultivated—and half wild beast. One of the challenges that Hesse wants to bring is just this very bifurcated notion of the self, but in terms of a unification of the self (something which Nietzsche praises Goethe for achieving); rather, further fragmentation of the self—in fact, giving up the notion of the self altogether.

The *Steppenwolf* concerns this character Haller, who has vowed to commit suicide when he reaches 55 because that is old enough. He is in every way a Nietzschian man. He considers himself one of the masters—not in any brutal way; he is a very polite and well-behaved good citizen. But he considers himself one of the masters in the sense that he is well educated, extremely creative. He is just the kind of character that Nietzsche himself aspired to be, and just the kind of character that Nietzsche represents in his discussion of the higher man. Like Kafka, Hesse challenges the very idea of Nietzsche's self, the idea of aspiration, the idea of taking life so seriously. The *Steppenwolf* has the thesis that what Haller is mistaken in is precisely his conception of himself as half and half, man and wolf. Borrowing from Buddhist philosophy, Hesse wants to say that Haller has "no self," or many selves.

He illustrates this in what is the most delightful part of what is otherwise a serious and sometimes somber novel called *The Magic Theatre*, in which Haller is invited into this place where, among other things, all of his values are turned upside down. Part of his extremely good taste as a good citizen of

Europe at the beginning of the 20th century was that he loved classical music and had no time at all for popular music, jazz in particular. The first person he meets when he goes into The Magic Theatre is a quite accomplished jazz musician who teaches him how to appreciate this, in a sense, vulgar kind of music.

Most importantly, what he finds is the values are turned upside down. In The Magic Theatre, murder is permissible—not necessarily desirable, but permissible. Most importantly, when he enters The Magic Theatre he learns of the story of the self. We think of the self, in the West especially, as a kind of a fruit—let's say a peach, in particular. Namely there is a lot of flesh around it, where the flesh can be construed in terms of physical flesh as well as in terms of the acculturations of society, the accumulations of one's education, what one has become as a member of this or that particular culture. If you peel off the flesh, what you are left with is a kind of rock hard pit—the self.

In contrast to that, what we get in *Steppenwolf* is the very Eastern idea of the self as an onion. If you peel off the outer layers of an onion, what do you find? More layers. As you peel off more and more of those inner layers, you find nothing but more layers. When you finally peel off the last layers in the onion, you are left with nothing. There is a very wonderful Buddhist picture, and it is one that the *Steppenwolf*, Haller, is encouraged to accept. In accepting it, what he can also accept is the kind of joy and happiness which he has not learned hitherto.

If you think about Nietzsche's story, and how Nietzsche talks about aspiration and the *Übermensch* and self-discipline, all this is admirable and enormously influential and persuasive. But, for all of Nietzsche's attempts at humor (and he has a very subtle sense of humor), something is obviously missing; that is, humor, joy, happiness. Nietzsche talks about these things, but we are never convinced. With Hesse and his Buddhist orientation, we suddenly become convinced that one can start with something very much like Nietzsche, but nevertheless come out on the other end with a genuine joy of life that Nietzsche himself only talks about.

Husserl, Heidegger, and Phenomenology
Lecture 15

Being and Time is not really about Being. It is a kind of preliminary work, a kind of preparation for asking the more serious questions that he simply anticipates. What goes on in *Being and Time* is the examination of a very particular kind of Being—what Heidegger refers to as "the being through whom the question of Being comes into question." That is, us.

Edmund Husserl (1859–1938) was the founder of phenomenology. Phenomenology was a new version of Cartesianism, carving out the special realm of consciousness or "subjectivity." Phenomenology is the examination of consciousness. Phenomenology might be defined as "the study of the essential (or 'intentional') structures of experience." Intentionality means that consciousness is *about* something. Husserl himself was a mathematician who was primarily interested in the nature of necessary truth rather than the problems of life.

One of the most vitriolic recent controversies in philosophy involves the question, "Who was Heidegger?"

Philosophy, according to Husserl, seeks certainty, as Descartes did, not empirical facts, as in natural science. Husserl sought an "Archimedean point" from which to establish such a foundation for all knowledge. (Husserl's enduring interest is always focused on the "necessity" of mathematical truths.) Husserl's "Archimedean point," the foundation of all knowledge, was the Transcendental Ego. Husserl's phenomenology provided the method for the existentialist investigation of the self, first in the philosophy of Husserl's prize student, Martin Heidegger, then in the work of the French existentialist Jean-Paul Sartre.

Martin Heidegger (1889–1976) was a student of Husserl's, but he was formerly a student of theology and more concerned with the deep questions of human existence than the more abstract questions that fascinated his teacher.

(Heidegger later commented that the purpose of philosophy was to "invent a new God.") Heidegger's early work is often referred to as "existentialist," although he himself rejected that affiliation. His first work, *Being and Time*, has existentialist themes. The central question of Heidegger's philosophy was the "question of Being." This must be distinguished from more particular "ontic" queries about the nature of beings, or entities. "Ontology" (or "fundamental ontology") was his effort to understand the nature of Being as such. Being is to be understood from a phenomenological point of view. Being has clear religious overtones. We are essentially ontological creatures, which means, in Heidegger's view, that we necessarily query the world about our own existence and identity. The being that so queries the world, the being that each of us is, is what Heidegger calls "*Dasein*," or "being there."

The quest for Being first of all requires an understanding of "that being through whom the question of Being comes into being," in other words, *Dasein*. Looking at *Dasein* from a phenomenological point of view, it is first of all Being-in-the-World.

Rene Descartes' philosophy was the ancestor of Husserl's and Heidegger's.

Unlike Husserl and Descartes, Heidegger says our primordial experience is a unified experience of being in the world. Heidegger would not describe us in the more naturalistic terms of "human being," because from the innocence of the first-person view, the question of what we are in nature remains to be determined. He does not talk about consciousness or subjectivity. *Being and Time* is largely devoted to the phenomenological description of what it is to be a *Dasein*. Although Heidegger believed that fundamental ontology was only possible as phenomenology, he rejects Husserl's emphasis on consciousness and the Transcendental Ego.

Heidegger sketches out the essential "existential" features of *Dasein*. Because *Dasein* is essentially "ontological," it is, by its very nature, self-questioning. On the one hand, the idea that we are essentially questioning creatures is common to almost all philosophers, culminating in Descartes. On the other hand, Heidegger refuses to talk about this questioning in terms of consciousness and subjectivity, as Descartes and Husserl did. Consequently, *Dasein* has an identity crisis. It wants to know "who" it is. What we think of as our identity is a false one.

One of the most vitriolic recent controversies in philosophy involves the question, "Who was Heidegger?" Heidegger committed himself briefly to National Socialism (1933–34). He served as Rector of Freiburg University under Hitler, was responsible for the firing of Jewish professors, and gave several well-documented pro-Nazi speeches. Heidegger never repudiated National Socialism but only bemoaned its failure.

Reconciling his life to his philosophy is a problem. But as Nietzsche suggested, to understand a philosophy, we must understand the philosopher—only then does a full picture emerge. Heidegger denies that he is doing "ethics" in his "fundamental ontology," but it is not so obvious that his philosophical views are entirely separable from his personal and political commitments. ∎

Essential Reading

Selections from Heidegger's *Being and Time* in Solomon, *Existentialism*, pp. 93–123.

Chapter 11 of Solomon, *Continental Philosophy Since 1750*, pp. 152–172.

Supplementary Reading

Although still difficult, the best exposition of Husserl's phenomenological "method" is Edmund Husserl's *Paris Lectures*, in Solomon, *Phenomenology and Existentialism*. These were rewritten as *Cartesian Meditations: An Introduction to Phenomenology*. For the very courageous, try Heidegger, *Being and Time*, trans. by Joan Stambaugh.

Some good overviews of Heidegger are: Dreyfus, *Being-in-the-World: A Commentary on Heidegger's Being and Time, Division 1*; Guignon,

Heidegger and the Problem of Knowledge; Metha, *The Philosophy of Martin Heidegger*.

For an overview of Husserl, see Solomon, *Continental Philosophy Since 1750* (chapters on Husserl and Heidegger), and *From Rationalism to Existentialism*, "Martin Heidegger: Being and Being Human," pp.184–244. For a lighter approach to Heidegger, see Solomon, *Introducing the Existentialists*.

Introductory Questions to Consider

1. For Heidegger, what is the difference between the "ontic" and the "ontological"? Why is it important that we (i.e., "*Dasein*") are "ontological"?

2. According to Heidegger, when is it that we begin to deliberate on the particulars of a project in which we are engaged and start to see things as "things," as "objects"? Think of yourself engaged in an everyday project. Do you agree with him? Explain.

Advanced Questions to Consider

1. How does Heidegger's approach to phenomenology differ from Husserl's "phenomenological method"? What are some of the different underlying presuppositions?

2. What does Heidegger gain by referring to "*Dasein*" ("being-there") rather than "human consciousness" or just "people," for example? Is *Dasein* an individual? The human collective? Both? Neither? Why talk in this novel way?

3. What, in general, is the relationship between a philosopher and his philosophy? Nietzsche comments (in *Beyond Good and Evil*) that every philosophy is "the personal confession and a kind of involuntary and unconscious memoir." What would count as "pro-Nazi" implications in a treatise such as *Being and Time*? How explicit would such implications have to be?

Husserl, Heidegger, and Phenomenology
Lecture 15—Transcript

In this and the following lectures I would like to move firmly into the 20th century. The two philosophers we are going to be talking about are Martin Heidegger, the first reductionist, then Jean-Paul Sartre for the rest of the course.

I want to begin with a philosopher who is not an existentialist at all, but whose philosophy so influenced both Heidegger and Sartre that we really can't understand what they did without him. I am talking about Edmund Husserl, a Moravian (or Czech/German) philosopher who wrote at the very beginning of the 20th century. What he did was to invent a method. The method is called "phenomenology." (Both Heidegger and Sartre began their careers as phenomenologists.) Phenomenology is a version of Cartesianism. Husserl, at one point, traces it quite explicitly back to Descartes. It includes a very strong emphasis on "subjectivity"—on consciousness. The idea is that whatever we know about the world, whatever we know about objective truth, basically begins with and is based in consciousness as such.

So, phenomenology very simply described is the examination of consciousness or, literally, the examination of phenomena—that which appears to consciousness. One can summarize what Husserl had in mind by saying that phenomenology is the study of the essential structures of experience. What he was interested in was what makes experience possible, what makes our knowledge of objects possible, what makes, most importantly, the necessary presuppositions of experience possible.

When he talks about the structures of experience, what he is talking about, among other things, is: "How our acts of consciousness," as he puts it, "relate to the objects of consciousness." There is one concept above all that defines consciousness for Husserl. It is a notion which is borrowed from the scholastics in medieval times. It is the notion of "intentionality."

Let me explain it very briefly by saying intentionality is the thesis that consciousness is always about something. If you believe, you believe something or other. If you perceive, you have to perceive something or other.

If you have an emotion—say, anger—you have to be angry about something or at someone. For Husserl, all consciousness is intentional in just this sense. This is also a notion which lends itself to a certain kind of move which in Descartes is absolutely central. Descartes talked about examining what we might call the ideas in consciousness, but with a kind of problem that surrounded this. One the one hand, you examine your own subjectivity. The question is how can you infer, on the basis of your subjectivity, to the reality of the world outside of you? This is sometimes referred to as the problem of "solipsism," the idea of being caught in one's own consciousness.

Husserl very often comes dangerously close to the same problem, except that whereas Descartes insisted that he doubt all of his objective leads until he could prove them on the basis of subjectivity, Husserl says that is going too far—the things of our experience are, in fact, the things of the world, and that it would be absurd to deny that. For the purposes of phenomenology, we are interested in them just as objects of experience and not as objects of the world. Or, to anticipate what I am going to say about Heidegger, Husserl thinks that phenomenology is one thing; "ontology" (a study of the things of the world) is something different.

In order to carry out his method, Husserl suggests that we make a couple of key philosophical moves. The first and most important of them is what he sometimes calls the "bracketing" of the natural world. The idea here is that instead of simply taking our experience as the perception of things in the world, rather what I do is I suspend any judgment about the reality of things, and I simply describe the objects of experience as such.

For example, I might think that what I see is a horse. On the other hand, I also can imagine a horse. I can also dream of a horse. Perhaps, under some very strange conditions, I might hallucinate a horse. Even though the status of the reality of the horse is very different in those different cases, in each of them I can describe what it is to experience the horse. So, phenomenology wants to talk about my experiencing of the object, and not particularly to talk about what it is for that object to exist as a thing in the world.

Husserl, as I say, was not an existentialist. He was interested in none of the questions about the meaning of life and so on that we have been discussing.

Rather, he came into philosophy from mathematics. His interest in phenomenology grew out of a concern for the philosophy of arithmetic and the status of mathematical truths. What is it that makes two plus two equal four true? Is it simply a matter of convention? Is it a truth about some Platonic realm in very peculiar entities? Is it simply a matter of logic? What Husserl says is "none of these."

Basically, phenomenology is a way of talking about mathematical truth in terms of necessity of a very key element, and necessity in terms of the structure of consciousness. What Husserl seeks, as did Descartes, is a kind of certainty. He thinks it is simply impossible to do what most philosophers have tried to do, which is somehow to derive certainty from our experience of the world. Instead, we have to understand certainty in terms of certain intuitions which are basic to those particular experiences of the world. You will see a move like this very much in Heidegger, too.

In order to get the necessity that he seeks, what Husserl needs is what we might call an "Archimedean point." Archimedes said, "Give me a place to stand and I will move the Earth." What Husserl wants is a place to stand in philosophy and to understand the nature of perception and mathematics and all the other things that we do. That place turns out to be what he calls the "Transcendental Ego," or more generally, "consciousness." He shifts between consciousness and the Transcendental Ego for much of his career. It is a method in its basic outline that, as I said, greatly influences first Heidegger, and then Sartre. The ways in which they use it are going to be very far afield from the concerns and the introduction that Husserl gave it.

Martin Heidegger was born at the end of the 19th century. He was a theology student as opposed to a mathematician. We can guess right from the start that his concerns were going to be very closely tied to the current concerns of human existence and the meaning of human life. The theological background is not insignificant; there is a sense in which religion is going to permeate all of Heidegger's philosophy. He writes very much in a theological mode. His writings are notoriously obscure and difficult. In the various interpretations that have been advanced of this very difficult work, one of them—and certainly one that predominates—is that there is something by way of a theological background—not necessarily the traditional notion of the monotheistic, Judeo-

Christian, Islamic God, but something more innovative. Heidegger often says in his work such things as: "Only a god can save us," and "What we must do now is invent new gods."

Heidegger is often referred to as an "existentialist." I think that this is to a certain extent true, and that is why he is included here. I should emphasize that it is really only due to his first great work, a work called *Being and Time*, which he never actually finished. (He gave it up and started turning in a new direction.) Nevertheless, I think *Being and Time* is so central to existentialist thinking that, although Heidegger himself rejected the term, I think we need to characterize Heidegger as one of the great existentialist thinkers of the century.

The concept that concerned him most, and what *Being and Time* is all about, is what he calls the "question of Being." Right away we get the sense that we are talking about something very profoundly philosophical. We get the sense that what we are talking about is something all embracing, and that is exactly what Heidegger intends. He distinguishes between Being and beings, or entities. He says through the history of philosophy, philosophers have worried about entities, what it is for them to exist and what they are really made of, and how they relate to each other causally.

What they haven't sufficiently pursued is the question: What is the ground of Being which makes the appearance of entities even possible to us? This is the question that he wants to ask. Even though I say that he changes his philosophy after *Being and Time,* it is something like the "question of Being" turned into later what he calls the "history of Being," which predominates in his philosophy.

Being and Time is not really about Being. It is a kind of preliminary work, a kind of preparation for asking the more serious questions that he simply anticipates. What goes on in *Being and Time* is the examination of a very particular kind of Being—what Heidegger refers to as "the being through whom the question of Being comes into question." That is, us. Here is where he, first of all, moves from what he calls the "ontic" dimension—namely, the study of mere entities—to "Being" more generally, and the concern with "Being" more generally, which he calls "ontology"—a very well worn, ancient philosophical term. Ontology is the study of Being, as such. It also includes the study of the being through whom Being come into question, and that is ourselves.

Like Husserl, he approaches philosophy from the first-person standpoint. Phenomenology as I just discussed it is the examination of our own subjectivity. With Heidegger, it takes on an added religious dimension. There is a sense always with Heidegger, which increases with his philosophy, that there is a sense in which we are not so much active in the world, much less producing the world; rather, it is a sense of passivity. Heidegger is fond of using words like: "The world disclosing itself to us." The question of Being becomes: Under what conditions can things disclose themselves?

It is phenomenology, in a sense, that begins with our immediate experience. Although, let me say right now, and I will say many times again, Heidegger will not use at all words like "experience," or "consciousness," or "mind." If we begin with what I will call, because I do not have a substitute without using Heideggerian jargon, "my basic experience," it is of a very different sort than what we find in a great many philosophers. In particular, the idea is that when I look at my experience, the first premise, the first realization is not, as Descartes suggested, that "I recognize myself as a thinking thing." My first experience is what Heidegger simply refers to as "being there." It is a sense of: "Here I am in a world."

This sense of being here in a world Heidegger gives the name *"Dasein."* *Dasein* is really the central feature of the whole of *Being and Time.* One might say that *Dasein* is us, and Heidegger says that *Dasein* is in each case "mine," suggesting the first-person standpoint that Husserl, and later Sartre, would refer to. He also suggests that *Dasein* is an important substitute for any such notions as say, human consciousness. I think this is actually an ingenious move. *Dasein* translated means simply "being there," "being here in the midst of the world."

There is a presumption in phenomenology and a presumption throughout the whole of modern philosophy, maybe through ancient philosophy too, that when we examine our own experience, our own perceptions of the world, what we are very prone to do is to generalize very quickly and say, "This is the truth about perception. This is how all people perceive." Perhaps even, "This is how all rational creatures or all creatures perceive." Phenomenology has this very real problem that, if what I am doing is studying the essential structures of my own consciousness, what grounds do I have for generalizing what I say, and presuming that everyone else has the same kinds of conscious structures?

To be a bit more pushy about it, why should I assume that—as many 18th century philosophers would say—what I am studying is human understanding, or human experience, or the human mind? Could the same structures be shared by the great apes, or by dogs? How far down the phylogenetic ladder does consciousness and its essential structures go? On the other hand, thinking multiculturally, why should I assume that the essential structures of my experience are the essential structures of any *Homo sapiens's* experience? Cultural differences may make an enormous difference, and Heidegger, especially in his later works, is perfectly willing to say that there are very different ways of perceiving the world, and some of them are much better than others. Ours is not among the best.

So this coinage, *Dasein*, is a very nice way of trying to do what Husserl wanted to do—namely get back to the basic, primordial experience and say in what it consists. Whereas Husserl, like Descartes, thought that our basic experience was an experience, one might say, of the experience, or our experience of the objects of experience, what Heidegger wants to say is, "No. Our basic experience is a holistic, unified experience of our being in the world." That phrase, "being in the world," is the first important character of *Dasein*.

The second, which in many ways precedes it, is the idea that we are ontological. That is one of our essential traits. To say that we are ontological here is to say that we ask questions, and, in particular, that we ask questions of Being. This does not necessarily mean asking the grandiose philosophical questions of being that Heidegger pushes us ultimately to ask. Rather, every time we question who we are, every time we are dissatisfied with the way we are performing, every time we are unsure about our place in a society or a group, every time we are unsure about the world and we ask scientific questions, for instance, we are being ontological—asking questions of the world. These are not just very particular questions, but questions which have as their basis some very global kind of conception or question.

Heidegger doesn't use the notion of "human being" for the reasons I just stated. Also, he does not use any of those notions, which I have just hinted at, as prescribed. He doesn't talk about consciousness. He doesn't talk about subjectivity. He doesn't talk about the Transcendental Ego or the mind. It is very important to see why he does not, because as soon as you use that language, the question is consciousness versus what? Transcendent Ego as opposed to what? In Husserl, we get this picture of, on the one hand, there is consciousness, then there are the objects of consciousness. Even if the objects of consciousness are in some sense *in* consciousness, then we raise the question, "What about the objects out there in the world to which the objects of our experience presumably refer?" Heidegger thinks this whole way of thinking is utterly corrupt and utterly hopeless.

The centerpiece of his philosophy is to reject all of this Cartesian tradition, and say the whole distinction between being in the world and something else—between consciousness and the world outside of us, between the phenomenological world with its intentional objects and the possibility of the objects to which that refers—all that way of thinking leads us to nothing but paradox. The truth is *Dasein* and the world are a unified phenomenon. To understand *Dasein* is to understand the world. To understand the world is to understand *Dasein*.

Furthermore, it is quite to the contrary of the idea that permeates a good deal of Western philosophy that, in some sense, the self or the mind or the soul could exist independently of the physical world. Philosophers have gone so far as to say there may be no material world, that all there is, in some sense, are minds which are informed by God, and that gives us the experience that we have. Any suggestion of that sort simply leaves us in an impossible situation.

What Heidegger wants to insist on is that there can be no *Dasein* without the world. At the same time, there can be no world without *Dasein*. So, what he is saying here is in a way it is a return to what used to be called "idealism." To call it idealism, however, really is to miss the point, because the whole distinction between realism—the idea that there is a reality which in some sense we can know—and idealism—which is that we know only in some sense the products of our own minds—really ignores the very bold move that Heidegger is trying to make, which is to say that *Dasein* already is being in the world, and being in the world cannot be separated into components: power being on the one hand; in the world on the other. Rather, we should think of being in the world like being in philosophy. It is not a spatial being in; it is rather: "I am engaged in the world." That is the first starting point of phenomenology.

The idea of being ontological and the idea of being self-questioning is nothing new in philosophy. It certainly goes back to Plato and Descartes and Aristotle and virtually every other philosopher you can think of. The idea of rejecting consciousness puts all this in a new light. One of the ways in which we tend to think of ourselves in philosophy is, not surprisingly, that we think of ourselves in terms of consciousness. The idea of rejecting consciousness means that a whole way of thinking about ourselves—for example, Descartes's thinking of ourselves as thinking things, or John Locke's thinking of ourselves in terms of our particular memories—all goes off the board. The question then is, where are we to find the self and self-identity? The old way of thinking about self and self-identity in terms of consciousness has now been displaced.

I emphasize that when we are being ontological, the questions that really push to the fore are the questions we raise about ourselves. Who are we? What are we? The nature of *Dasein* as simply being in the world in a way does not allow any easy answer to that question. In fact, it almost blocks it because the whole picture of *Dasein* as nothing, but engaged in the world, raises the question whether *Dasein* has a particular identity. If so, what might that identity be? As we will see in the next lecture, what Heidegger wants to suggest is, what we think of as our self-identity is a false self-identity. What we think of as *Dasein* is something very different from the individual self that we normally ascribe to ourselves.

Talking about identity crises raises a question which is to me the most uncomfortable question in talking about Heidegger's philosophy. I guess the simple way to put it is: Who was Heidegger? On the one hand, Heidegger was an indisputably brilliant philosopher, however obscure, who introduced some bold new ways of thinking into philosophy at just the right time. He was a young man, coming out of theology, who was very ambitious. In fact, he started succeeding at those ambitions at a very early age. *Being and Time* was published in 1927, and he was already on his road to fame. Another man who was born not in Germany, but in Austria, the same year that Heidegger was (1889), was also now on his road to fame. That was Adolph Hitler. The two came together in the 1930s. Heidegger at this point was a successful academic with ambitions. Hitler was just about to become the Fuhrer of Germany. In 1933, Heidegger was made rector of the University of Freiburg, with the support of the Nazis.

What is more, Heidegger himself joined the Nazis. He gave many speeches in favor of the Nazis and the National Socialist Program. He characterized it as "the great new move" in the world, not just in Germany. It was not just German society that was to be saved. Heidegger perceived Germany as literally the center of the Earth. It was from Germany that the entire Earth would be reformed by way of the Nazi party. Heidegger quit the Nazi party by 1934 and, in that sense, it was clear that he was already becoming disillusioned with some of its policies. The reason this causes me so much trouble, and anyone else who reads and especially likes Heidegger, is that following the war he never repudiated the Nazi program at all. While he was still in the university and during his life, during the war, he never questioned Nazi policies. At the end of his life, the most he really said was that the Nazi movement never achieved its potential greatness. It became too much like the other technological societies—America and Russia.

This raises some very serious questions. One of them is this: What do we think of a philosopher who has brilliant ideas, but nevertheless has what I will simply call a despicable past? Nietzsche said the philosopher should be an example. In particular, he should be an example of the philosophy. In Nietzsche's own case, as we saw, there is some question about how well he fulfilled that role. Nevertheless, I would argue that Nietzsche's writings and his personality were very much in tune with the sorts of things he wrote, however polemic and overstated they may have been.

With Heidegger, it is a more difficult problem. It is often said that Heidegger's philosophy prefigures his Nazi enthusiasm. That perhaps has some basis, and in the course of these lectures, I will say something about how that linkage might be made. In general, it is greatly overstated. Heidegger's philosophy is so abstract, and in many ways so abstruse, that it is very hard to pull out a specific political program to which that philosophy is directed. On the other hand, there are philosophers who say the philosophy is one thing; the ideas can be defended independently. Heidegger the man, hateful as he might have been, is really a side issue. It has nothing to do with the philosophical issue.

Here, I want to go back to Nietzsche and take him very seriously. The idea is that when we understand a philosophy, we have to understand the philosopher. Who the philosopher is has a lot to do with what the philosophy is. I don't take this to be the kind of translation between ideas written down and ideas put into practice so much as it is a holistic picture, something that Heidegger would certainly endorse. The idea is that to understand the writings, we have to understand when they were written, the context in which they were written, the personality that produced them. To understand Heidegger, therefore, is to make some sort of connection between his Nazi sympathies and his actual writings.

It raises a more general question, too, about ethics. This is particularly difficult with Heidegger because Heidegger greatly enjoyed making fun of ethics and making fun of those who fished in the muddy sea of values. He claimed that *Being and Time* was in no way an ethical work, nor did it have any ethical implications. The truth is it is impossible to read *Being and Time* without seeing that it has some very powerful ethical implications and tells us in a very special way how we should live our lives. Heidegger would utterly reject this. Because he rejects that, one also has to ask the question how much this stance of not doing ethics and not even implying ethics has to do with his own sense of not wanting to come to grips with the implications that his philosophy actually has.

In talking about Heidegger, what I am going to be trying to do is to simplify a very difficult philosophy. Let me give you one concept in particular which I think is going to rule much of what he writes including *Being and Time*. It is a distinction that comes back from the 19th century especially. (One thinks especially of Hegel.) It is the idea of alienation. What bothers Heidegger from his early days in theological school is this problem of alienation, although he hardly ever talks in those terms. The term he uses is the ideal of "feeling at home in the world." The truth is, Heidegger did not feel at home. The truth is, he claims that modern man doesn't feel at home—that mass consumerism and technology have made it impossible for us to feel at home on the Earth.

Somehow making good this concept and this notion of feeling at home is going to be, in many ways, the motivating force behind Heidegger's philosophy. It is not surprising that in his life in the Black Forest, after he finished with his professional career, he often emulated the life of a simple German peasant—which by the way, is how he interpreted the Nazi party as well. To use that as the image behind his very difficult thinking, I think, will give us a handhold on a way of understanding Heidegger that is not always evident in the prose itself.

Heidegger on the World and the Self
Lecture 16

We can say *Being and Time* is basically a concern about ourselves and the world and how we fit into the world. There are two features I want to talk about—two existential structures in this lecture. The first is the nature of knowledge, which has been the focus of philosophers since at least the Greeks. The second is the notion of the self, which, at least in the terms that we are going to be speaking in, essentially has been the main concern of philosophy since at least Descartes.

From the point of view of *Dasein*, the world is no longer a mere object of knowledge. Philosophers think of the world and the things that make up the world as, first of all, something to be known. But Heidegger says we are not first of all "knowers." We are, instead, engaged in the world, faced with tasks. Kant or Wittgenstein, for example, describes the world as the totality of objects and states of affairs—but that isn't obvious to Heidegger at all.

The world, accordingly, first appears to us as "equipment," not as an object of knowledge. For Heidegger, the world is knowing *how*, not knowing *what*, as in the example of using a hammer in a workshop. So, too, the appearance of "things"—even something as basic as a hammer—becomes a phenomenon to be explained, not an obvious philosophical starting point. Paying attention to the task itself (reflection) can interrupt the very process of doing it. Heidegger questions the ultimate benefits of technology, suggesting that our view of the world as "resource" betrays both our own nature and the nature of our relationship to the world. Competition and consumerism make us diminished beings, no longer authentically engaged in the world.

From the point of view of *Dasein*, it is no longer clear what the self is. Descartes's famous "I think, therefore I am" is a misleading paradigm of self-identity. It suggests a disastrous split between the mind ("I am a thinking thing") and the body, which Heidegger rejects. It also suggests that self-knowledge is immediate and transparent. Heidegger tells us that the self is neither immediate nor transparent, and self-recognition is rare and special rather than philosophically routine.

This need and capacity to clarify our own mode of being, to be "ontological," raises the questions of what it is to be genuinely one's own self—or authentic (*eigentlich*)—and in what way can we then properly approach the question of Being. It also raises the question of what it is to be inauthentic (*uneigentlich*). Most of our lives, we are not our genuine selves, not authentic but inauthentic, what Heidegger calls the *das Man* ("one is") self.

From the point of view of *Dasein*, it is no longer clear what the self is.

Heidegger develops the concept of the self as *das Man*. The ordinary self is not the self of Cartesian reflection. It is not an individual self. It is an "anonymous" self, a self defined by other people. The ordinary self is, thus, inauthentic. When we describe ourselves, we refer to the roles we play or social categories. The *das Man* self is the social, comparative self. Although it is essential to life, it is not our genuine self. This view harks back to Kierkegaard's and Nietzsche's attacks on the "herd mentality" of contemporary society, but Heidegger doesn't accept the extremity of their rejection of everyday social life. Heidegger's contrasting notion of authenticity comes to play an enormous role in existentialist literature.

Heidegger encourages us to be authentic, to "take hold of ourselves." Heidegger dramatically announces that we are "thrown" into the world, suggesting a dimension of involuntariness and fatalism. To take hold of one's self, one doesn't reject society but resolutely accepts one's historicity and reasserts the self in traditions and "destiny." ∎

Essential Reading

Selections from Heidegger's *Being and Time* in Solomon, *Existentialism*, pp. 93–123.

Dreyfus, *Being-in-the-World: A Commentary on Heidegger's Being and Time, Division 1.*

Heidegger, *Being and Time* (New York: Routledge, 1997), pp. 39–48, 59–70, 77–82, 107–122; and *The Question Concerning Technology and Other Essays.*

Solomon, *From Rationalism to Existentialism*, pp.184–244.

Introductory Questions to Consider

1. How does Heidegger's approach to phenomenology have ecological overtones? In what sense can he be construed as attacking the very idea of the earth as a "resource"?

2. What (who) is *das Man*, the *das Man* self? To what is it opposed?

Advanced Questions to Consider

1. What is the nature of "existence" for Heidegger? Does this say anything more than affirm the fact that we have choices and make decisions?

2. In what sense are we "thrown" into the world? What images does this violent choice of words suggest? What does it imply about the nature of our lives?

3. "The word 'I' is to be understood only in the sense of a non-committal formal indicator, indicating something which may reveal itself as its 'opposite' in some particular phenomenal context of Being. In that case, the 'not-I' is by no means tantamount to an entity which essentially lacks 'I-hood' but is rather a definite kind of Being which the 'I' itself possesses, such as having lost itself" (Heidegger, *Being and Time*, "The 'Who' of *Dasein*"). What is Heidegger telling us about the nature of "self-identity"? Contrast this notion of the "I" with Husserl's more "Cartesian" approach.

Heidegger on the World and the Self
Lecture 16—Transcript

Being and Time is the study of *Dasein* and its essential structures. In simpler language we can say *Being and Time* is basically a concern about ourselves and the world and how we fit into the world. There are two features I want to talk about—two existential structures in this lecture. The first is the nature of knowledge, which has been the focus of philosophers since at least the Greeks. The second is the notion of the self, which, at least in the terms that we are going to be speaking in, essentially has been the main concern of philosophy since at least Descartes.

What concerns me is the way that Heidegger wants to examine—again, I will make the apology—the basic structures of experience are a term which he would reject. What he wants to say is that if we look at the basic structures of experience or what he would call our primordial take on the world, what we find, is, as I said in the last lecture, that we don't find ourselves as a consciousness, a thinking thing. Rather we find ourselves as Being in the world in which the world and ourselves—*Dasein*—are utterly inseparable.

To even talk about knowledge is to enter into a domain which philosophers, according to Heidegger, have not understood at all. Philosophers from their armchair stance, or what one of Heidegger's very good contemporaries, the American philosopher John Dewey called "a spectator view of the world," essentially tend to think of the world as something to be known. Thinking about the world as something to be known, one thinks about, for example, the categories of knowledge, the question of what it is for something to be a thing, the question of what it is for things to be in causal relations, and so on.

For Heidegger all this is very late in the game. To think of this as our primordial experience of the world is to miss something very basic. Instead, what Heidegger wants to say is: "We are not, first of all, knowers." We are not spectators. Our first-of-all experience of the world is as engagement. What does engagement mean? It means that what we are involved in are tasks, things to be done. What we are involved in is a world with other people in which we know we must obey them. We have to get along with them. We have to cope with them. In most of this, to talk about knowledge in a way is beside the point.

Heidegger wants to make it into a kind of puzzle. How is it that we come to have anything like the "knowledge" that philosophers talk about? What are the conditions that make that knowledge possible? What are the conditions of our talking about ourselves? What are the conditions of talking about things? In a philosopher like Kant, the idea that the world consists of objects—or of someone like Wittgenstein where the world is everything that is the case (states of affairs, and so on)—we might think that what they are talking about is something that, on the one hand, is obvious. What Heidegger wants to say is it is not obvious at all. In fact, it is a mystery how we can talk in such language at all.

What does it mean to be engaged? The first thing to say is to be engaged is to care. In Heidegger's philosophy in *Being and Time,* caring takes the place of all those more cognitive notions that appear in most philosophers; in particular, the notion of knowledge. We live in the world because we care about things. We act because we care.

Caring is a concept that has a long history. One should be very careful not to confuse caring with caring for others or about others. Heidegger himself was not a particularly caring person. Nor should we think of caring in the sense of anxiety and worry. One should remember that the use of that word "Sorge" was also a major piece of Goethe's famous play *Faust,* in which Sorge explicitly refers to the burdens of worry and the world. Caring in Heidegger means something much more general. It has to do with being involved, being concerned, having ends, having purposes. He therefore talks about the world not in terms of things, and not things that we know. Instead, he talks about the world in terms of things that he calls "equipment." You might say that it is a matter of knowledge, but it is knowing *how* rather than knowing *what.* It is not observing or being a spectator; it is being engaged in tests.

Let's take a very Heideggerian example. I walk into my workshop, and there are a couple of planks that need to be nailed together. I reach up, and I pick up the hammer, take the nails, and I hammer. If I describe the phenomenology of that experience, what I will describe is not a hammer, nails, planks, and my behavior in hammering the nails into the planks. It is, as Heidegger puts it, all of a piece. There is a kind of totality of equipment: the workshop as a whole. What I focus on is simply the task to be done. The hammer is not a hammer. It is something I use for a purpose. The nail is not a nail, but something I use for a purpose. The plank is not a plank. It is the material I am working with.

One might talk well here about knowing how to do something. Notice in this description: to think about the items which I am using in the tool shop for this task as "things" is a kind of mis-description. What is it to see the hammer as a thing? To see it as a thing means that I stop hammering first of all. I hold it up, and I look at it. Then it becomes a piece of wood with a slab of metal on the top. I can now analyze it into its components. Perhaps, I can explain why it is so useful in terms of hammering nails into planks. What I have done is a very special piece of behavior. It is not part of my engagement into tasks, but it is looking at the hammer as something separate, something distinct. That is something we don't find in my treatment of the world as equipment, in my involvement in tasks.

You watch children at play or doing their routine tasks. There is a sense in which they don't see anything as a thing. What they are doing is they are completely involved—completely engaged—in their activities. Just as Heidegger wants to say that all of the items in the equipment are a totality and they are functioning together, he also wants to say that I, as the actor, am nothing but part of that same totality. To think of myself as something separate, as the agent who is doing this task, is, again, too much of a stretch. It is something that enters into our vocabulary only as a very special step. One way to address the question is: Under what circumstances do we stop simply involving ourselves in tasks and pursuing purposes, and instead, start seeing the things that we use as things? That means as not part of the totality of equipment, but as individual instruments or individual items.

Think about the hammer example. When I am hammering, there is a point at which I will very likely hold the hammer out and take a look at it. For example, if the head flies off so I can no longer hammer, I will look at it and I will say, "What is wrong with this picture?" At that point, I will notice that the hammer doesn't have a head. Or, if you are taking notes and your pen runs out of ink, you will look at your pen, and you will realize it is a pen and it is malfunctioning. When I watch people write—and when I write myself, I reach into my pocket and I pull out a pen. I never look at the pen. I don't think, "Where is the pen?"—unless I can't find it, which is a different kind of breakdown. Basically, the pen is part of the equipment I am using to perform certain kinds of tasks.

One of the ironies here is that paying attention, making something into a thing, can actually interfere with the task at hand. One obvious example, if you ask someone who is typing, "Where are the different keys? How do you know what is what? How do you figure out which finger to use on which key?" (I am assuming someone who has been typing for years and does it by touch), the truth is, they will find themselves at that moment incapable of typing, because in what is normally a completely involved activity in which one does not stop to think what one is doing, suddenly one is asked to focus on his or her fingers, the typewriter, as a thing—then suddenly we are incapable of behaving. In a different kind of example, there is a childhood poem I remember about the centipede who is asked, "How do you manage to coordinate all those different legs?" The centipede at that point becomes essentially paralyzed because he can't figure it out, whereas before the question was asked he was perfectly happy just walking along.

One can think here about a point I made about Camus and the kind of antithesis between, on the one hand, lived experience (now let's talk about engagement), and, on the other hand, reflection. The one can actually interfere with the other. But, to think that reflection is the basis of human consciousness and human life is to get it all wrong. What we will see in Sartre, as well, is prereflection, is more important—what we do, in a way, unconsciously; that is, without stopping to look and think and take in these things as things.

A different kind of example is Arthur Conan Doyle's stories about Sherlock Holmes and his friend, Doctor Watson. There is one question that Holmes is rather fond of asking Watson, by way of embarrassing him. That is, "How many steps do you take up to my flat?"—a walk which Dr. Watson has made hundreds of thousands of times. Watson is terribly flustered and embarrassed to realize that he does not know. Of course, Holmes then criticizes him for his powers of deduction (actually, one would say induction, but that is a different matter). The idea is that Holmes has seen things, noticed things that Watson has not, even though he has done the same stair climbing that

Holmes has done—the same stair climbing that Holmes has done for all those years. I want to side with Watson on this one, even though Watson does not try to defend himself. It seems to me what Holmes is saying is something which is, if not wrong, slightly neurotic.

I walk up the steps of my office every day and I have for 20 years, and I haven't a clue how many steps there are, and I don't care. There are people who are just natural counters. The truth is that when we walk up steps, do tasks, do all sorts of things in which we are engaged, we don't notice, in an important sense, what it is we are doing. We don't have that kind of consciousness which spells itself out as knowledge of "things," or knowledge that such and such is the case. What we are concerned with is getting the task done.

This spells itself out in a number of ways in Heidegger's philosophy. One of the more fascinating ones, which I am just going to jump to a bit out of sequence, is the idea that this way of thinking about the world, in terms of active engagement, is something which, in his kind of celebration of peasant life, is very much the paradigm of his philosophy. When he thinks about peasantry—and later in his career, he will actually say things like: "Peasants really have the answer to the questions of being in a way that philosophers since Plato do not," because peasants are actively engaged in their world. They don't stop much to think about it. They don't necessarily label things. Consequently, there is a kind of ideal of pre-reflective engagement that Heidegger entertains.

This is to be contrasted with something which may easily be confused with it, mainly the sense of using the world as a kind of resource. I mention this because one of the main targets of Heidegger's later philosophy certainly is the whole philosophy of technology. The alienation I mentioned at the end of the last lecture comes about in the modern world, according to Heidegger, more because of technology than anything else. It is a way of thinking about the world, not in terms of our place in it and our activities in it, so much as it is thinking of the world as something alien, merely a "resource." Consequently, even apart from the ecological issues, it is a way of seeing the world which loses the charm and immediacy that our simply behaving in the world tends to capture.

Technology also makes everything the same. This is a very old criticism, going back at least to Marx, whom Heidegger would have despised, but the idea that money reduces everything to the same level. Consumerism in the 20th century is something that Heidegger despised. It is interesting and important to see just why, because what these things do is quite the contrary of simply going back to the idea of being engaged in the world. What they do is they separate us from it, and from each other. The whole notion of competition, of consumerism, basically makes us greatly inferior and diminished beings. Heidegger's original flirtation with the Nazi party had to do with the Nazi promise to capture, in a sense, the old rural Germany, even though, as we said, the Nazis very quickly turned to the same kind of technological obsessions that the Russians and the Americans displayed.

What I want to conclude this part with is to say that what Heidegger is concerned with here is not just a narrow set of philosophical issues of what counts as knowledge, experience, how we should understand ourselves in a phenomenological way. He has much bigger fish on the line. What he is ultimately interested in is a question about what it is to be a human being, even if that is a term that he does not use.

This brings us back to the question about what the self is. The starting point, I think, must be Descartes's notion: "I think, therefore I am, and consequently, I am a thinking thing." We have already seen that this leads to a split between mind and body—something that Heidegger is going to reject immediately, because it is not as if I have a mind distinct from my body. When I am engaged in the world in tasks, what I am doing is using my body, not as (to use a Cartesian metaphor) a captain running a ship, but I am using my body, and it is me as my body that is engaged in the activity. One might notice also that there is a sense in Descartes with his "I think, therefore I am," that self-knowledge is immediate, and, one might add, it is also unmistakable. Descartes uses this as a proof that here is at least one proposition which is absolutely self-evident and undoubtable.

The truth is, according to Heidegger, that we don't know what our selves are, and anything resembling true self-recognition is a rare thing, which leads us to the most famous single concept in Heidegger's philosophy. That is the concept of "authenticity." This will be the subject of the next lecture, so I am just going to mention it here. Let me say that authenticity, first of all, doesn't mean, as it does in English, simply "genuine." It also means something which is quite obvious in the German word, *eigentlich*, something having to do with being one's own—authentic, the authentic self. To be a true human being, if I can use that language, is to be one's own person.

By contrast, there is also "inauthenticity." Inauthenticity is not being one's own self—not being a true person. Again, Heidegger introduces as coinage—the coinage is what he calls *das Man*. It is a word which is derived from perfectly ordinary German—*Man* with one "N" is the word that is used in such phrases as "there is," or "one is." We say, for example, "One doesn't do that sort of thing around here." What is interesting about that kind of expression is that it does not refer to anyone in particular. It does not refer to the authorities. It does not refer to the law. It doesn't refer to the person who is speaking, or any particular group that they represent. "One doesn't do these things around here" is a reference to the anonymity of the group. This is what Heidegger wants to say is the way most of us, in fact, think of ourselves.

He talks about the *das Man* self, where the *das Man* is an "anonymous" self. It is not an individual self. It is not really a reflective self—not the self of Cartesian reflection, anyway. It is inauthentic through and through. Let me say something about why that is the case. The first thing to notice is that when we talk about ourselves, we almost always talk about ourselves in terms of our place in a group—our roles. So, in American society, the question, "What do you do?" is really the question, "Who are you?" The answer usually has to do with your job, or your position in your company, or the fact that you are a student, or the fact that you are a student studying classics, or whatever. We give our identity in terms of our social roles. In an important sense, our social roles aren't us.

If you type up a brief biography—a resume, perhaps, applying for a job, and you write down where you went to high school and what awards you won, and then where you went to college and what you have done there, and perhaps some of your extracurricular activities—what you are listing, essentially, are your social roles and your social rankings. I think there are few of us who have not done such a task and then pulled it out of the typewriter or the computer, looked at it and said, "That is not really me. That is just some of my accomplishments, some of the things I have done." The truth is, when we describe ourselves, what we inevitably describe are precisely the roles that we play—our status compared to other people.

When I say of myself, for example, that I am intelligent, I am implicitly comparing myself with others—perhaps on the basis of one of those tests like an IQ test, perhaps on the basis of my ability to perform well in school. In any case, intelligence is not something that I myself have. Rather, it is a way of comparing myself with other people. If I say of someone that they are good looking, or they are charming, these are obviously social categories. It has to do with not only the values of a particular culture or subculture, it has to do with relations and comparisons between people. In short, when we talk about ourselves, we tend to talk about ourselves in terms of roles, or position, or statuses which someone might occupy instead of us. If I were not a student at The University of Texas, say, then that slot would be filled by someone else. None of my teachers would miss me because they would not know that I existed or did not exist.

The same argument can be made in an extreme way. If you had not been born, someone else might have been born in your place. We can play with this in science fiction, and say they might even look exactly like you and been raised exactly like you—that doesn't matter. The important thing is that they are not you. The question is, what is missing from the world? Your parents wouldn't notice anything, because they have the child they have in your place. None of their friends or your current friends would notice, because there is someone else that they have to play with. There is a sense in which nothing is missing except you.

What is that you? That is where the question of authenticity is going to come in. The *das Man* self is nothing but this social comparative self. It is not the real self. Nevertheless, Heidegger is going to say it is an essential part of life because, when in our pre-reflective engagement in tasks we often tend to be engaged with other people, that sense of being engaged with other people is going to be precisely the idea that we are part of a group in which we fit ourselves in terms of being part of the group. To take a different kind of example, if I go to a football game, and I am there cheering with thousands of other people, I am generally not aware of myself as an individual, as a self. Rather, I am aware of myself only as part of the cheering crowd. So, the idea of *das Man*, here, is to give us a picture of the self, which most of us take to be our genuine selves—which Heidegger wants to say is really not that at all.

There is a sense in which one can detect here a return to two of Heidegger's greatest influences. Those are the two philosophers Kierkegaard and Nietzsche. He read both of them carefully. He was actually rather fond of them both—Kierkegaard, because of his religious sensibilities; Nietzsche, in a way, has to do with volumes of Nietzsche misinterpretation, which I don't want to get into here. Nevertheless, Kierkegaard and Nietzsche, one thing they had in common was a rejection of what they referred to as "herd mentality." Nietzsche, in particular, rejected with some vigorousness the whole idea of being part of the herd. The idea is that one has to be an individual.

In Kierkegaard, one is not a Christian because one lives in a Christian community, because one is surrounded by Christians. One is not a Christian because other people think you are a Christian. You are Christian all by yourself. It is a personal relationship with God. It is a mere matter of happenstance that there are other Christians in the world with you. It is an extremely individualistic philosophy, as we saw.

In Nietzsche, while the notion of the individual there tends to become more ambiguous; nevertheless, Nietzsche's reaction against "herd mentality"— and what he calls "slave morality," which is again the whole idea of fitting in with the crowd, finding safety in the crowd, the idea of exercising values which are protective of the crowd—is something diametrically opposed to what he obviously prefers in terms of "master morality" or his image of the *Übermensch*. The idea is that to be a real person is to be, in a very important and powerful sense, independent, and in particular, independent of other people's opinions and influence.

The strong emphasis on individuality, as I have said, is going to permeate all of the existentialist figures we are talking about. In Heidegger's language, it has to do with "taking hold of yourself." Let's not leave it there. That notion might very well be Kierkegaardian, or Nietzschian, or, as we will see, Sartrian. The idea of being authentic and taking hold of yourself—in a way, lifting yourself by your own bootstraps—is at most half the picture in Heidegger, and even there I would say, subject to many qualifications which I will try in the next lecture.

He also has a notion that we are "thrown" into the world. It is a very dramatic notion. It is an idea which has real charm because we have all imagined, for example, what it would be like if we lived in the 13th or the 19th century, or what it would have been like if we had been born 10 years earlier or 10 years later. When we imagine that we realize the contingency of our existence— the fact that we didn't choose exactly when and where we were going to be born we didn't choose our parents. So, the idea of being thrown into the world in a certain time and place is itself very dramatic. This is going to compromise the notion of taking hold of yourself, because you take hold of yourself not in a vacuum, but you take hold of yourself within a very particular historical and cultural context.

Moreover, Heidegger is going to say—and here is where I think one can make some of the linkage to his Nazi attachments—that when one takes hold of oneself, one does not break free of society. That would be the height of alienation, and that is very much what is wrong with contemporary technological and consumer society. Rather, one takes hold of oneself and appreciates one's traditions, one's history, or what Heidegger refers to as one's "historicity." One essentially embeds oneself back, as a matter of what he calls "resoluteness," in one's culture and one's time. One can easily see, given what his culture and time was, that he saw national socialism and he saw German culture, in general, as not just "herd mentality" that he should escape, but quite to the contrary a way in which he should take hold of himself and reassert himself into it.

There is a sense, too, in which to talk about the self in this way is to talk about the self in time—the second term of Heidegger's famous book. To talk about time is not simply to talk, as philosophers often do, about what Heidegger refers to as "clock time"—the sort of time that is talked about by physicists, the sort we measure in making appointments. To understand yourself is to understand the sense in which you are yourself in time, and in many ways definitive of time.

We talk about living in the moment—living in the present. The truth is, we never do. The present, in fact, is nothing but a razor-thin line between the past and the future. When we think about ourselves, what we are always doing is thinking about ourselves in terms of our past and our history and our tradition, and, at the same time, in terms of our future, and our future projects in particular. To understand this is to understand that what we are as *Dasein* is, first of all, as creatures in time. Second, and more important, to understand authenticity is going to be to understand how this attitude toward time enters into what it is to find and take hold of oneself.

Heidegger on "Authenticity"
Lecture 17

To think about authenticity is to think about living a certain kind of life. It is to think about living what most of us call a very serious kind of life, or a very profound kind of life, in which the larger questions about being, and our being in particular, are always in some sense in front of us.

In Nietzsche's description of master and slave morality, he clearly prefers the former. So, too, does Heidegger, who gives us an ethics of authenticity. Heidegger encourages us to be authentic (*eigentlich*), to "take hold of ourselves" or comport ourselves toward the world in a certain way.

Among the various "existential" features of *Dasein*, Heidegger highlights three: existence, facticity, and fallenness. Existence (*Existenz*) is that which is essentially *Dasein*. *Dasein* has no essence other than the fact that it exists. "Existence precedes essence." *Dasein* has "possibilities." *Existenz* is that feature of *Dasein* through which we envision our possibilities, our future. It is the capacity to make choices. (Heidegger's later philosophy will question this existential concept of choice.) It is our necessary ability to look into the future and disclose to ourselves the three interwoven dimensions of time, the present, the past, and the future. Our moods (not to be conceived as merely transient mental states) are ways of being "tuned" into the world, in which our *existenz* is disclosed to us. Heidegger says our moods are shared. They are not "in our minds" but out there, in the world.

Facticity consists of the brute facts that characterize us, such as height, weight, date of birth, and so on. Here is where Heidegger says that we are "thrown" into a world not of our choosing. Our "historicity" is our historical situation.

Fallenness is the "pre-ontological" way in which *Dasein* fails to face up to its ontological condition and "falls back" to daily inauthenticity, *das Man*. It is the everyday core of inauthenticity, falling back into tasks. It is what we experience in our everyday lives and should be respected as such. But fallenness alone is just one dimension of human life and not yet authentic. Heidegger goes on to distinguish various authentic and inauthentic modes of being: Understanding is opposed to curiosity. Thinking is opposed to calculation. Speech is opposed to chatter. Heidegger marks these distinctions as the structure of conscience. We cannot help but ask questions about what we are and feel anxiety about our existence.

The most dramatic suggestion in *Being and Time* is that we are all "Being-unto-death."

The most dramatic suggestion in *Being and Time* is that we are all "Being-unto-death" (*Sein-zum-Tode*). The recognition of our own mortality is that it is a necessary fact about us. But we normally don't take this seriously. Our mortality prompts us to "take hold of ourselves" in an authentic "resolution" of our own existence. It also forces us to appreciate our limitations and immerse ourselves in our "historicity," our historical situation. Being-unto-death forces us to see ourselves and our lives as a single unity.

This last point is immensely problematic because of Heidegger's own place in history. Does his philosophy make an excuse for his flirtation with the Nazis in the name of "historicity," his historical situation? Why did he never repent for his involvement in the National Socialist cause? Facticity? Fallenness? Or bad faith? ∎

Essential Reading

Solomon, *Existentialism*, pp. 93–123.

Supplementary Reading

Solomon, *From Rationalism to Existentialism*, pp.184–244. For a good analysis of Heidegger's own "historicity," see Sluga, *Heidegger's Crisis*. For a good defense of Heidegger, see Young, *Heidegger, Philosophy, Nazism*.

1. Define the following Heideggerian terms: "facticity," "thrownness," "existence," and "fallenness."

2. Who is "*das Man*?" Is it you? Or "partially" you? Explain.

3. What role does death, or more precisely, "Being-unto-death," play in the realization of authenticity?

1. Heidegger asserts that "fallenness"—which is the result of losing oneself in the idle talk, curiosity, and ambiguity of "the they"—"does not express any negative evaluation, but is used to signify that *Dasein* is proximally and for the most part alongside the world of its concern." Is it true that Heidegger doesn't view "fallenness" normatively? If so, why should we try to live "authentically," especially given that Heidegger tells us that fallenness brings "tranquility"?

2. What would it mean to live "authentically" in the world? Is there any way that "you" could live authentically in a world that is otherwise "fallen," or does individual authenticity depend on living in a more "authentic" context?

Heidegger on "Authenticity"
Lecture 17—Transcript

I'd like to hone in on the notion of authenticity and describe some of the existential structures of *Dasein* that Heidegger thinks are essential to it. There is a sense in which what we are going to be talking about is ethics, despite Heidegger's disclaimer. I think it is very hard to read what he says about authenticity without coming away with the conclusion that authenticity is a good thing to have and inauthenticity is, if not a bad thing, inferior to authenticity. It is the same kind of conclusion I came to when we talked about Nietzsche.

Nietzsche describes master morality and slave morality as two different perspectives on morality appropriate—two different people with different personalities in different situations. There is no question, on reading Nietzsche, that Nietzsche strongly preferred master morality. The way he describes slave morality and herd morality, often in extremely disdainful terms, makes it obvious that this is something to be avoided. Heidegger won't go that far. As you will see, inauthenticity is an essential part of human life, and in that sense not condemnable at all. Nevertheless, I think there is a very strong argument to be made that what Heidegger is giving us is ethics of authenticity, and trying to say that authenticity is something that we should try to achieve.

In talking about Heidegger's ethics, to think in the traditional ethical terms of good, bad, right, wrong, really is beside the point. There is a sense in which the term I used at the very beginning of my discussion of Heidegger—the notion of feeling at home—is much more central. The way I would describe Heidegger's project in terms of authenticity is something more like this: There is a choice we have to make, and Heidegger does describe it as a choice, between authenticity and inauthenticity.

Inauthenticity, if what I just said has any correctness, is something which is inferior. Just going along with the crowd, living only in the eyes of others, just being what other people expect you to be is, in some sense, an inferior mode of existence. The alternative, authenticity—taking hold of yourself in this kind of very individualistic way that Kierkegaard and Nietzsche both praise—

that is really identical to alienation. One of the problems that Heidegger has with modern societies, of which he has many very nasty things to say, is the fact that people are generally alienated. They think of themselves simply as individuals. They pursue their own self-interests. If we think about modern, industrial, consumerist society, this is elevated to the point of an ideology. Heidegger wants to reject that.

The question that I want to begin the lecture with is the question: Inauthenticity or alienation? Is that the choice we have? Heidegger would say, "No. That is not the choice. There is a third alternative." With that, I think we will better understand both what he means by authenticity, and how he could, in his philosophy, already orient himself toward the Nazi movement he would join a few years later. The notion of authenticity, or again to use the German notion *eigentlich*, is taking hold of ourselves. It is thinking about ourselves in a certain way—more accurately, Heidegger would say comporting ourselves, behaving ourselves in a certain way. To understand how this way is to be defined, let's look at three of the existential, essential features of *Dasein* that Heidegger outlines. He calls these "existential" as a way of emphasizing that they are essential aspects of our existence.

The first of them is called *Existenz*. Here, Heidegger is hawking back to Kierkegaard with his very special notion of existence—the idea that human beings don't just exist the way a coffee cup exists or a tree exists. Human beings have, or have the capacity for, a very special kind of existence which involves, among other things, appreciating who you are. It is not so much reflection in the abstract theoretical sense; rather, it is reflection in the sense of being ontological—asking basic questions about your own existence. Heidegger says that *Existenz,* in some sense, precedes the notion of essence here. The notion of essence—how we think about ourselves as particular individuals and so on—is something that follows from, does not precede, our notion that we are, first of all, existing creatures—questioning, asking creatures, creatures who in a way have to take hold of ourselves.

It is within the context of *Existenz* that Heidegger says *Dasein* has possibilities. It is important to explain what he means by this. There is a sense in which acorns have possibilities. An acorn has the possibility of turning into an oak tree. An acorn has the possibility of being eaten by a squirrel. An acorn has the possibility of being stepped on by an undergraduate. Heidegger would say acorns don't have possibilities. Acorns are not *Daseins*. There is no perspective, no first-person standpoint for an acorn. We always see our world in terms of possibilities. This goes back to the analysis of time, which actually takes up quite a bit of Heidegger's first book, and which I discussed at the very end of the last lecture. We see ourselves never simply in terms of the present. We always see ourselves in terms of the future. Since the future is as yet unsettled, we see ourselves in terms of our plans, aspirations, hopes, fears.

I was at dinner alone the other night while on a business trip, and as I always do, I took out a pad of paper and was just sort of jotting things down. I keep lists. I am at the age where I tend to forget what I am supposed to do. So, I was jotting down my notes about myself. It was very interesting. The notes fell into two different categories. First of all, there were things to do on Monday, things to do when I got back to Texas, things to do in my upcoming classes. On the other hand, there were notes to myself, things that I wanted to tell my wife about what I had done. The notes fell into the categories of the future and the past. That was what defined the present. If someone had said, "Why don't you just keep track of what you are thinking right now," I might come up with a very narcissistic and uninteresting stream of consciousness. Nevertheless, there is a sense in which, even then, what I would be doing would be very quickly recapturing the past. Probably I couldn't do that without already referring in all kinds of ways to the future.

Existenz is this sense of the future. It is the sense that we have the capacity to make choices. While I don't want to make it sound as if freedom and choice is an important part of Heidegger's philosophy, his later work really eliminates most of what the existentialists, such as Sartre, will defend in that capacity. Nevertheless, in *Being and Time*, it is clearly the case that *Existenz* is in part a kind of freedom to make choices, an openness in the future, and to see the future as an essential dimension of time. One thing to note is that Heidegger talks, at this juncture, a great deal about moods.

I have said throughout my discussion of the existentialists that an emphasis on the passions is very often a key to how they see themselves and see human nature. That would be too strong in taking about Heidegger. I think something along those lines is very much a part of his philosophy. I said in the first lecture that for Heidegger, our attitude toward the world is not knowledge or curiosity; it is, first of all, caring. Caring might be thought of as a special kind of mood or something that is general to all moods. But, our moods here are not to be construed as we usually construe them as transient internal weather. We feel this now, but I'll be over it in an hour, or "I am just sad right now, but it is not really about anything."

What Heidegger says is, first of all, our moods are always about something, as Sartre will later say about emotions. Our moods, in a very clever sort of punsical coinage, are what tune us into the world. So, when Wittgenstein says that a depressed man lives in a depressed world, one might transfer that to Heidegger in much the same sense. Our moods are ways of seeing the world, experiencing the world, engaging in tasks. What is more, moods are not simply individual. They are necessarily shared, or to use a phrase that Sartre likes: they are out there in the world.

Moods are, in this sense, a part of our existence, because it is moods that tune us in not just to the present and the past, but moods that gear us toward the future—moods that involve ambition, hope—and certainly that is something that would be definitive in Heidegger's own time, in the late 1920s when Germany was in such terrible condition. You look at this overall picture of existence, and what one wants to say is that our existence is our openness to the future, and it is not just the fact that in the future we will do such and such, or even just the fact that we have plans, but our very existence itself is something that is defined in terms of our possibilities.

The second existential structure of what will turn out to be a trio is what Heidegger calls "facticity." We are going to see this term again, because Sartre borrows it directly from Heidegger. The meaning in Heidegger and Sartre is very much the same. Facticity might be thought of as simply the facts that are true of us. We are thrown into the world, Heidegger says in his very dramatic coinage. When we are thrown into the world, we are thrown into the world in a particular time, place, culture, and history. Being thrown into the world gives rise to our historicity—the idea that we are born into a particular historical situation and a particular tradition. As I have already suggested, where Heidegger is going to compromise his own individuality (borrowed from Kierkegaard and Nietzsche) is where he says, "What we do once we have achieved a kind of authenticity, is we re-insert ourselves into our historicity and our traditions." This is going to be, to anticipate again, the third way beyond inauthenticity and alienation.

The third category here is what Heidegger calls "fallenness." This is a very difficult concept, and I actually have some trouble seeing exactly how it ties in with the other two. Fallenness—and the language here is very strongly reminiscent, intentionally so, of The Fall in the Bible; the same allusion that Camus makes in the title of his last novel—fallenness refers to the fact that we "fall back" from a kind of reflective and authentic position to something that Heidegger refers to as "pre-ontological."

In other words, what we do is stop asking questions for a while, we stop wondering who we are, and just as the beginning of *Dasein* told us, we fall back into tasks. As opposed to thinking this is something hateful or something to be avoided, Heidegger makes the very strong case that this is how we live most of our lives. It is a kind of inauthenticity because we are not taking hold of ourselves; we are simply doing what we have to do—joining in with the others and doing what they expect us to do. Nevertheless, fallenness is part of human existence. It is to be respected as such. Nevertheless, fallenness by itself, remaining on a preontological level—not taking hold of oneself and asking the kinds of questions that Heidegger thinks we should ask—is in some important sense to be something less than fully human, although that is not a language that he would ever give us.

He talks about authenticity in terms of three different contrasts; I think this will help us get a clue as to what this notion involves. First of all, he contrasts understanding versus curiosity. Modern science, he thinks, is simply curiosity. Most people when they ask questions are simply being curious. They want to learn facts. They want to learn how something works. There is a sense in which this is a clearly inferior form of cognition.

Understanding, by contrast, is really just being ontological. It is trying to ask those kinds of questions that Heidegger suggests are definitive of being a human being. It is asking those questions about oneself and who one is that are essential to gaining authenticity. The notion of understanding has a long standing in itself in German philosophy. In the 19th century, many philosophers were talking about *verstädnis*, understanding, as a way of understanding other people, empathizing with them. That, too, is involved here. What we understand is not just ourselves and our world. What we understand is other people along with us.

The second contrast is thinking, as opposed to calculation. Again, one can see here a reference to technological society. In a late essay called "What is Thinking?" Heidegger makes this contrast all the more dramatic. The technological society is, in one sense, utterly brilliant. The thinking involved in the manufacture of computers and software is something to be hugely admired, but not by Heidegger. The truth is the kind of thinking it involves is really just calculative thinking. Thinking, properly understood, is thinking philosophically.

One might think here back to the great German sociologist Max Weber, who at the beginning of the century was talking about what he called "instrumental rationality." He clearly thought it was something very dangerous, and he talked about the disenchantment of the world with this kind of thinking. Heidegger, I think, is following in these footsteps very closely. The idea is the kind of thinking which just calculates, figures things out, the kind of calculating that just tries to get means adjusted to ends, and get things done—all of this is very different from "real thinking"—philosophical thinking—in short, the kind of thing that Heidegger is doing in *Being and Time*.

The third opposition is speech, as opposed to what Heidegger calls "idle chatter." We all know what this difference refers to. If you are in a conversation with a friend, you may well just gossip, talk about the news of the day, chitchat about fashion, hairdos, philosophical periphera, what this professor is doing or that professor is doing, or what they did to a student, or something of that sort. This is all chatter. It is talk, but it just fills in time. It entertains us. True speech is something very different.

You think, for example, you meet an old friend, and you get into a conversation. Instead of talking about what you hoped you would talk about, namely, the origins of the friendship, and how you have grown up together, and how you have so much to say and so much in common, instead of that kind of conversation which can often be very moving and very edifying, instead, what you end up doing is chitchat. We all know what that difference amounts to. Most of us spend most of our lives—even those of us who are engaged in the highest kind of thinking and philosophy—actually spend most of our time just chitchatting.

We should always keep in mind that there is something else. Chitchat is not what Heidegger means by speech. Speech is something that is profound, ontological, philosophical. It is tied to real thinking and understanding.

To think about authenticity is to think about living a certain kind of life. It is to think about living what most of us call a very serious kind of life, or a very profound kind of life, in which the larger questions about being, and our being in particular, are always in some sense in front of us. That is not enough to make us authentic. Heidegger adds to this two essential structures, which are very dramatic as opposed to the last three I mentioned, and they are very much in tune with the kind of existentialist angst which Heidegger, among others, has made so famous.

The first is what he calls "conscience." It is the idea that there is in us a constant reminder. We remind ourselves that we are not all we would like to be. We are not authentic. We are just going along with the crowd, and as we are going along with the crowd, there is this quiet voice that reminds us that we could be something more, something authentic. Conscience gives rise to guilt. It is very important not to think here of the notions of conscience and guilt—for example, the notion that Christianity has often given us that conscience is the voice of God within us, although Heidegger would not completely reject that. Nor should we think of a conscience, as Freud talked about it, as the superego—the voice of our parents reminding us what to do.

Conscience is something built into our very existence. It is the constant reminder that we are not being all that we can be. Here again, we go back to someone like Nietzsche, or talking about Camus who follows. The idea is that the guilt that we feel is not guilt for any particular transgression, or even guilt for any particular omission. Guilt comes by virtue of the fact that we are human. In this case, it comes not so much by the fact that we are reflective, but that we are ontological.

We can not ask questions about being and about who we are—and when we stop asking those questions, when we fall back into a very comfortable mode of existence, whether a comfortable job, neighborhood, or marriage—there is still always going to be this nagging conscience that we have that reminds us there is something else, and you should start to think about who you really are. That does not mean you should quit your job, or move from one neighborhood to another, or break up your marriage.

As we will see with Heidegger, it is very much a status quo philosophy, despite all of the radical existentialist element. What we find is that to be authentic, to listen to the voice of conscience, to pay attention to that mysterious guilt, is to start to think about your job in a new way, to start to think about your neighborhood in a new way, to start to think about your marriage in a new way. In a sense, it is taking hold of those and making them your own rather than simply being in a job, living in a neighborhood, being in a marriage.

The second notion here, perhaps even more dramatic, is what Heidegger calls "Being-unto-death." It is one of the best-known features of Heidegger's philosophy. It has often been exaggerated to a kind of absurdity. The idea is that Being-unto-death has been taken as a kind of death fetishism. One thinks, for example, of some recent French authors who have really turned death into a kind of cause of celebration, not to mention some rock musicians in the United States.

Being-unto-death for Heidegger means something quite different. It is not a celebration of death. It is simply a recognition of death. It is a recognition of death as what he says is "a necessary fact about us." It is a necessary fact which is sometime in the future; we don't know when. He says, "Among our various possibilities, is our most necessary possibility." There is a sense in which "Being-unto-death" means living with death in mind. That sounds pretty morbid, but let's see what he means by it.

The first thing to say is that we all know we are going to die. Teenagers know they are going to die, just not for another 50,000 years. There is a sense in which we think about death and the inevitability of death—our own mortality—in an abstract way. We think, "Of course I am going to die. All mortals die. I am a mortal, so I am going to die." The truth is, we don't face death. We don't take it seriously. Facing death is something very different.

When one faces death—and here I am talking not so much about the modern way of facing death, mainly a very close call in a fast moving automobile— instead, I am talking about the kind of facing death that has some time for reflection built into it, even something as quick as drowning. I remember reading a Walt Disney comic when I was a kid. Pluto the dog falls into the water, and is in the process of drowning (of course, he gets saved). But as he is drowning, before his eyes in little cartoon balloons, his entire life passes in front of his eyes. He sees himself as a puppy, his first bone, his first doghouse, and so on. It is a cartoon version of something which we have often heard. The recent movie, *American Beauty*, makes this into the main concluding theme—the idea that in the moment of death, your whole life passes before you. To think of this as a kind of video biography is to misunderstand what is going on.

There is a sense in which when you face death, what you ask yourself are some very basic questions about the nature of your life. You see your life as a whole. Most of the time, we are caught up in particular tasks, we are caught up in questions about who we are and how we stack up, but we don't think in terms of our life as a whole. We all know how easily we can get sucked into this or that obligation, or this or that obsessive task.

What death does—that is, the prospect of death—is it shakes us out of this. This is no longer abstract, no longer a syllogism; namely, "Everyone is mortal, I am mortal, therefore I am going to die." Rather, it is something very concrete and very individual. Heidegger says that it is death that individuates us. It is death that makes us into true individuals. It is death that shakes us out of our concept of our *das Man* self, because when you are on the brink of death, you don't think of yourself in terms of your roles, in terms of your social functions. There is a sense in which you think of yourself just as yourself.

In the example I gave, when I said, "Suppose you were never born, but someone else was born in your place," I said there is a sense in which no one—including your parents and your friends—would ever miss you, because you never were in the first place. The only one that would miss you, and this is a very odd locution, would be you. You are not there.

When you face death, what you face is the sudden realization that you might not be there. In addition to all the other things you might worry about with death—how your loved ones are to be taken care of, or how your loved ones will react to your death, how you might manage funeral expenses, how you might look after you die—in addition to all those rather concrete affairs, there is one very abstract philosophical fear. One might put it in terms of perceiving for the first time true nothingness. When you die, you will cease to be a *Dasein*. The world will cease to exist for you, and because the world depends on *Dasein*, the world, for you, will cease to exist.

I have a very close friend who was/is a doctor, and spent the first five to seven years of his medical career doing something that most doctors don't have the nerve to do. He practiced medicine in some of those far-flung and medically questionable parts of the world. He was a doctor in Ethiopia and Eastern Turkey, on a Navaho reservation in the west. In these various circumstances, he found himself quite literally surrounded by death. One day, he had an accident while camping, and he was rushed to the hospital and was, for a while, in very serious condition. I talked to him later, and he said, "Interesting. I have seen people die by the thousands in my life. I realize there is a sense in which I never thought it would happen to me. Now, for the first time, I find myself facing my possible death, and suddenly it is a different way of looking at myself." That is the kind of transformation that Heidegger has in mind. When you actually face death, it shakes you up and makes you see your life as a whole in a way that nothing else will do.

Being-unto-death is not the same thing as authenticity, although it is one aspect of authenticity. It also acts as a spur, a kind of probe that throws us out of our fallen condition, our of our in authentic existence as a *das Man* self, and forces us to see ourselves and our lives as a single unity. That is the sense in which we learn to take hold of ourselves, because once we have seen our lives as a unity, and we have seen ourselves in terms of our mortality, then we start making what Heidegger calls "resolutions of a profound sort." It has often been complained of Heidegger, and later for Sartre, that this ethics, if we call it ethics, doesn't tell us anything that we should do.

In that sense, I think Heidegger is right that he is not giving us an ethics in a usual sense—namely, make your bed every day, keep your promises, and so on. What he is giving us is a picture of what we should be as human beings, or *Daseins*. That is, we should be resolute where resolute means making commitments, taking hold of ourselves. What should we do? It is not as if Heidegger doesn't give us an answer. Here is the solution to the problem: Are we to be alienated as authentic or inauthentic and, in that sense, not living a full life? He says once we have become authentic, what we can do is "resolve" ourselves to immerse ourselves in our own historicity—to essentially put ourselves back into our traditions and admire them with our newfound authentic self.

It is not too hard to see here a possible excuse for his Nazi affiliations. That is what was going on in Germany at the time. To immerse himself in his times and traditions and the hopes that all Germans had at the time was, perhaps unavoidably, to join the Nazi party. Nevertheless, I am not going to let Heidegger off. Even if that were true in the 1930s, why continue to support the Nazis in the 1940s? Why no repentance after the war was over? Is this simply a matter of Heidegger himself, making himself nothing but his own facticity and ignoring his own possibilities? Is it a matter of Heidegger's own fallenness and never achieving the authenticity he talks about? Or, to borrow a term from Jean-Paul Sartre, was it simply a matter of "bad faith?" That question I leave to you.

Jean-Paul Sartre at War
Lecture 18

Sartre wrote voluminously. It is said that he wrote as much as 20 pages a day every day of his life, and he lived into his 70s. The idea is that what he wrote was so varied and so, in a way, all over the place, that to talk about Sartre's philosophy is really just to talk about a piece of a very grand campaign.

Jean-Paul Sartre (1905–1980) is the ultimate existentialist; he concentrates on the issue of responsibility. His voluminous writings amount to a huge *oeuvre*, a true testament of "engaged literature." He named the movement and popularized it, first in France, then throughout Europe and America. The characteristics so often identified with existentialism are his own. Only his most faithful companion, Simone de Beauvoir, has stuck with his philosophy, while correcting him on important points and arguing all the way.

It is Sartre's philosophy, condensed in his great tome, *Being and Nothingness*, that can best be summarized in the phrase "no excuses!" His analysis of human nature was solidified during the horrible years of the German occupation. He spent time in a Nazi war prison—not a concentration camp. Nevertheless, he borrows much of his language from Heidegger and earlier German philosophers. Sartre's vehement denunciations were mainly aimed at his fellow Frenchmen for their cowardice, hypocrisy, and collaboration with the Germans.

What bothered Sartre was the way that everyone disclaimed responsibility for not helping the Resistance, for living their lives as normally as possible, and for collaborating with the enemy. This context prompted the question "What is human nature?" Their excuses during the war included: "What can I do about it?"—an appeal to individual impotence. "I didn't start the war, did I?"—an appeal to personal innocence. "Everyone else is doing it"—an appeal to the "herd," to the diminution of responsibility by dispersal. "I'm just looking out for myself (the same way everyone else is)"—an appeal to human nature, the instinct for self-preservation. "I couldn't help it; I had no choice"—the appeal to helplessness. "I couldn't help it; I was afraid"—the appeal to emotions (as determining behavior).

Against all such excuses, Sartre wants to argue that we are "absolutely free." We are responsible for what we do, what we are, and the way our world is. This does not mean (what is absurd) that everyone can do (succeed in) anything they choose. It does mean that there are no ultimate constraints on consciousness, on our ability to undertake (or try) to behave in the most eccentric, courageous, or perverse ways. Our choices aren't unlimited, but choices are always available. Meursault experienced a kind of freedom while in jail in *The Stranger*. Though imprisoned, he discovers freedom of thought and, in a sense, of choice about how he will die. Sartre gives the example of a mountain—is it a sacred object, an obstacle, an insurance against invasion? How we see the world is a function of our chosen project. Moreover, our motives and emotions do not determine our behavior. We determine what motives we will follow and how we see the world through our emotions.

> **Sartre's harsh view is that everyone is responsible for his or her situation.**

Sartre's harsh view is that everyone is responsible for his or her situation. He famously says, "Everyone gets the war he deserves." War inspires fear, heroism, greed, opportunism. Though a war is chosen by no one, it requires one to make choices, and "the war" is the outcome of those choices. Whatever the situation, Sartre argues, one has choices. Not all of them are conscious. One makes of the situation and oneself what one can. One may adopt an attitude of defiance, or resignation, or escape. Whatever we do is to the exclusion of other alternatives. Many choices are made by default.

The threats to freedom are often thought to be internal, such as the intrusion of strong emotions. Emotions and motives, for Sartre, are parts of the situation. To say that something was merely said in anger is false—it may be closer to what one really feels than years of polite conversation. In a sense, anger is a choice—one decides whether to react to something or repress it.

"Falling in love" is also a series of choices we make. Shyness is usually presented as a structure of the personality. But is shyness—or cowardice, for that matter—a given that determines us or a sequence of choices we exercise individually? Thus, we are all responsible for what we do, what we are, and the way the world is. ■

Essential Reading

Solomon, *Existentialism*, esp. "Existentialism Is a Humanism," pp. 196–205.

Supplementary Reading

Sartre, *The Wall and Other Stories*, trans. by Lloyd Alexander, and *The Age of Reason* (a novel), trans. by Eric Sutton.

Solomon, *From Rationalism to Existentialism*, pp. 245-324.

Introductory Questions to Consider

1. In what senses can we be said to be responsible for ourselves? Is the limit of our responsibility the reach of our voluntary actions? Or can we be held responsible for things outside our control---for example, the way the world is?

2. Consider Sartre's contention that we are "absolutely free." What, exactly, does he mean by this? Does he mean that we can achieve whatever we want at any time? If this is not the case (and it clearly is not), how could we be "absolutely free"? Explain.

3. What would it mean to say that a person in prison has a multitude of choices? What might they be?

1. Sartre maintains that "the first principle of existentialism" is that "man is nothing else but that which he makes of himself." What does he mean? Is every aspect of ourselves within our own personal control? If not, what sense can be made of Sartre's claim?

2. If you were a Frenchman in Paris during the early 1940s, what would you have done? What factors influence your decisions? To what extent do basic questions of survival dominate your thinking?

3. If you were a German soldier in Paris during the early 1940s, what would you have done? What factors influence your decisions? To what extent do basic questions of survival dominate your thinking?

Jean-Paul Sartre at War

Lecture 18—Transcript

Jean-Paul Sartre is the ultimate existentialist. He named the movement, and when people talk about existentialism it is typically his philosophy they have in mind. The characteristics that I have mentioned previously—the emphasis on freedom, choice, and responsibility, in particular—are very much the centerpieces of his philosophy. As I pointed out, with some of the members of the movement, Nietzsche for example, they aren't particularly central, and with someone like Heidegger they are also problematic.

Sartre's existentialism really does focus on one concept above all else. That is the concept of responsibility. Perhaps the only person who followed him through and considered herself an existentialist along with him was his equally remarkable life-long partner, Simone de Beauvoir, and of their relationship I will have something to say a bit later on.

Sartre wrote voluminously. It is said that he wrote as much as 20 pages a day every day of his life, and he lived into his 70s. The idea is that what he wrote was so varied and so, in a way, all over the place, that to talk about Sartre's philosophy is really just to talk about a piece of a very grand campaign. He wrote literature. Some of it I would consider excellent. He wrote a great many journal articles, magazine pieces, and newspaper pieces throughout his life. He was very deeply politically engaged, and perhaps he is best known among writers for his defense of what he called "engage literature," which would include philosophy—the idea that philosophy must be nothing if not practical. That meant for him, political.

One does not write for the enjoyment of it, the prestige, and the external rewards. As evidence of this, when he received the Nobel Prize in 1964, he rather dramatically turned it down. Sartre's writings in politics are very often, I think, eccentric. His writings in philosophy deserve to be recognized as some of the greatest in the 20th century. He follows very closely on Martin Heidegger, and you will see there is a good deal of influence there.

Unlike Heidegger, who was often a bit vague on such notions as freedom and responsibility, Sartre is absolutely straightforward. It is from him that

I essentially take the notion "no excuses!"—the idea that one is always responsible, one cannot beg off. One cannot push the blame on someone else, but one is always responsible for what one does, who one is, and perhaps more problematically, for the state of the world.

Much of Sartre's writing, and in particular his great book, *Being and Nothingness*, which will form the core of most of what I will be saying, was written during the German occupation. Sartre was in a prison camp for a short time. One should carefully distinguish this from the horror of the German concentration camps. He had access to literature, books, and writing materials. Consequently, it is really from his place in the German camp that he begins the ideas of *Being and Nothingness*. We have a rather full set of letters between himself and Simone, and I will say, despite the rather coldness of some of Sartre's writings, in those letters he shows himself to be a warm, caring human being.

It is through the German occupation that he writes this. It is the occupation itself that gives Sartre the impetus for his basic thesis. There is an irony here, and that is that he borrows in his language and ideas very heavily, not only from Heidegger, but from other German philosophers as well. His target really is not the Germans. The target is his fellow Frenchmen. He denounced them for their cowardice, their hypocrisy, their collaboration.

Much of this is becoming evident really only in the last 10 years as some of the files are opened up and we can see how the average Frenchman did behave during the war. Sartre was particularly bothered by the disclaimers and the excuses that people made about why they did what they did. Why they did, for example, join that movement called "The Resistance"—the French underground, which was trying to undermine the German occupation—or why people collaborated and pursued their careers, perhaps to their own advantage, but very often to the clear disadvantage of the French community.

In general, the idea of excuses must have weighed very heavily on him. What is more, it is an excellent test for an age-old philosophical question. That is, "What is human nature?" If you go into some aspects of philosophy, that question gets answered in a very armchair sort of way. We imagine human beings before the advent of society. We imagine human beings in the so-called "state of nature." Then we kind of make up, on the basis of our casual experience, what people must have been like.

One set of theories says people are basically selfish and not very nice to each other. Another set of theories says that basically people are content and indifferent to one another; that it is society that causes them to have traits that they have. And another theory yet might be that people in the state of nature really are already looking for recognition from others. This is armchair philosophy, and it has very little to back it up, except for one's rather casual experiences of people in ordinary life. In recent Oxford philosophy, analyses of human nature often take the form of people keeping promises and what people do as good citizens of a civilized state.

Suppose you take the question of human nature in a different way. Suppose you think that human nature betrays itself not in everyday behavior, rather in something that you have to discover only by putting human beings under stress. You take the analogy from chemistry—if you have a bit of stuff that you want to analyze, you don't just look at it. What you do is you see what happens if you subject it to enormous pressure, or heat it to boiling point, or treat it with acid or a strong base, or perhaps bombard it with neutrons, or put it in liquid nitrogen and see what it does. In other words, by putting it under enormous stress, what you discover is what it really is. Sartre has this view, which he shares with Camus, that if you want to understand human nature, you can't just look at people in their daily bourgeois existence; rather, you have to look at people under the greatest stress. Perhaps there is not greater stress than being occupied by an army during the midst of one of the most horrible wars in the history of humanity.

What he saw as he watched his fellow citizens and dealt with them in his own minor role in the Resistance is that people would do what they did—collaborate, or in any case cooperate—and what they said about what they did, almost in any case, came out in terms of excuses. For example, "What can I do?"—the kind of excuse that comes from impotence. The idea is that the forces of history and the German army are so overwhelmingly powerful, and here, "I am one lone individual"—perhaps even without arms—"what could I possibly do?"

There is the argument for innocence. "I didn't start the war." The idea of innocence here is one that we have run across in Camus, who at this time is very much a colleague of Sartre. It is a notion that we have run across in perhaps other philosophers too—notably, for example, in Heidegger, who in a very different sense talks about innocent guilt. With Sartre, the idea of innocence takes on a rather striking notion. It is not the abstract metaphysical notion you get in Heidegger. It is not the very generalized notion of original sin that you get in Camus. It is a notion of innocence which has to do with making excuses. One begs off by saying, "I am not responsible, therefore. ..."

There is a notion of "Everyone else is doing it." There is the appeal to a kind of "herd" instinct, going back to Kierkegaard and Nietzsche. There is the idea that everyone else was collaborating. There is the idea that one's friends were not doing anything to aid the Resistance. That, in itself, seemed to be an adequate excuse for a great many people. We hear it today in all sorts of contexts, for example, people in business who say, "I really know this is wrong, but everyone else is doing it." It is another excuse, and it is just the kind of excuse that Sartre wants to get rid of.

There is the "I'm just looking out for me" excuse—the appeal to self-preservation, the idea that each of us is a selfish or at any rate self-interested human being, so what I am doing is just natural. It is what anyone would do in a similar situation. If they are not, then it is their problem.

There is the "I had no choice" excuse—the appeal to helplessness, the idea that we all didn't have any alternatives. Here we are, we are stuck in Paris, the Germans are all around us, and so, what we have to think about is simply what we have to do. The emphasis is on "have to do." We don't have choices.

Finally, there is a kind of emotional appeal, the idea of "I was afraid." "I collaborated because I was afraid of what would happen to me or my family if I didn't." Or, "I didn't cooperate with the Resistance because I was afraid of what the Gestapo would do if they caught us," and so on.

To all of these excuses, Sartre wants to say, "No." The central thesis of his philosophy put in one way is that we are absolutely free. That means that we don't have excuses. We are responsible for what we do. Before we go any further, let me just put aside one very common misunderstanding and criticism of Sartre's philosophy. Philosophers will very often take someone with whom they have problems—and Sartre gives us lots of problems to cope with; for example, he is always throwing responsibility back in our faces—this causes lots of philosophers to resist him. One of those philosophers was Martin Heidegger, but on that story more later.

What we get with Sartre is the idea that we are "absolutely free," not in the absurd sense that we can do anything, or we can do anything that we choose to do; rather, it is the idea that we always have choices. What is dramatic about Sartre's philosophy, and what makes it so challenging and appealing, is the way he extends this thesis into all sorts of realms of human life, and shows us that we have choices in many ways that we never considered ourselves to have choices before.

To interpret the notion of absolute freedom, I would suggest something like the notion of the absence of any ultimate constraints. Sartre makes it very clear that we are always in some sense constrained by our situation. We are always given a limited number of choices in one sense. There is the idea that we are never free from our circumstances. As Heidegger says, and Sartre uses this language: We are thrown into our world in a particular place, at a particular time, in a particular political situation, and so on. Within those circumstances, we often don't have a very wide range of choices. Nevertheless, we always have choices.

The important thing about Sartre's philosophy is to appreciate just what those choices are, and how we are responsible, even in the most minimal situations. Let me give you an example. There is a scene that is very popular in French literature in illustrating just this thesis. We saw it in Camus's novel *The Stranger*. It is the idea of throwing a young man in prison, and in that sense absolutely limiting his freedom in one sense, but using it as a device to show just how much freedom we really have. In prison, Meursault learns about freedom of thought—the freedom to reflect. He reflects on the possibility that he might have a one-in-a-million chance of escaping, rather than facing the certainty of execution. He reflects on the meaning of his crime, his imprisonment. He reflects on the overall meaning of his life, and tries to ascertain what that is. He thinks about the execution and comes up with the decision that he really has choices regarding the execution itself—namely how to face it.

Let me take an even more extreme example. There is a cartoon that has been popular for quite a few years called "The Wizard of Id," which contains a character called "the Spook," who is a man thrown in prison, presumably for a very, very long time. The Spook is not only in the dungeon of this medieval situation, he is also shackled to the wall, so he is spread eagled and can hardly move. The question is, does it make any sense whatsoever to talk about him as free? Sartre would say "Yes, indeed."

He has a number of choices. He could see himself as rightly condemned and consequently spend his life feeling penance. He can see himself as wrongly condemned and spend his life feeling resentment. He can resolve to be a martyr for whatever cause it is that he might choose to be a martyr for. He might choose to be an example of an exemplary prisoner, or the example of a terrible prisoner. He can rail and shout and make himself utterly obnoxious, even if no one will hear him. He can try to escape, perhaps absurdly, by simply trying with his fingernails to carve his way through the iron of the shackles. It probably would not work. This highlights what Sartre has in mind with absolute freedom. It is not the freedom to accomplish—to achieve—anything we choose. It is always the freedom to try, and the freedom, first of all, to form our attitudes and senses in which we will approach and deal with the world.

He gives an example of a mountain. In a sense, a mountain is just a fact of nature. It is there. Yet, people who live near the mountain have all sorts of choices, which they probably make collectively. For example, they can choose to see the mountain as a sacred object, as the center of the universe. They can choose to see the mountain as an obstacle, something that blocks their easy progress to get to the other side. They can choose to see the mountain as an aesthetic wonder, something beautiful to look at. They can choose to see the mountain as protection from dangers on the other side. They could adopt several of these attitudes, more or less, at once. The idea is that the options, alternatives, the different ways we can deal with the world, are always open to us. Even though the situation might seriously limit what those options might be, there are always options.

Sartre says, extremely harshly, "We all get the war we deserve." One imagines being caught in the middle of the Second World War during the German occupation, and one can see, in Sartre's countrymen, the different kinds of choices that they made. One looks at the war as a source of profit. One thinks of Cottard in Camus's novel *The Plague*, another looks at the war as a great misfortune. Still another looks at the war as an opportunity to pursue journalism, to write a great novel. Or, the same character might think the war is a good time to lay low and disappear from society, so one hides in the basement for five, six, seven years. One might see the war as an opportunity for heroism. One might see the war as a source of great obligation. One could go on at some length.

The idea is that even this horrible situation, which in one sense was not chosen by anyone, at least not by any ordinary person, nevertheless presents us not with a choiceless situation; rather, precisely a situation which requires, demands, any number of choices. That is the idea. We have a choice here about how we are going to live our lives—what we are going to make of ourselves—even in the direst and most constricting of situations.

Toward the end of his life, in an interview Sartre says, "One is always responsible for what one makes of what is made of one." It is a bit convoluted, but when you think about it, it makes perfectly good sense. We don't choose our situation. In an important sense, we don't even choose ourselves. Namely, we are subject to all sorts of forces starting from the circumstances of our birth, background, and upbringing, and peer pressure, our jobs, and our world. Nevertheless, within those circumstances we are responsible for making the choices, which include, among other things, the choices which will change the circumstances and allow us to make something else of ourselves in the future.

This is really the heart of what Sartre is trying to tell us. This is the sense in which one is often tempted to say that the constraints on human freedom are not necessarily those that are external; for example, the threat of German soldiers or the threat of some sort of external sanctions. The threats against our freedom are often from the inside—for example, in compulsion, the sense that we have to do something and we can't escape that impulse, or the idea of strong desire, or perhaps most dramatically, the intrusion of strong emotions.

Sartre's thesis, here at first, is going to sound a bit confusing and counterintuitive. To summarize it very quickly, it is not that one is caused to behave by his or her emotions or motives. Rather, emotions and motives are really part of the situation in which one chooses what to do. In particular, let me focus on emotions for a minute because that is going to be, as you will see, an essential part of Sartre's argument. We often say, "I couldn't help it; I was just afraid," or "I didn't mean what I said; I was just very angry," or "I'm sorry I was so foolish; I was falling in love." What is dramatic here is that in each and every case, emotions are being used as excuses. We did something and now we want to take away our responsibility for doing it, and instead, blame it on the emotion.

Once again, we have this picture of emotion as something inside us, but at the same time foreign, a kind of intrusion on our rationality—the Freudian "It" if you like. Thinking about it, we realize something very different is the case. Take anger. We say, "I didn't really mean it; I was just very angry." The friend whom you insulted knows, and you know, that what you said was not just the product of anger, but a very deep, cutting insight that perhaps you had sort of thought of for a very long time but never said before. The fact is that you were, in truth, telling something much closer to the way you really feel than you have in perhaps months or years of casual friendship. Instead of the anger talking and contradicting your own preferences and choices, there is a sense in which the anger itself is a choice.

One thinks about how one gets angry, and we talk about this as if it is something that just hits us. It is true; sometimes the circumstances that make us angry happen very suddenly. When we get angry, what we do is make a decision. There might be that first flush as you recognize that you have been gravely offended. Then you have to decide—often we do this very quickly—what can/should we do about it? You decide at that point whether to forget it or whether to dwell on it, whether to say something back increasing the odds of increased hostility, or whether to just keep your mouth shut.

Let me take the example of love, because perhaps that is the most dramatic. We talk about "falling in love." Is there such a thing? I believe in love at first sight. I do believe that you meet people who are just almost chemically dazzling to you. There is a sense in which you meet someone and get very excited. Is that the same thing as falling in love? I think not at all. It is not even an infatuation. It is just being excited. Then you have to make a choice. You make a choice whether or not to continue to look at this person; whether or not to talk to this person. Later on, you have to decide whether or not to date the person; whether or not to marry the person. In short, when you think about falling in love, it is actually a gradual, or a rather quick, step-by-step process which involves choices every bit of the way.

Put this together and one comes away with the conclusion that emotions are not simply things that happen to us. They are not excuses, such as "the train got derailed." Rather, they are choices that we make in a very subtle way which very strongly influence both the way we see the world and the way we act. That is precisely what Sartre is after.

This emphasis on choice as opposed to things happening to us extends to other realms as well. For example, consider someone who is shy. The way we generally think about shyness, like most character traits, is it is something like a structure of the personality. The structure of the personality causes us to behave in certain ways, to perform certain acts. What Sartre suggests is that the causal relationship (if we want to talk about a causal relationship) goes just the other way. In fact, we are shy because we engage in certain behaviors, because we act in certain ways.

This is perhaps most important in the context of the situation he faced in the war, looking at his fellow countrymen and their reactions to the Germans; also in one of his best plays, a play called *No Exit*, which I will talk about in a few lectures. That is the question about cowardice. People are often quite happy to make an excuse for themselves and say, "I didn't or won't do something because I am a coward." The picture is here is this structure of one's personality causing us to make certain choices, causing us to perform certain actions. Sartre would say just the opposite. You are a coward because you choose to behave in certain ways. Once again, the whole emphasis gets turned around. Instead of talking about what we are forced to do, have to do, or determined to do, what Sartre puts the emphasis on is the choices that we have within the situation.

It is in this sense that we are all responsible for the world. When he says we all get the war we deserve, he is referring not just to that particular circumstance and the different options that one can choose with regard to the war. He is also talking about the consequences of those choices, and he is talking more generally about the kinds of choices we have all the time.

A very important point here, which I will later bury in some very heavy Teutonic terminology, is the choices we make are not always self-evident to us. We think of a choice as something which is essentially deliberate and reflective as when, for example, you are talking with a friend about which restaurant you will go to tonight, and you give the different possibilities, weigh the options and the different prices, and you talk about it, think about it. The decision, in some way, emerges from the discussion.

We make other kinds of choices too. We are making choices all the time, not only in behaviors which Sartre will call "unreflective" or "pre-reflective"— behaviors in which we are not reflecting as such, we just see that something must be done and we choose to do it—perhaps more importantly, we also behave in those ways when there are all sorts of choices which we never think of. This is absolutely essential to Sartre's philosophy, as you will see, because it is an essential part of the political wing of the "no excuses" issue.

Consider, for example, as I say to my classes, the number of things you could be doing right now instead of being in this class. Some of them are not particularly productive—drinking coffee in the local student café—but others. Could you at this point be helping the Red Cross, or serving the homeless downtown, or doing any of a number of other things that you might all think of that would really benefit humanity in a major way? This is not to say you should do it, but you could be doing it. According to Sartre, it is also to say that you are responsible for not doing it. There is a sense in which what we are doing all the time is making choices to do what we are doing, to the exclusion of all sorts of other alternatives which you simply choose not to think about.

There are some serious questions that come in here, and Sartre's colleague, Maurice Merleau-Ponty, raised some of them in his continuing conversations with Sartre as well as in some of his other books. Is it really fair to people to charge them with responsibility for situations of which they are utterly ignorant? One thinks about the problems that missionaries sometimes face when they are dealing with overseas tribes—people who have never heard of Jesus Christ—and they face the rather awful thesis that, despite the fact that these people have never heard of Christ, nevertheless, they are responsible for them not taking him in. It is a similar thesis here. What do we say about children who are too young to understand what is going on? What do we say about a peasant in some far-flung country who does not have any news, does not know how other people live, does not know the options that are readily available to us?

Perhaps we want to modify the thesis in certain ways. Let me simply emphasize what is most important to Sartre. If he is to say we are responsible for the world and the state of the world, then it must be the case that we are not just responsible for those choices which we make deliberately and reflectively, but we are responsible for all sorts of choices that we make—in a sense, out of default or neglect—which we don't think about, but which we are capable of thinking about, and perhaps should think about.

The idea, as always, is no excuses. The fact that you did not think of it is no excuse. The fact that it is inconvenient or has a great cost is no excuse. As always, what you choose is not just the act, but also its consequences. What you choose, therefore, *is* the cost. If you say it is too expensive, it is too inconvenient, too difficult, then you are responsible for making that choice too. The idea is you are responsible for yourself, and you are responsible for the world. What I would like to do in the subsequent lectures is to try to make that thesis as plausible as possible.

Sartre on Emotions and Responsibility
Lecture 19

By the time he had written *Being and Nothingness,* Sartre was also evolving a notion of his own of psychoanalysis. It was not Freudian psychoanalysis. It was what he would call "existential" psychoanalysis. The principal difference with Freud was that it was not mechanistic. To put it all into another slogan: Where Freud says, "I cannot," Sartre would say, "I refuse."

In an early essay on emotions (1938), Sartre argued that emotions are choices, "magical transformations of the world." He wanted to get away from the mechanistic picture of emotions as brute forces or mere physiological disturbances. He tried to defend the emotions as choices, strategies for coping with a difficult world. They are also, accordingly, our responsibility, not mere excuses.

One of his targets is the great American philosopher-psychologist William James. James argued (though not consistently) that an emotion is merely a set of sensations caused by a physiological disturbance that is itself caused by a disturbing perception or image. The beauty of James's theory, for psychologists and philosophers, is how specific it is. Sartre argues that emotions (and all acts of mind) must have "intentionality," direction toward the world, and cannot be mere sensations or "feelings." Emotions, then, are always about something. James, on the other hand, suggests that some emotions are instinctual in nature—thus, perception gets short shrift. Furthermore, Sartre argues, emotions have "finality" or purpose. There are reasons for one's emotions. An emotion is a strategy for dealing with the world. In Aesop, the fox's perception transforms the world when he can't get the grapes he wants. The fox refuses to see himself as a failure, thus escaping from the humiliation of defeat. In the story of the fainting woman, emotion reflects a choice to evade an intolerable situation. Even through love and joy, one chooses to absolve one's self of responsibility.

A second target is Freud. Sartre rejects "the unconscious." But is there really a difference between this concept and Sartre's "pre-reflective" consciousness? Sartre also rejects the very idea of "psychic determinism," the notion that human emotions, thoughts, and decisions are caused by antecedent conditions and external events. They are not to be construed as forces "within us," the Freudian "id," acting upon us against our will (and apart from our knowledge). Emotions are strategies, knowingly and willfully (but not reflectively) undertaken.

Sartre's view of the participation of the body in emotion anticipates some of the most interesting recent work in neuropsychology.

Sartre's view of the participation of the body in emotion anticipates some of the most interesting recent work in neuropsychology. Emotions are not just bodily reactions or sensations. Nevertheless, Sartre develops his own brand of psychoanalysis, "existential" psychoanalysis. The essential difference with Freud becomes not so much the existence of the unconscious but the rejection of the supposedly mechanistic, impersonal workings of the mind. ∎

Essential Reading

Sartre, *The Emotions: Sketch of a Theory*.

Supplementary Reading

Fell, *Emotion in the Thought of Sartre*. For various readings on the nature of emotion (including William James's classic "What Is an Emotion?"), see Cheshire Calhoun, ed., *What Is an Emotion?*

Soll, "Sartre's Rejection of the Freudian Unconscious," in *The Philosophy of Jean-Paul Sartre*, ed., Paul A. Schilpp.

Solomon, *The Passions: Emotions and the Meaning of Life*.

———, "Sartre on the Emotions," in Schilpp, ibid.

1. What does Sartre mean when he refers to emotions as "magical transformations of the world"? What leads us to "magically transform" the world in one particular way as opposed to another?

2. What does Sartre mean by the term "intentionality"? What role does "intentionality" play in Sartre's theory of the emotions? How does it enable Sartre to respond to the skeptic?

3. Why is Sartre intent upon rejecting Freud's notion of "the unconscious"?

Advanced Questions to Consider

1. According to the American philosopher William James, an emotion is nothing more than a sensation that is caused by a physiological manifestation (which, in turn, is caused by a perception). Sartre has several major problems with this view. What are they?

2. Consider Sartre's introduction of "that face which appears at the pane" at the end of *The Emotions*. In response to this face, Sartre tells us: "the behavior which gives emotion its meaning is no longer ours; it is the expression of the face, the movements of the body of the other person which come to form a synthetic whole with the disturbance of our organism." What do you make of this description? Can it be reconciled with Sartre's position throughout the book that our emotions are voluntary and, therefore, ultimately our own responsibility?

3. By calling emotions "magical" transformations of the world, is Sartre negatively evaluating them? Are they always some form of "sour grapes"— some evasion or distortion of the world by consciousness because of its inability to change the world to meet its ends? If so, do you agree with Sartre? Are all (or some) emotions necessarily evasions?

Sartre on Emotions and Responsibility
Lecture 19—Transcript

The idea that emotions are choices informs one of Sartre's first philosophical publications. In the late 1930s, more than five years before he would publish *Being and Nothingness,* he writes a huge manuscript (I don't think Sartre writes any small manuscripts) which was to be called *The Psyche.* Of that work we only have one piece, the piece he published in 1938, which is called "The Emotions: Sketch of a Theory." It is a fascinating essay, and one can see in it all sorts of theses which will emerge full-blown five or so years later. The central thesis, though, is that emotions are choices. Emotions involve alternatives, options, and most importantly perhaps, involve a kind of purposiveness which most scholars and psychologists have simply ignored.

The key phrase of that early work is a very dramatic phrase. Sartre says that emotions are "magical transformations of the world." What I would like to do in this lecture is try to understand what that means and to try to see how that fits into his overall philosophy. What he wants to do with this thesis is, first of all, to get away from a mechanistic picture of emotions as physiological disturbances, the idea that emotions are bodily upsets which we then experience. Instead, predictably, he wants to show that emotions are choices, and particularly that they are strategies for coping with difficulties. They are there for our responsibility and not the source of excuses.

His first target is the great American psychologist/philosopher William James. James's views on emotions are quite complex. They are often oversimplified. His religious writings—for example, the essay "Will to Believe"—involve a really subtle notion about the ways in which we can choose our emotions, choose our attitudes towards the world, something that would be very much in mind with what Sartre is arguing. The target that Sartre focuses on is a very famous essay that James wrote in the late 19th century called "What is an Emotion?" which he then reworks later for a book, and it finds its way into his principles of psychology as well.

In that work, James has one formulation which psychologists ever since have used as the basis of a great deal of their research. It simply goes like this: An emotion is an upsetting perception, which causes in us a physiological disturbance. James at one point says a "visceral disturbance," and we are quite aware of what that means. The idea of our stomach tightening up, the idea of feeling flushed, the idea of feeling sometimes cold—the various kinds of very easily specifiable operations of the body, which then give rise to, or cause, a set of distinctive sensations—the feeling of a visceral upset, the feeling of a chill, the feeling of being flushed.

In short, what James argues is that "This perception of the physiological upset IS (he both italicizes and capitalizes the word "is") the emotion." In other words, an emotion is a set of sensations, which are caused by a distinctive set of physiological responses, which, in turn, are caused by some upsetting perception. Nietzsche once said, "It is not the least charm of a theory that it is easily refutable." The truth is that the beauty of James's theory has often been the idea that he is so specific that it is very easy for a theorist to come around and say, "The theory is right. The theory is wrong. Here is the evidence, and here is the counter-evidence." It doesn't involve such vague terms as "effect," that philosophers can argue about for ages without ever pinning it down.

In James's own time, he was challenged by some fellow physiologists who claimed that the number of physiological phenomena that gave rise to sensations just wasn't expansive and broad enough to account for the huge number of emotions that we experience. On the other side, it was argued that although it is true that emotions are sensations with a physical origin, they must be something else besides. It is this side of the argument that Sartre wants to weigh in on. What Sartre wants to say is that James ignores at least two very important features of emotion. First of all, he will argue that emotions, like all mental phenomena (and here we see Sartre's debt to Husserl), are necessarily intentional. They have "intentionality." That means that they are not simply "feelings" or sensations, they refer outside of themselves to the world.

To refer to it rather simply, emotions are always about something. You don't just love; you love someone or something. You don't just hate; you hate someone or something. You can't just be angry; you have to be angry at someone, about something. You can't just be sad; you have to be sad about something. Even those cases with what we might call mysterious objects—

for example, in dread what we are worried about is perhaps the unknown, or there is what Freud later calls "free-floating anxiety"—the idea of being extremely disturbed and upset about something, someone knows not what. There is the question of mood, when sadness expands beyond being sad about this particular thing. I think it is not a stretch of our language or our conception of mood to say that when one is sad or depressed or joyful, one is nevertheless depressed or joyful about something, perhaps just the state of the world as a whole, or one's own position in it.

In short, all emotions are "intentional," in that they are always about something. What this means is that they can't be mere sensations and feelings, because feelings are not about anything. Or, perhaps one can say feeling is a very vague, general notion, which encompasses within it both feelings which are intentional—namely emotions—and perhaps those feelings—merely sensations—which are not. A headache is not about anything. It might be caused by something, for example, your mother-in-law coming to visit. We don't say that the headache is about your mother-in-law. Certainly, if you have a pain in your toe, it might be because you stepped on a nail, but nevertheless, the pain is not about the nail. Nevertheless, if you are caused to be angry by somebody insulting you, it is not just the cause—it is also the intentional object of the emotion. You are angry about the offense. You are angry at the person.

This is what James leaves out. Of course, one can try and save James by saying he doesn't really leave it out. It is in the realm of perception. Then we have a new set of problems. James says very little about the perception that causes emotion. In fact, sometimes, very much in tune with the psychology of his times, he suggests that these are basically instinctual in nature. At least some emotions are caused by instinctual reactions, which involve really very little thought and very little of what we would normally call "perception," at all.

There is a kind of natural fear of snakes. There is a natural revulsion to vast quantities of blood. Whether or not these instinctual theses are true, it is pretty clear that in James, in the account of emotions, perception gets very short shrift. One could say that perceptions are always about something, that perceptions are intentional and precise, Sartre says. In that sense, one can say that James captures the notion of intentionality in the perception part of the thesis. Then we have some other problems, because it is not the emotion itself that is about something—it is, rather, the perception. To say that a cause is two steps removed from the emotion is intentional; it is not necessarily to say that the emotion itself is intentional.

It gets worse than that. For example, a bear steps out from behind a tree as I am taking a walk through the woods. This is one of William James's own examples. I have this familiar sensation of queasiness in my stomach, and my knees feel weak. I feel rather flushed and tense. What I feel is fear. What is the fear? It is that set of sensations which is caused by the physiological upset, which is caused, in turn, by my sudden perception of the bear. Not so fast. Let's ask a question. How do we know that the emotion is fear? Just suppose: I have just broken off a relationship with a particularly hairy lover. As the bear jumps out from behind the tree, my thought is "No! I am in love again." I interpret all these sensations as falling in love. Absurd? Of course.

If you think about some of the arguments that James's own contemporaries in physiology had made—for example, that the sensations and the physiological upset accompanying a great many emotions were the same yet we distinguish the emotions quite sharply—you can see that what I have just given is an extreme example of that same doubt. How do we individuate and identify emotions? You can't just say on the basis of perception, because the perception as far as we have it here is, namely, the perception of a fact—that is, "here is a bear." It can't be in the physiology and it can't be in the sensations that make up the emotion.

One has to say that something else is going on here. Sartre just jumps in with two feet and says, "Of course. The fact that emotions are intentional means that what distinguishes an emotion and identifies it is precisely the kind of thing that it is about." One might again modify James, and say, for example: "Instead of thinking of perception as just perception of a fact, namely 'here is a bear,' what one actually perceives is already deeply value laden. What I see is not a bear, but what I see is a great danger in the shape of a bear." That gives us some mileage. Even then, it has often been argued by cynics that love and the feelings of love are, in part, compelled by the sense of danger. In this case, my absurd hypothesis, that I might be falling in love again becomes at least a little bit plausible. How are we to understand this? It seems to me that the basic idea is that what James is doing is over-physiologizing the emotions.

In James's defense, I should say that at the time he was writing at the end of the 19th century, this was a bold and very important move. There were a great many psychologists, both American and European, who were focusing on psychology in terms of the measurement of very particular differences in perception and such. What they were doing was often ignoring the body. What James was doing was, much in turn with some people today, was trying to remind philosophers that they had bodies. If you think about what an emotion is, you can't get away from the body. James famously and plausibly says, "You can't really imagine anger without the urge to vigorous action." So, the concept of emotion for James is firmly tied to bodily response and bodily behavior, which for the purposes here, he does not adequately distinguish. The idea is that if you are to understand emotion, you must understand the body.

While Sartre doesn't disagree with this, he thinks that that is the wrong emphasis. To understand the body and the role of the body in emotion is not to understand the essence of emotion, but rather to understand one of its most interesting and important consequences. Before I get to that, let me introduce the second way in which Sartre wants to correct James. He says— contrary to not only James, but also to almost every thinker on the subject of emotions—emotions have what he calls "finality." Here, what we should understand is the word "finality," not in the sense of ending, rather the sense in which "finality" refers to an end. The word comes from Aristotle, who talked about the final causes of behavior, where the final cause is basically the purpose.

What Sartre is arguing here is that emotions are purposive. It is a bold thesis, because we typically think about emotions as being caused in us, and consequently, they don't have a purpose, or if they do have a purpose, it is not our purpose. Sartre, to the contrary, wants to say that a person who has emotions has reasons for that emotion, whether or not he or she manages to articulate them, or he or she understands what the emotion is. I want to talk about this at great length later on. The basic idea is that an emotion is a kind of strategy. An emotion is way of dealing with the world. An emotion, consequently, is chosen, and is chosen for a purpose. For purposes of this essay, the reasons tend to be virtually all the same. What one does is make a choice to escape from a painful situation. The way in which emotions do this is something I will talk about in a bit of detail.

Let me give Sartre's own examples. First of all, there is an example that comes from Aesop, the ancient fable teller. It is a very persuasive example of Sartre's thesis. He talks about "The Fox and The Grapes," a story we all know. We still use an expression that comes straight out of Aesop, the notion of "sour grapes." This story very briefly is the fox sees some yummy, delicious grapes, and craves them, but even with all his fox-like ingenuity, he can't reach them. So, he turns away in disgust and says, "They are probably sour anyway." Sartre rather wryly suggests that it is not the chemistry of the grapes that has changed, but what has happened is what Sartre calls a "magical transformation of the world." Now let me explain that phrase.

First of all, notice that in one sense it is not the world that changes. The grapes stay exactly as they have been. The fox never touches them. What he does is change his attitude. He changes his way of seeing the grapes. He now comes to see them as sour. That is the transformation. One might say that what is transformed is not the world, but the fox's way of seeing the world. That is okay, because remember, what we are aiming toward (the next lecture will make this fully explicit) is Sartre as a phenomenologist, in which, like Heidegger, phenomenology and ontology—the way in which we experience and the way in which the world is—are firmly tied together. From a phenomenological point of view, it makes perfectly good sense to say that what the fox does is transform the world.

What about the magical? That is where it gets really fascinating. There is a sense in which the fox might actually change the grapes. For example, we can imagine a very spiteful fox, who, unable to reach the grapes, takes a spray can and makes them sour by putting a chemical on them, in which case it is true that the chemistry of the grapes has changed—that the grapes now are sour. Sometimes we behave like this, ruining what we can't have so that no one else can have it. Often what we do is this kind of magical transformation, which is, instead of actually doing something to change the world or the situation, we transform it as if by fiat in our minds. What the fox does here, exemplifying the emotion of resentment, something that Nietzsche talks about at great length, is he refuses to accept himself as a failure. He refuses to accept himself as having been not up to the difficulty of acquiring the grapes. Instead, he sees himself now as a wise fox who is not willing to expend any more energy on such a wasted project.

That idea of escaping from a difficulty, of using one's emotions to escape from the world, is the heart of Sartre's thesis in this early essay. He says emotions are basically a mode of escape behavior. What that means is that we have our emotions, not because they are caused in us by frustrating circumstances, but rather, we have our emotions because they are a way of dealing with the world, in which we come to see ourselves as better off than we would otherwise.

Let me give another example from Sartre—this one not nearly so plausible; nevertheless, I think it illustrates the thesis in a very dramatic way. He is concerned with a young woman in Victorian times who finds herself caught in a ball with a bunch of men who are telling off-color jokes. This puts this proper young woman in a very awkward position. If she walks away from the men and the jokes, she will be labeled as a prude. If she laughs at the jokes, she will labeled as who knows what. If she abuses the men for telling the jokes, then we all know what they will think of her. In short, all of her options are unacceptable, because in all of them, she comes out being much worse off then she is.

What does she do? Sartre suggests she faint dead away. This is not a phenomenon that we see very often in the world as it approaches the new millennium. Certainly, in the last century or so, such phenomena were well documented and frequent. One can try to explain them through the side door by saying that what such women wore were much too tight, depriving them of oxygen. That is probably true. Nevertheless, one has to explain away: Why did they faint dead away at precisely that moment? One can add to that a kind of Jamesian thesis: Because they were flushed with excitement, and that made it all the more serious—the lack of oxygen. It still doesn't explain what we want to explain.

Here is what Sartre says. The young woman faints dead away as a way of escaping from her extremely awkward situation. She can't face it. She can't walk away from it. She can't do anything about it. Instead, she, in a very concrete sense, disappears. I don't find that a particularly plausible example. I have actually never known anyone who has fainted in such a circumstance. Nevertheless, we can see what Sartre has in mind. What is important here is that it is not as if the woman decides in a conscious, deliberate, reflective way to faint. She just chooses. She just does it. For Sartre, most of our emotions are not reflective. Most of our emotions don't involve deliberation. Nevertheless, they do involve choices. In this case again is the choice to evade a situation which one no longer finds tolerable.

There are other examples which I find not so plausible either, but I think Sartre is on to something very important. Let me give the two other examples so you get the range. He considers someone who has fallen in love, and one thinks of falling in love in our society, as in Sartre's society, as a very positive thing. Sartre, who has a very strong skeptical streak regarding human behavior, puts this into question. "What do you do when you fall in love?" he asks, as some songs have asked. The answer is what you do is act like a fool. You are irresponsible. Ironically, or even paradoxically, the person to whom you are most irresponsible, most inconsiderate, sometimes even cruel, is the person whom you love. How to explain this? Sartre's argument again, I think, illustrates the thesis, whether or not plausible, in this particular case. That is the idea that one chooses love as a way of absolving oneself from responsibility for one's behavior.

So, too, with the emotion of joy. Again, we think of joy as a very positive thing. Sartre, who was a reasonably gloomy fellow at times, says that joy, too, is a kind of escape behavior. When you feel joy, what you do is throw off the world; you throw off your cares. In particular, you throw off all those political responsibilities and obligations with which Sartre himself was so concerned.

We can think of examples that bear this out. People whose good moods, in fact, are very obnoxious, and you might wonder, "Why—why should I resent somebody being in a good mood?" You watch the behavior and you say, "Because the good mood is, in fact, acting as an excuse for them not to be doing the sorts of things they are supposed to be doing, and not to be behaving the way that they ought to be behaving." In short, the idea is that what emotions do for us is act as choices—as ways of transforming the world, our world, such that difficulties disappear, or at least, in an important sense, that they are mitigated.

Sartre has a second target, and this is a target that will carry him through virtually his entire philosophy. That is Sigmund Freud. The arguments here are somewhat complicated—we will see them again when we get to Sartre— on what he calls "bad faith." There are basically two points of utter rejection. The first is that Sartre rejects the idea of the unconscious, but one is to be very careful here. Notice that I have already said that for Sartre, emotions for the most part are not reflective. They are pre-reflective or unreflective. One might rightly challenge whether there is a real difference between the unconscious and merely being pre-reflective. In neither case is it open to conscious awareness, is it articulable or readily articulable. So the question is: In what sense does the unconscious differ from a thesis that Sartre clearly wants to defend himself?

One answer is the rather technical answer that comes from Freud. That is, unconscious mental events are not just those that are not conscious, but they are those that cannot be made conscious. They are repressed. Consequently, it is not simply the fact that they are not in mind or reflective at the time, but it take enormous effort, and perhaps enormous expense and time to make the unconscious conscious. To understand the source of Sartre's objection, one has to look at a second idea. That is the notion of what is called "psychic determinism."

What the unconscious does for Freud is it gives him a way of explaining human behavior, including behavior which previously seemed inexplicable or meaningless, by pointing to the causes which the person him or herself may not be aware of at all. The idea here is that every conscious event has its unconscious determinant, its unconscious causes. If this were to include decisions and choices, if this were to include emotions, then we find that Sartre's thesis is firmly contradicted. What Sartre rejects here is any idea that the psyche can be determined by forces outside of it, or within it. What we will see in Sartre is that consciousness involves virtually no dimensions at all. It is, as he will say, "a nothingness." That means that the idea of causal relations between it and the world, or within it, are simply incomprehensible.

Back to the idea of emotions. They are not forces within us, as Freud might argue. Rather, those strategies, taken up willfully, even if pre-reflectively—and that raises the question: If they are strategies, and if they are in that sense conscious (Sartre will say consciousness has no place for emotions to hide), then where do we fit in the body? How do we take account of the very good and plausible arguments that James makes about the necessary participation of the body in emotions? I think the important thing is to say, first, that while emotions involve the body, it is not primarily a matter of bodily sensations, which is where James puts the emphasis. Rather, we might say it is a matter of bodily responses. It has often been argued, by biologists for example, that if you take the physiological disturbances that happen to us in emotion, one can easily see these as part of a pattern. They would add some of these are more or less automatic, part of the autonomous nervous system. Others are willful; they are part of the voluntary nervous system.

Nevertheless, the idea is that if you look at all these sensations and the physiological disturbances that James was referring to, most of them have to do with preparedness for action, getting ready to do something. In fear, it is getting ready to flee. In anger, it is getting ready to fight. There is a sense in which James is perfectly okay with this, which is why I mentioned before that when James talks about the body, he doesn't make a very clear distinction between physiological reactions as such, and actions as such. The idea is that one can put oneself in an emotion by, for example, acting it out. James famously says, "A woman is sad because she weeps. She doesn't weep because she is sad."

How does Sartre account for this? He does so by not taking the sensations in emotions as the primary focus; rather, by taking the bodily responses and preparation for action as the focus. What he says, basically, is that part of the magical transformation of the world is a magical transformation of one's own body. One might take as an extreme example of this the young woman who faints away upon hearing some dirty jokes. More realistically, I think, one can understand why one feels the way one feels in fear, by seeing it all as complex—in which one, among other things, is getting ready to flee. One can understand the emotions—heat, tension and anger—by understanding those not as mere sensations, but as preparation in action for doing something. In short, what Sartre wants to say is that the bodily sensations we are talking about (and more generally, bodily responses), follow from the emotion and are not causes of it.

Before we dismiss Freud too quickly from this discussion, let me repeat not only the similarity about what Sartre says about pre-reflective emotions, and what Freud says about the unconscious, but let me also note that, by the time he had written *Being and Nothingness,* Sartre was also evolving a notion of his own of psychoanalysis. It was not Freudian psychoanalysis. It was what he would call "existential" psychoanalysis. The principal difference with Freud was that it was not mechanistic. To put it all into another slogan: Where Freud says, "I cannot," Sartre would say, "I refuse."

Sartre's Phenomenology
Lecture 20

The starting point of Sartre's great work, *Being and Nothingness*, is phenomenology. More particularly, it is a phenomenology of consciousness. This would indicate that Sartre is going back to Husserl and saying what Heidegger refused to say: that the subject matter (and what we are going to be examining in phenomenology) is consciousness itself.

In separating consciousness and the world, Sartre is a Cartesian. Freedom and responsibility have their source in consciousness. Sartre tells us that consciousness is freedom. Responsibility is the (necessary) awareness of being the incontestable author of an event or situation.

Sartre tells us that "consciousness is nothingness." Consciousness is not a thing (an object of consciousness). Introspection cannot make an object of consciousness. Consciousness is always "behind" the things of our awareness; it is the activity that discloses them. Consciousness is intentionality. It is always about something other than itself.

Consciousness is therefore outside the nexus of causal relations. If consciousness could be caused, the deterministic thesis would be true and the result would be the loss of responsibility. Consciousness is freedom from external determination. This does not mean that Sartre denies the scientific view of the mind as explicable (at least in part) in terms of neurophysiology. Sartre adopts a "two standpoints" view, much like his illustrious predecessor Immanuel Kant. From the first-person phenomenological perspective, we cannot see ourselves as anything other than free. But from a naturalistic (scientific) standpoint, we can view ourselves as creatures that can be explained by biology and the other natural sciences. Sartre uses the word "spontaneity" to carve out a middle range between deliberate agency and mindless habit.

Consciousness has the power of "negation." We are not simply passive receivers. We have expectations, which can be thwarted. We impose values on our world. We can say "no!" to the situations in which we find ourselves. Or, we see things in terms of what we can do with them. When we perceive through negation, we construe the world in terms of what's *not* there. We are always able to "distance" ourselves, "step back" and adopt an attitude toward objects of consciousness, even with pain. Whether or not we do it deliberately, we do something like this all the time.

Sartre's phenomenology of human nature is intended to take the place of traditional philosophical argument.

By way of negation, we can distance ourselves from our mental states. In pain, we not only suffer. We also ask, "What does this mean? Do I deserve this? Can I take this? Should I cry out or complain?" So, too, in anger, real wisdom can be found in the simple motherly advice to "count to ten." We can reconsider our anger, its cause, its warrant, its expression. We can ignore anger, or overcome it, or give into it. We say that we "fall" in love, but we also encourage it, provoke it, decide whether to follow through on our impulses or not. However strong the attraction, one can always ask, "What am I to do about this?" Finally, cowardice, like courage, is not simply a vice or virtue one is born with. A person decides, through his or her actions, to be a coward or to be courageous. This was of particular concern to Sartre as he observed his compatriots during the war.

Sartre's phenomenology of human nature is intended to take the place of traditional philosophical argument. Arguments derive conclusions from premises. But often the premises themselves are more controversial than the conclusions. Since Plato, the linearity of logical argument too easily eclipses the multidimensionality of experience.

Phenomenology presents us with experiences so "essential" that they prove the point beyond any possible argument. Three examples follow. First, nausea is an experience of the pervasiveness of Being. This is the thesis described in Sartre's novel *Nausea*. His character, Roquentin, finds existence intrusive. The novel shows being (by way of the being of particular entities) to be utterly undeniable, whatever arguments skeptical philosophers may produce. Second, anguish is an experience of our own freedom. Anguish is different from fear. (The latter concerns what might happen to us; the former, what we might do.) In a dangerous situation, we realize that nothing stands between us and our own willful self-destruction. Third, shame is an experience of the existence of other people. We do not primarily know of the existence of others by way of perceiving them. We know of the existence of other people primarily because of our experience of their perceiving us. ■

Essential Reading

Solomon, *Existentialism*, pp. 194–205; *Continental Philosophy Since 1750* (chapter on Sartre); *From Rationalism to Existentialism*, Chapter 7, "Sartre and French Existentialism," pp. 245–324.

Supplementary Reading

For the curious and very industrious, Sartre, *Being and Nothingness*, and *Nausea*. See also Barnes, *Sartre*.

For a lighter approach to Sartre, see Solomon, *Introducing the Existentialists*; Sartre, *Notebooks for an Ethics*; Murdoch, *Sartre: Romantic Rationalist*; Anderson, *Sartre's Two Ethics*.

Introductory Questions to Consider

1. What is "nausea" as Sartre uses the word (in *Nausea*)? What does the experience of "nausea" signify for Sartre? (How would you compare it with Camus's experience of "the Absurd"?)

2. Why does Sartre single out "anguish"? What does Sartre mean when he categorically states that "man is in anguish"? Consider one of Sartre's more compelling examples, the person who walks dangerously close to the edge of a precipice. How does this situation highlight the fact that "man is in anguish"?

1. In "Existentialism as a Humanism," Sartre stresses the "atheistic" nature of his brand of existentialism. Yet Sartre and Kierkegaard do not sound dissimilar when speaking on such matters as choice, commitment, and anguish. In what ways does the belief in God cause Kierkegaard's brand of existentialism to differ from Sartre's?

2. In *Nausea*, what do Roquentin's rather grotesque descriptions of his own body (his limp hand, the saliva in his mouth) signify about the role of the body in experience?

3. Compare Sartre's Roquentin with Camus's Meursault (*The Stranger*) and Clamence (*The Fall*). Although Meursault and Clamence seem in many ways to be polar extremes, it would seem that Roquentin, depending on his perspective at any given moment, has certain experiences or attitudes in common with each. Explain this if you can.

Sartre's Phenomenology
Lecture 20—Transcript

The starting point of Sartre's great work, *Being and Nothingness*, is phenomenology. More particularly, it is a phenomenology of consciousness. This would indicate that Sartre is going back to Husserl and saying what Heidegger refused to say: that the subject matter (and what we are going to be examining in phenomenology) is consciousness itself. Nevertheless, Sartre wants to join with Heidegger in some of his basic critiques of Husserl. What he wants to say is that if in examining consciousness, in doing phenomenology, we are not just examining the objects of conscious. What we are also doing is examining the world. Just as Heidegger wants to say the world and *Dasein* are one and the same thing—just two different aspects of one unity, Sartre will want to say that there is no separating consciousness from the world. Consciousness in the world or of the world is a unified phenomenon, and it cannot be separated.

With this in mind, let me explain, if I can, what I take to be the source of the almost insufferable difficulty of this very large book. There is a philosophical problem behind this. I think probably there is something else going on too. Sartre set out to write a great book in philosophy. If you look at history, the great books in modern philosophy have tended to be German. I think the philosophical problem is subtle and profound. On the one hand, Sartre is a Cartesian through and through—what this means is something that is often debated. Essentially, I take it to be starting with the base distinction, dichotomy.

On the one hand, there is consciousness. On the other hand, there is the world. How one sees the link between them, or whether or not one identifies them as Sartre and Heidegger try to do, is a more specialized point. The basic point is that by separating the discussion into two terms—consciousness on one hand, the world on the other—Sartre puts himself rather firmly in the French tradition in which he was raised. However, Sartre read Heidegger. He was convinced by the arguments and sometimes even uses the word *Dasein* in his discussion. If you look at these two—on the one hand, the Cartesian dualism of consciousness and the world, on the other hand, the Heideggerian insistence that there is no valid distinction to be made here—it is pretty clear that what Sartre has to do is some pretty fancy dancing to come out with a philosophy which is coherent, and at the same time, embraces both of these viewpoints.

An awful lot of what, in Sartre, comes off as a kind of very complicated doubletalk really is an attempt to get these two different views together. We should never lose sight of what the ultimate aim of the philosophy is and its ultimate point. With Heidegger, there continues to be enormous discussion, essentially about what his philosophy is about—what its point is. With Sartre, there really is no debate at all. He makes it very clear, and it is clear to everyone who reads it—the idea is freedom and responsibility. What he wants to say as the beginning of his phenomenology is that consciousness *is* freedom. He rather emphasizes the point that this is an identity relationship. This is what characterizes consciousness. It is not as if freedom is one of the aspects of consciousness or freedom is a property of consciousness. Rather, consciousness itself must simply be defined as freedom. Conversely, freedom itself is nothing other than consciousness.

Responsibility, on the other hand, is something which is more concrete and, in a way, more political than philosophical in this very ethereal sense. Responsibility is the idea that we are the incontestable author of our passions. That means that we are always responsible for them. They are our doing. We must take the consequences, and again, there are no excuses. What Sartre does in *Being and Nothingness*, right from the start, is he gives us a characterization of consciousness. Keep in mind as I discuss this that his aims are two-fold. First and foremost, it is to make out this thesis that consciousness is freedom. Secondly, it is to join with Heidegger in rejecting what would seem to be a starting point; namely, the dualism between consciousness and the world.

The problems that follow Cartesianism and dualism are pretty straightforward. Basically, once you find yourself in consciousness, it is very difficult to argue that what you know is the world outside of consciousness. Philosophers have tried many ingenious strategies to try to get from within consciousness out to the world. Sartre responds by a striking thesis. What he tells us is that "consciousness is nothingness." Consciousness is nothing.

What he means by this is a number of different theses. First and foremost, in terms of phenomenology, when you describe your experience, you describe all the objects of your experience—perhaps how you feel, your orientation. There is a sense in which what you don't describe is your consciousness as a thing. Rather, consciousness is such that so-called "introspection" cannot make an object of it. You might say consciousness is always behind our awareness. The thesis here, as in Husserl, is that consciousness is always intentionality. It is necessarily and always about things.

To understand what this means, we don't have to look at consciousness, as Husserl sometimes did, as a realm, much less as a transcendental ego. Rather, we see consciousness as a kind of activity, pure activity. One might envision this as looking around a dark room with a flashlight. Consciousness is the beam of the flashlight. What it does is illuminates the things in the room. To complete this picture for Sartre, one has to take away the flashlight and leave only the beam.

What consciousness is, is essentially nothing but the awareness of the things in this world. This is going to be very complicated, because it is an awareness which is not just passive and not just receptive. In that sense, it is not like the flashlight beam because it is going to be very dynamically active with reference to its perceptions, and with reference to the nature of things it experiences. One goes back to his essay on the emotions and thinks about how, in an emotion, one dynamically transforms the world by being dynamically conscious of it. It is not just a matter of perceiving things as they are. Rather, it is a way of perceiving things according to a scheme which one imposes—for example, whether one is in a situation of great difficulty, or one is looking at something as an aesthetic phenomenon. It is also a matter in which consciousness transforms the world that it perceives.

Part of the importance of talking about consciousness is "nothingness," with reference to Sartre's part-dominant thesis, a thesis about freedom. Saying that consciousness is about nothing allows him to say that it is, therefore, outside of the causal relations of the world. If this was not so—if the deterministic thesis that our minds are the effects of causes, whether in our brains, or in the world, or perhaps even of God putting ideas in our minds—then we would not be free. It is important to see consciousness as something independent and distinct from the causal relations in the world.

One can, here, take on a fairly straightforward Kantian interpretation. Sartre had read and knew his Kant. Kant said, for example, much the same thing at one point. He said that insofar as we see ourselves as agents, actors, as opposed to seeing ourselves simply as creatures in the universe, what we do is we separate ourselves from the kinds of causal relations that we usually apply to things, and see ourselves as something different. Kant's thesis here, I think, will serve as a very good slogan for understanding what Sartre is all about. Kant says, insofar as we consider ourselves agents, we can't imagine ourselves anything other than free. To put it in another way (also Kantian), he might say that what consciousness does is it imposes causal categories on the world. It is by seeing the world in a certain way, let's say a scientific way, that we see things in terms of cause and effect relations.

When we examine ourselves and examine our consciousness, that is not the way we see ourselves. He doesn't deny the scientific view of the mind. One can examine, as many philosophers and psychologists are now examining, the neurology of the mind and the psychology in such a way that one does talk about causal ideas of all sorts. Nevertheless, one has to separate here, as Kierkegaard did, between the objective scientific view and the phenomenological, first-person, action-oriented view. What Sartre is doing is insisting that, for the purposes of his phenomenology, what we always adopt is this first-person, action-oriented view of ourselves. From that point of view, consciousness is nothingness, at least now in two senses. First, it is not a possible object of consciousness. It is not a thing. Second, consciousness is not caused. From there, it is a short step to saying: If consciousness is not caused, it is free.

The word Sartre often uses here, and again it is prone to misunderstanding, is the word "spontaneity." Some philosophers have interpreted spontaneity as a kind of indeterminism. They have applied, for example, the free will question to current science and pointed out that in quantum theory, causal relationships break down, and whether something happens is purely a matter of chance. This is not going to work if we are talking about freedom, because if I acted simply by chance we would not talk about my actions being free.

We want to talk about my actions being chosen, and that is the very opposite of being undetermined.

Talking about spontaneity, on the other hand, allows him to carve out a middle range between determinism and indeterminism; and talking about agency on the one hand emphasizes the thesis he has already made in his essay on the emotions—that much of what we do is pre-reflective. It is not conscious in the full-blown sense. It is not articulate. It is not the subject of thought. It is not the subject of the kind of reflection in which we name what we are feeling or what we are doing. We just do it.

Spontaneity is the freedom of consciousness, which is to say that to understand consciousness is to understand from the outset that consciousness acts. It acts in such a way that it acts without any prior causality. What Sartre will also have to say, if he is hold this thesis, is that all the questions psychologists have asked about motivation and the like have to be absorbed, if not on the causal side of consciousness, then on the object side of consciousness. In fact, that is just what Sartre does. Many of the questions about motivation and emotion that are usually attributed to a causal account of consciousness and action, what Sartre will say is that motivation and emotion now lie on the object side of emotion, and they are considerations in terms of which we make the choices that we do.

I might add that by the time he wrote *Being and Nothingness*, five years after his essay on the emotions, one of the things that he has given up is the rather oversimplified thesis that emotions are always a mode of escape behavior. That might work still for some kinds of emotions. I think the fox example with the grapes would be a good example of that. There are times when we have emotions and it is pretty clear that the purpose is to save us from some kind of embarrassment or humiliation, even in our own minds.

Sartre, by the time he writes *Being and Nothingness*, is also aware that emotions have many different purposes and many different ends. Among other things, he is, by now having been through the war or a good chunk of it, well aware of the heroic functions of emotions too. So, what he wants to say here is the emotions are not to be construed as causes of behavior. That he holds with his old view. Rather, emotions are to be construed as spontaneous outpourings of consciousness in which one takes the world in a certain way. We are not talking about emotions in consciousness, just as in the early essay we didn't talk in Jamesian terms about emotions and sensations. Rather, we are talking about emotions as ways of structuring consciousness, but now as one way among many of structuring consciousness.

The idea that consciousness is nothingness has a further meaning, and one that makes Sartre's thesis about freedom all the more plausible. One of the most remarkable things about consciousness is the fact that it has the power of "negation." To put it very simply, consciousness spontaneously says "no." This is not just a matter of denial. That would be pathological. That would be a more pervasive feature of consciousness, which Sartre feels is absolutely essential to understand the nature of consciousness itself, as well as the nature of the freedom he wants to celebrate. In a way, you might say, it is prefigured in Husserl.

Husserl gives a sample of perception, and points out to us that when we look at something, say that coffee cup, in one sense what I see immediately is the coffee cup from a certain perspective. At the same time, what I see is a coffee cup, which means, among other things, that it has a backside which I don't see. It has an underneath which I don't see. It has weight, which I am not now feeling. It has a texture. One can imagine if I were to reach for the coffee cup and discover any of these things not being so, I would be shocked and surprised. There is a sense then in which what I see is not just what I see. It has to do with a host of expectations which are built into the perception itself. There is a sense in which what I see, is always more than what I see. What I see is already defined by expectations of all sorts, including those built into the perception itself, but also more generally having to do with my values and expectations. For instance, I gave the example earlier of a mountain, which might present itself as an obstacle to one people and as protection for another, as an aesthetic object for still another, as a point of recreation for still another.

In the same sense, when we see, we are never simply passive receivers. I gave the flashlight example a minute ago, but let me correct that one more way. It is not just that there is no flashlight, but one can't look at the beam as itself simply picking up the reflections that the objects give off. To the contrary, the beam itself is dynamically active, and it structures the way we see things. So, to talk about negation here is to talk in a very powerful way about consciousness as an activity, which is not simply a matter of receiving, as many of the early empiricists suggested. Rather, it is a matter of shaping, as the early essay on emotions made quite clear.

This has a number of different manifestations for Sartre. For one thing, any situation in which we find ourselves, we can say, "I refuse to accept this." In fact, that is very reflective, what I just said. We have one set of instances which permeate our lives, in which the power of negation is evident right at the basis of consciousness, even in its most primitive forms. That is the notion of desire. When you think, what is a desire actually? It is not just seeing the world. It is seeing the world in terms of something you want. If you look at that delicious piece of chocolate cake, it is not just a factual perception. It is not just the recognition that there is a chocolate cake. Rather, it is looking with desire. It is looking with the expectation or hope that one will, quite literally, internalize that chocolate cake as soon as possible.

We see things in terms of what we can do with them and in terms of how they fit into our plans. One might look, for example, at a notice from the IRS as an opportunity to express oneself, explain oneself, or, more realistically for most of us, one might spy the same invitation with a kind of horror as something that is going to interfere with our lives. There is nothing in the fact of the matter that dictates this, but how we perceive it and the indications are all what Sartre builds into this notion of negation.

There is a sense in which our perceptions are always filled with negation, in another sense as well. Take, for instance, I walk into a bar, and I am supposed to meet my friend Peter. But I walk in, and look around, and what I see is that Peter is not there. One can construe this in terms that many philosophers would find plausible, along the lines of: "What I see is . . ."—and now we make a list of: all the people in the bar, all the furniture in the bar, all the bottles and glasses in the bar, and, perhaps, the architecture of the bar. One examines that list and notices that Peter is not on it. That is not the way we experience things. When we go into the bar, expecting to see Peter—or hoping to see Peter—there is really just one thing that we notice as we walk in and perceive the bar. That is, that Peter is not there.

This strange kind of perception, the perception of an absence or lack, is something we experience all the time. Desire might be construed as nothing but the perception of such a lack. Plato at one point suggests that. There is also the idea that when we perceive a negation, when we perceive and absence or lack, what we are doing is already construing the world in terms of what is not there. Here we find another interpretation of the notion of nothingness. One might say in quasi-logical terms, among the features of the world, which we must take into account, is the nothingness of the world. At extremes, one can understand all kinds of ways in which this might be the case.

In particular, there is a sense in which we can perceive ourselves with a kind of dissatisfaction of what we are. Or, we can perceive our situation, including our psychological situation. We can take a step back and distance ourselves. We can think of ourselves not simply in terms of what we are given, but what we insist upon as our own ideals. To take an extreme example: if you are in pain, there is a sense in which the pain is a given, but another important sense in which it is the perception, and possibly the reflection on the pain, that we distance ourselves from. We negate it. Not in the sense that we simply make it go away. It would be nice if we could do that. Rather, we negate it in the sense that we put it at arm's length and now consider how to respond.

Whether or not we do this reflectively and deliberately, we do it, in fact, all the time. Am I going to give in to this pain? Am I going to express it loudly and perhaps embarrass myself in front of my friends? Or, am I going to be heroic and pretend as if all is well, and present myself as a kind of hero to my friends? Or, to the contrary, should I use the pain to get out of an obligation? Or, should I consider this a lesson in life or the punishment of the gods?

Again, this idea of setting one's attitude toward one's situation and what one experiences is absolutely essential. In the last lecture, I gave a number of illustrations from the emotions in anger. We can determine, in many ways, whether or not we are to get angry, and how to use that anger. We can, in many ways determine whether we are to fall in love. It is not just a matter of falling, but in many ways, deciding. With a trait like cowardice, it consists of a whole series of decisions. In short, all this has to do with the nothingness of consciousness, because of the idea that consciousness is nothing but an activity directed toward the world—intentionality. What we fall back into is something like Freud's psychic determinism, which is what Sartre always wants to get away from as much as possible.

A word on phenomenology, or a number of words on phenomenology: Philosophers today, in the analytic tradition, often complain that in Heidegger and Sartre there is not much by way of argument. They simply seem to present their views, or their perceptions of the world, as truth. In analytic philosophy, and in philosophy in the West, what we often find is philosophers arguing rather outrageous conclusions on the basis of premises that sometimes are hard to reject. Alternatively, we find longstanding philosophical arguments that have to do, ultimately, with an argument over what is self-evident or not by way of premises.

There is a sense in which logical argument often threatens to overcome the multi-dimensionality of experience. One way of talking about phenomenology, and in particular, Sartre's phenomenology, is that what he tries to focus on are those kinds of key, essential experiences that define our experience in general. He wants to use this in place of the kinds of arguments which philosophers have often given. What I would like to do for the rest of this lecture is to outline three such examples.

The first appears in the early novel that he wrote, before he had fully formulated his phenomenological thesis in *Being and Nothingness*. The early novel was called *Nausea*, which is a wonderful title, and an example (perhaps a rather perverse example) of the intentionality of emotions—in that nausea is construed not just as a physical feeling (which we all know too well), nausea has an object. Nausea is a way of construing the world. In particular, much in line with a good deal of existentialism, especially thinking back to Kierkegaard, what *Nausea* is, is a kind of dissatisfaction and revulsion with the apparent meaninglessness of the world.

Let me put it in a broader philosophical context. Philosophers have often argued that the status of the external world, or our knowledge of the external world, is in question. This follows from a set of arguments which we have anticipated many times in these lectures—the idea that somehow we are stuck inside our own experience, or stuck inside our own consciousness. Sartre, as we have seen, is going to deny this by taking the contents out of consciousness and turning it into nothingness, so one can say there is no *inside* of consciousness to be stuck in. Again, the kind of beam analogy comes to mind.

How do philosophers get into this pickle? Certainly, it is a pickle. Not even insane people believe there is no external world. Rather, this is a pure philosophical fabrication. It follows from, basically, the Cartesian position, which says that it is possible to know only one's experiences, then the question: "How do we know the world?" Even with a revised notion of consciousness, one has to ask the question: "Is it true that we know that we see the actual world? Might it be possible that the world that we see is simply the world of our own construction? The world is simply idea?"

To answer this, what Sartre does in this rather remarkable early novel is he gives us a character who is, in one sense, rather like Camus's Meursault in that he is a very kind of eccentric, strange person. Unlike Meursault, he is a highly educated, extremely reflective person, more like Dostoevsky's underground man. So, what we see is a person who is overburdened by reflection on the world. In one critical scene late in the novel, Sartre has this character go into a park where he sees a tree. He sits down by the roots, and what follows is a description that might be fodder for some contemporary horror movie producer. The tree becomes ominous, and it forces its existence on us. The idea is that existence is not something which is in any way inferred from the experiences we have. It is not added to, or a point of speculation. Existence simply forces itself in our experience in a way that is absolutely undeniable.

A different example—Sartre talks about walking along the edge of a precipice, and one looks down at the fall beneath, and suddenly, one is ceased with anxiety. What is anxiety? It is not just fear. One might be afraid of the ground giving way. One might be afraid that one's companion will give one a push, and one will go hurtling over the edge. Anguish is something different. Anguish is the sudden, spontaneous realization that at any moment, I could just, intentionally take an extra step—give myself a little push, and I would go hurtling to my death. So, I take a step away from the edge. What experience anguish gives me is the basic experience of my own freedom. Or, to put it in a Sartrian way: Nothing stands between me and my self-destruction, except my own decision.

A third example is one that appears later in *Being and Nothingness*, and we will talk about it in some detail. Philosophers have wondered how I know that other people exist. After all, I know only my own experience. Could all these other people be androids, robots, and have no consciousness at all? What Sartre says is, there is an experience that devastatingly shows us that other people cannot be questioned, cannot be denied. If I find someone looking at me as I am doing something embarrassing, I suddenly experience embarrassment, or shame. What I experience is the other person not as an object, rather, the other person as "looking at me." Such experiences, Sartre says, are sufficient to undermine any possible philosophical argument to the contrary that we don't really know other people.

What we will see in what is to follow is how phenomenology is going to highlight other experiences, which are going to give us a good outline about what it means to be human.

Sartre on "Bad Faith"
Lecture 21

Perversely, Sartre, like Heidegger, says he is not doing ethics. Nevertheless, I think there is no question whatsoever that any reader can raise that that is exactly what he is doing

In *Being and Nothingness*, Sartre elaborates his "phenomenological Ontology," a phrase borrowed from Heidegger. It is phenomenological because it steadfastly holds to the subject matter of experience and the first-person standpoint. This leads to conclusions at odds with science and "objective" thinking, although Sartre does not reject science. It is an ontology because Sartre, following Heidegger, insists that the content of experience is and must be the content of our reality.

The key to the Cartesian structure of *Being and Nothingness* is the basic distinction between being-for-itself and being-in-itself. Being-for-itself (*pour-soi*) is the being of consciousness. Being-in-itself (*en-soi*) is the existence of things. Later in the book, Sartre will introduce a third basic category, being-for-others, as in his examples of shame and embarrassment.

Sartre distinguishes between consciousness and the self. In an early essay, "The Transcendence of the Ego," Sartre argued that consciousness is not the self. The self is "out there in the world, like the consciousness of another." The self, he goes on to argue, is a product, an accumulation of actions, habits, achievements, and failures. Sometimes other people know us better than we do. Sartre also distinguishes self-conscious reflection from ordinary "prereflective" consciousness. He distinguishes between consciousness and self-consciousness. Running for a bus, I am not conscious of myself but only of the "bus to be overtaken." Consciousness doesn't contain the "I," the self.

Human existence is both being-in-itself and being-for-itself. As embodied in a particular place at a particular time in particular circumstances, we have what Sartre (following Heidegger) calls "facticity," or facts that are true about us. As consciousness, we have what Sartre calls "transcendence" (Heidegger's "existence"). The term "transcendence" means "outside of" but serves several very different uses for Sartre. It refers, first of all, to our transcendence of the "facts." Desires or plans reach beyond facts. It also refers to our transcendence of the present into the future. We are to be described by our personalities and our plans—"I am what I am not." The desire to be both in-itself and for-itself is the desire to be God. The very notion of God, for Sartre, is a contradiction.

> **One's self turns out to be negotiable—our freedom makes the facts about us vulnerable.**

When we talk about possibilities, we are limited by our facticity. Facticity and transcendence limit each other. Confusing facticity and transcendence is what Sartre calls "bad faith," a kind of self-deception. In his discussion of bad faith, Sartre provides us with four of his most often quoted examples: the waiter in the cafe, a young woman on a first date, the frigid wife, and the hesitant homosexual. One's self turns out to be negotiable—our freedom makes the facts about us vulnerable. In all of these examples, Sartre attempts to take on Freud—"I refuse to" versus "I cannot"—but the examples, at least all but the last of them, have serious problems. We falsify ourselves by subscribing exclusively to facticity—or transcendence. Either alone leads to bad faith, but bad faith is inescapable.

Sartre raises serious questions about what should count as an "ethics." Sartre does not in fact reject morality. He establishes an ethics of what is more commonly called "integrity." ■

Essential Reading

Solomon, *Existentialism*, pp. 194-247.

Supplementary Reading

Danto, *Sartre*.

Fell, *Heidegger and Sartre: An Essay on Being and Place*.

Fingarette, *Self-Deception*.

Jeanson, *Sartre and the Problem of Morality*.

Natanson, *Critique of Jean-Paul Sartre's Ontology*.

Sartre, *The Transcendence of the Ego: An Existentialist Theory of Consciousness*.

Introductory Questions to Consider

1. What is the difference between "being-in-itself" and "being-for-itself"? Pay special attention to the question of personal self-identity ("one is what one is" or "one is what one is not"). In what sense(s) is personal identity a function of time (past-present-future)?

2. Describe an incident or circumstance (perhaps continuing) in which you were or are in "bad faith." What sorts of steps did (could) you take to get out of bad faith? In what sense was (is) this impossible?

3. Consider Meursault, Clamence, Rieux, and Roquentin. Are any or all of these characters in "bad faith?" Explain.

Advanced Questions to Consider

1. Why does Sartre describe *Being and Nothingness* as a "phenomenological ontology?" Does this "synthesis" create a tension in the work? Explain.

2. "I think, therefore I am," declared Descartes. Why does Sartre attack this famous slogan? Why does he take such pains to separate the self from the fact of consciousness? What's wrong with the idea that the self is "in" consciousness?

3. According to Sartre, "the essential structure of sincerity does not differ from that of bad faith…" What does he mean by this? Is all sincerity in bad faith or simply the objective of being sincere?

4. In terms of the "double property of the human being, who is at once a facticity and transcendence," compare Sartre's "flirtatious woman" and "the waiter." Have they both entered bad faith by the same route? If not, what is the difference between them?

5. Sartre contends that "man fundamentally is the desire to be God." What does he mean by this? (Put your answer in terms of the two human properties of "facticity" and "transcendence.") In connection with the last question—is it only God that can avoid "bad faith"? Does "bad faith" smack of the "doctrine of original sin"? Explain.

Sartre on "Bad Faith"
Lecture 21—Transcript

Sartre subtitles *Being and Nothingness*: *An Essay in Phenomenological Ontology*. That is a phrase he borrowed directly from Heidegger, indicating two things. First, it is phenomenological, which, in Sartre, has a very precise meaning. The idea of phenomenology is that it is all from the first-person standpoint. Sartre, unlike Heidegger, has no hesitation stating an examination of consciousness—or more properly speaking, the objects of consciousness. On the other hand, it is an ontology. Like Heidegger, he wants to insist that when we examine what we experience (although Heidegger would not use that term) we are describing the things of this world. A Nietzschian twist—when we describe the things of this world from the first person, we are quite clearly describing them always from a perspective. It is a very particular, and sometimes peculiar, perspective.

Most notably, when we describe things from the first-person perspective, what we are doing is coming up with conclusions that are very often going to be at odds with science and objective thinking. As I stressed in the last lecture, it is not as if Sartre rejects science any more than Kierkegaard does. He, too, would probably say something like, "All power to the sciences, but . . ." And then go on to say, "Here is what is really important, our understanding of ourselves," and that has to be through the eyes of phenomenology.

Sartre introduces an ontology, but one has to be very careful here. He uses the word "being," but I think this is, in many ways, a kind of copycat behavior because Heidegger was, in many ways, his model. Since he thought of himself as doing ontology, it seemed to follow that being was the subject matter. Nevertheless, I think we would go wrong not taking very seriously what Sartre calls "being," and instead, talking about that, too, in terms of perspectives and aspects.

He distinguishes, as I indicated in an earlier lecture, primarily between consciousness on the one hand, and the world on the other. The first he refers to as being-for-itself. The essential idea here is that when we reflect, we necessarily recognize that we are conscious. Descartes makes this quite explicit in his much-quoted statement "I think, therefore I am." For Sartre, it is not necessarily reflection that does this. There is a sense in which consciousness is always aware of itself, or, more properly speaking, aware of itself aware of objects all the time. It is not something which is prone just to reflect the recognition.

On the side of the world, what Sartre says is, here we find "being-in-itself." The notion of "in-itself" has a long philosophical tradition. Kant had talked about the world in itself. Many philosophers following Nietzsche attacked the world, the idea of the "world-in-itself." The idea of "being-in-itself" seemed to capture for Sartre the idea of simple physical existence. He really doesn't worry about the kinds of questions that bothered Husserl, about the being of numbers or abstract entities.

One should add here, for completeness, that Sartre adds a third category, so it is not going to be on one hand or the other hand; it is going to be, rather, a dramatic form—a kind of trio of concepts. That third concept which I very scantily alluded to in the last lecture is what he calls "being-for-others." The example that I gave that might be a good example for that is the example of shame or embarrassment. Since he doesn't introduce that for a good 200 pages into his book, I am going to stick for the time being just with the categories of "being-for-itself," "being-in-itself," and how they relate to each other.

In an essay that he wrote just prior to *Being and Nothingness*, called "The Transcendence of the Ego," Sartre argues what will turn out to be an extremely important thesis for him. It makes a distinction—which Descartes, for example, did not make, which Husserl did not make—between the self or the ego on one hand, and consciousness on the other. About the self, Sartre says, it is out there in the world like the self of another. In other words, we talk about ourselves in philosophy all too often as though it is something deep down inside.

The true self—and of course, there is a long Christian tradition which takes the self as the soul—what Sartre wants to say is the self is something very different than that. The self is an accumulation of actions and experiences. It is who I am in a way that is determined by the world, that is determined by my activities in the world. It is an accumulation of all my achievements and failures, in such a way that the way I describe myself as a self is no different from the way someone else would describe me as a self. In fact, as we all know to our embarrassment, it is sometimes the case that other people know ourselves better than we know ourselves. There is a sense in which we can tell that someone is arrogant, when he or she can't tell him/herself that he/she is arrogant.

There is a sense in which the self, then, is not something to be found directly in phenomenology, and certainly in no sense inside of consciousness or equivalent to consciousness, as Husserl suggested. To find out who you are, you have to really review the tapes and videos of your life; you have to look back to see what you have done. Very often, that picture will be very different from your perception of yourself from a momentary bit of introspection.

Consciousness, on the other hand, as I talked about in some detail in the last lecture, is nothing but an activity. It is an activity directed toward the world and its objects. It is an activity which is not just passive in the sense of receiving information, but very active—not just in terms of understanding, but in terms of transforming the world according to our desires, according to our expectations, according to our ideals. Furthermore, as we saw in our discussion of the emotions, Sartre also wants to distinguish between self-consciousness in its reflective mode, and self-consciousness or consciousness as pre-reflective.

I should say that, in Sartre's text, this gets enormously complicated, partly because of the fundamental idea of "being-for-itself," which seems to presuppose some sense of self-awareness even on the pre-reflective level. I am not going to try to sort out those paradoxes here. What is important for our purposes is really to say that when we understand consciousness in Sartre we should not think necessarily in terms of reflective consciousness, but oftentimes it is consciousness without being, in some reflective sense, aware of itself.

Let me give an example, and it is Sartre's example. Suppose I am trying to catch a streetcar—or to get away from old technology, suppose I am trying to catch a bus. If I were to describe my experience at that time as a phenomenologist would, it would not be "Here I am trying to catch a bus." It would be something more like, "Bus to be caught up with, there goes the bus"—the number of feet between where I am and the bus. My perceptions, my consciousness would wholly be caught up in the need to catch the streetcar.

The "I," Sartre says, doesn't yet appear. When the "I" does appear it is not necessarily as an agent, but sometimes, it is a kind of formal indicator of the person who is doing the talking, the describing, the thinking. The important point here is that consciousness itself in no sense contains the "I," in no sense contains the self. Our experience has to be understood in terms of, as Heidegger put it, tasks to be completed, people in the world to be appealed to, a sense of things to be done. What counts as the self, on the other hand, is going to be the sort of thing that we find in a biography. Autobiography is just one instance of biography. We should not assume that we are in a better position to know who we are and what our lives look like than anybody else.

Human existence is a curiosity. It is a curiosity in that we are not simply consciousness, and sometimes Descartes talks that way. We are all people. People have bodies. People perform actions with their bodies. People are subject to the material cause-and-effect relationships in the world, which is a way of saying, in Sartre's jargon, that we are both being-in-itself and being-for-itself. There is a sense in which we are not simply bodies, not simply creatures.

Sartre, by the way, would abstain from questions about where consciousness enters into the evolutionary chain as being irrelevant. Like Heidegger, he starts with the phenomenological fact of my own existence in the world. The question is wholly: "How then must I see myself?" What are the essential structures of that consciousness as Husserl tried to pursue the question? Because I am both being-in-itself and being-for-itself—because I am both a body and a mind—I have two different sets of attributes. On one hand, what I have is what Heidegger called, and what we will call following Sartre, "facticity." Facticity should be construed as the sum total of facts that are true about us.

Examples of my facticity include the fact that I was born on a certain date in a certain year, the fact that I am now a certain height, the fact that I am living in the 20th century, the fact that I am born of the parents who are my parents, the fact that I was raised as I was raised, the fact that I went to school and got degrees and learned such and such. That is all part of my facticity. My medical health is part of my facticity. My situation in general is part of my facticity. The fact that I am now standing in Virginia is part of my facticity. In short, you might say everything that is factual about us, is constitutive of my facticity.

One can understand this in terms of, for example, my past—the idea that everything that is past is now, in a sense, a fact. I can't alter it. The fact that everything about me presently in some sense is now a fact. I can't alter it. There may be facts about the future too. For example, Heidegger pointed out one rather notorious and problematic fact, and that is the fact that we are all going to die. That might not be a fact in the sense of what has already happened, so I can't say when it is, but we all understand exactly what it means to say that it is a fact that I am going to die.

Contrasted with facticity is that aspect of ourselves that Sartre calls "transcendence." Transcendence is a rather unfortunate term here, because it has such a rich, philosophical history, particularly in the German philosophy that Sartre is in many ways following. "Transcendent" sometimes means outside of the world, or other times it means outside of experience. In the first instance, God is often referred to as transcendent, outside of the world. In the second instance, people like Kant would talk about the world as it is in itself as being transcendent, in the sense of being outside of our experience. Sartre doesn't have either of these meanings in mind. It is problematic that he uses a term which is so rich in philosophical history.

I think we can talk about transcendence in Sartre in two ways, and they are both rather concrete. First, my transcendence is the sense in which I overreach the facts about my life. For example, I have aspirations, plans and desires. They reach beyond the facts of my life and the facts of the matter, and they are possibilities; they are not yet facts. I can choose between them. As you can guess, transcendence is going to be absolutely essential to Sartre's notion of freedom. Not only do we transcend the facts, we also transcend the present. This is again a Heideggerian point, the idea that time is not simply the specious present, the momentary present, that line between the past and the future. Time, my time, described from the first person, is already full of the past and pregnant with the future. So, I transcend the present into the future all the time.

I am always seeing the world in terms of my expectations, my hopes, my plans, my fears, and so on. In a sense, to say that I am transcendence is to say that I am not what I am. Sartre puts it, as one of his more frequent little paradoxes that the very nature of being-for-itself, and consequently, the hallmark of transcendence is the fact that I am what I am not, and I am not what I am. It sounds straightforwardly paradoxical, but I think we can now understand it quite clearly.

What I aspire to be is, let's say, a lawyer. I am not now a lawyer. Nevertheless, my plan, my aspiration, is to be defined in terms of becoming a lawyer. My activities from now until then can be understood only in terms of that plan. Am I a lawyer now? No. To describe me, you would have to say what I am not yet. The sense is that we are always to be described in terms of our possibilities and our plans. Again, to go back to a plan I made very early in the Sartre lectures, this is not necessarily something that I am fully conscious of in the sense of being reflectively articulate about it. Sometimes my possibilities are there, and I deny them or ignore them, or I am simply unaware of them. Nevertheless, what I want to be determines what I am in a very obvious and profound way.

This distinction between facticity and transcendence—the ideas of, on the one hand, being what the facts about me say I am, and, on the other hand, being what I am not yet; namely, what I plan to be or hope to be—don't fit together very conveniently. Let me point out two problems that Sartre points out in great detail. The first is that what we all want in a strictly neurotic sense is to be both pure facticity and pure transcendence. Sartre sums this up by the conscientiously blasphemous comment that what we really desire is to be God. Going back to some medieval characterizations of God, what we find is that God is described, first of all, complete in himself. One might say that everything that God can be, he is. At the same time, because God is all-powerful, one wants to say that God can do anything that he wants.

Now, think about the way we think about our lives. There is a sense in which we talk with some compulsiveness about getting ourselves together and defining ourselves, determining exactly who we are, and knowing, with some certainty, what is ourselves. At the same time, we have what philosophers often refer to as this desire for negative freedom, to be free from constraints, to be able to do anything we choose to do. When we put these two together, you get a kind of contradiction. Of course, Sartre doesn't mind the notion that the very notion of God is there for a kind of contradiction.

The other problem is much more far-reaching and will give rise to the rest of this lecture. That is, I just described facticity and transcendence in a pretty straightforward way. Mainly, facticity is everything that is now true of us, and transcendence is just that which is not true of us, or not true yet. Take some of the examples I cited, for example, my birthday. That would seem to be a fact written somewhere in the annals of the universe. Nevertheless, when I look at it from the first-person point of view, it is not simply a fact at all. For instance, I might look at my birthday as being too early. I'd rather be younger.

Many of my undergraduates who are only 19 or 20 look at their birthday and think it is too late. What is more, they take active steps to change it. They find false ID cards. They lie about their age. Although they might change their minds about which direction the lie should go in subsequent years, there is a sense in which they are not accepting this fact about themselves. Rather, they are trying to replace it with a different fact. One can, of course, get very complicated here and say, "Suppose one of my students not only gets a false ID, but actually goes back to the hospital in which he was born, and goes to the records in the halls of records where he was born, and changes the date on significant documents. Would that change the birth date?" The metaphysical view, the third person view we might have of this is "Of course not. What he is doing is lying about the date, but the date, no matter what he does, remains the same." The truth is, in a very important sense, how the date plays in his life is subject to his transcendence—his expectations, hopes, plans, and so on.

So, too, we talk about transcendence as our possibilities, but what our possibilities are must be understood in terms of what the facts are. I can't simply want to be an angel. I can't simply want to be, at my age, a great basketball player. I am too short, and I am too old. There is a sense in which when we start talking about possibilities, even though we are free to imagine almost anything we want, we are quite limited in the choices we have.

Facticity starts to look as if it is going to be corrupted and compromised by transcendence. Transcendence looks as if it is going to be constricted by facticity. But, it gets worse.

Sartre introduces a concept which has become quite famous. It is the concept of *mauvais-soi*, "bad faith." It is something like self-deception, but more particularly, it is self-deception about oneself, about who one is. We can see, from what I have already said, the form in which this will probably appear. I can lie to myself about who I am by claiming to be just facticity. In other words, my self is defined by what facts are true of me. Not only my self will be so defined, but I will go into bad faith by pretending my consciousness is so defined, too. So, I can say that I am a certain age. That is a fact about me, and that defines what I can do. I don't plan to be a basketball player. I refuse to even consider the possibility. One can lie to oneself about the facts in a different way by ignoring them. One can simply live through wishful thinking, through one's hopes or one's fears, and in so doing deny the facts that are true of oneself.

The difficult thesis is that we are necessarily both of these, and both of them in a kind of tension which ultimately is going to characterize Sartre's view of human nature. Let me go through several of his examples. Most famously, since Sartre wrote in Parisian cafés, and one can see him there scribbling his 20 pages a day, one can imagine him watching the people walking around him. In particular, here is the waiter who is serving him. He sees the waiter behaving rather oddly in a sense. He walks kind of like a military man, makes very sharp military corners. If you have been in a Parisian café, you know the picture. He is acting out a role, Sartre says. The question is, what is the role? Sartre tells us he is trying to *be* a waiter. In other words, he is acting as if he is nothing but a waiter.

Let's take a more dramatic example. A Nazi soldier is given an awful assignment. Let's say, as an example that Camus uses, he is asked to shoot a couple of children. Challenged on the awfulness of his behavior, the Nazi officer might well say, "Look, I am just following orders." In other words, I am a Nazi soldier, and I cannot do otherwise. Of course, we can very quickly point out that he can do otherwise. The cost of doing otherwise may be lethal.

He could be court-martialed. He could be shot on the spot. Nevertheless, what he is, in a sense, is negotiable.

This notion of confusing one's facticity (what is now true of one) as one's essence (what one must be) is the most obvious form of bad faith, and the one that Sartre plays with through a great deal of his philosophy. The truth is that our freedom, our transcendence, always makes the facts about in clay, and makes it possible for any fact about us—no matter how critical and unavoidable—any fact can be dealt with in a number of different ways.

Sartre gives the example of a young woman on a date. I would argue that there are several confusions embedded in this example, so I want to spend a fairly short time on it for now. The young woman on her first date is talking of fairly high intellectual matters (let's say discussing Heidegger) with her companion. She is acting as if she is just this intellect, this brilliant and witty mind, when in the middle of the date, the young man reaches across the table, puts his hand on her and rather tenderly caresses her as he is talking. The young woman, at this point, doesn't want to get involved. She is rather enjoying her intellectual existence.

So, what Sartre says (and I think one can argue this is a very sexist interpretation) is that she denies what is, in fact, happening to her. She, as he puts it, disowns her hand, just kind of leaves it limp under her companion's, and instead, goes on as if she is nothing except this intellectual mind. I think there are a number of problems. For one, how does Sartre know, during his phenomenology, what this young woman is thinking? Secondly, if you imagine being a young woman on a date with an unwanted advance, one might say what she does is exactly the right strategy. Nevertheless, the idea is that the young woman is in bad faith because, in this case, she is disowning an obvious fact about her situation.

The third example that Sartre gives has to do with a frigid wife. Sartre points out that, during sex, she finds herself thinking about her household accounts. What Sartre says rather bluntly to the psychoanalysts who had talked about such examples, is that thinking about the household accounts is a choice, and it is the way that one makes oneself frigid. It is not a psychodynamic beyond one's control, but quite the contrary. It is a choice not to get involved.

The best example perhaps is the example of the hesitant homosexual—someone who has had many homosexual encounters, who finds in himself many homosexual desires, and nevertheless resists being called a homosexual. Sartre provides us with an example of just this sort in an early novel he writes called *The Age of Reason*. The homosexual's problem is that, looking at the facts of the matter (the number of encounters he has already had, the way he finds his desires oriented), one has to say (as what Sartre says) the champion of sincerity would insist on saying, "I am a homosexual." To say, "I am a homosexual," is to define myself as essentially a certain kind of being. The truth is I still have choices.

One of the best-known gay intellectuals of our time, Gore Vidal, has often said there is no such thing as homosexuality and there are no homosexuals. There are only homosexual acts. I think that is very much in a Sartrian mind. The idea is that to say, "I am a homosexual," is to turn myself into just my facticity. On the other hand, to pretend that I have not done what I have done, or that I don't have the desires that I have, is bad faith of a different sort.

In all these examples, Sartre takes on Freud. What Freud says is essentially that there is a psychodynamic here. There is a sense in which we cannot do certain things, we cannot take certain positions. What Sartre wants to say in every case is we *will* not. We refuse to take certain positions. Or, we choose to look at ourselves in one way rather than another way. The idea is that when we are in bad faith, what we are doing is misperceiving, misjudging ourselves. As we noticed in the essay on emotions, this is something that we do for a purpose. Often the purpose is pretty straightforward. One does not want to take responsibility. When one emphasizes facticity, one is full of excuses: the facts of the matter, one's age, circumstances, upbringing, parents, anything which is a fact can somehow be used to wriggle out of our claim to responsibility.

On the other hand, to think of ourselves as pure transcendence—as Sartre gives in the rather curious example of joy, and also of falling in love, in the essay on emotions—what we notice is that a person chooses a kind of irresponsibility too, because by just focusing on the possibilities, on the fantasies, what one does is one does not pay attention to the actual facts of the matter. There is a sense in Sartre, which comes through fairly clearly in his discussion of the homosexual's dilemma, in which we are damned if we do and damned if we don't. We are always prone to emphasize either our facticity or our transcendence. If that is so, we are bound to bad faith. Sartre does sometimes give us the suggestion that bad faith is something that we cannot escape. We are creatures that are, by our very construction, as being-in-itself/being-for-itself, are caught in the necessity of bad faith.

This raises some serious questions about what should count as ethics for Sartre. Perversely, Sartre, like Heidegger, says he is not doing ethics. Nevertheless, I think there is no question whatsoever that any reader can raise that that is exactly what he is doing—ethics. If we can't escape bad faith, that makes it sound as if bad faith is just an excuse in itself. There is no doubt as he goes through his examples, his many plays and novels, that bad faith is something that admits of all sorts of variations and degrees. There is no question that bad faith is bad. It is something to be avoided.

I want to suggest that what Sartre does is, he does not reject or neglect ethics or morality. What he does is, he rather takes on a different kind of view of these matters. To use a simple word—to put a label on it—we can say what Sartre is really after is a theory of "integrity."

Sartre's Being-for-Others and *No Exit*
Lecture 22

As always with Sartre, who we are is an ambiguous notion. It is who we are in the eyes of the person who has caught us.

Nearly halfway through *Being and Nothingness*, Sartre introduces his third ontological category, being-for-others. Though last in his formulation, it is equal to the others in importance. "Being-for-others" has a more paranoid ring than Heidegger's "being with others." In Cartesian philosophy, with its primary emphasis on consciousness, skeptical problems arise concerning our knowledge of the "external" world and our knowledge of the existence of other people.

Many philosophers have argued that we know of the existence of other people through an obvious kind of inference. The inference is from our knowledge of our own minds and behavior and our observation of others' behavior to the contents of others' minds. Sartre rejects this approach. It wrongly assumes that we have a way of verifying the analogy between our minds and behavior and others' minds and behavior. It wrongly supposes that we can know ourselves independently of the recognition of other people. This last thesis Sartre borrows directly from Hegel, from whom he also borrows substantial portions of his view of being-for-others.

Sartre insists that our primary knowledge of other people comes not from observing them but rather from being looked at by them.

Sartre insists that our primary knowledge of other people comes not from observing them but rather from being looked at by them. Thus, shame is our conduit into the interpersonal world. He takes the case of writer Jean Genet. Caught in the act of stealing, Genet's decision to accept the label "thief" will determine his future existence. As in Camus, our experience with other people is not happy. We are all, in essence, always on trial. What other people think of us is a powerful determinant of who we are. We are necessarily influenced by the way other people see us—and the way we see ourselves. Being-for-others is being objectified according to their judgments. Bad faith is seeing ourselves only as others do—or only as we do.

Sartre, like Camus, seriously considers the prevalence of guilt as a necessary outcome of human awareness and being-for-others. For Sartre, however, the notion of responsibility takes priority over the more pathological notion of guilt, a secular notion of original sin. Sartre goes on to argue that our relations with others are essentially confrontations and relations of conflict. In his dramatic play *No Exit*, one of his characters sums it up: "Hell is other people." One character is dogged by the question of whether he is a coward or a hero. Another is an upper-class murderess; still another is a lesbian. Relations between people are essentially struggles for self-definition, struggles for authenticity. My conception of myself is largely the result of others' views of me. Others' views of themselves are largely the result of my (and others') views of them. Consequently, we are perpetually engaged in a kind of tense negotiation over how we will judge one another. Being-for-others is, thus, a critical part of our being. ∎

Essential Reading

Sartre, *No Exit.*

Supplementary Reading

Sartre, *Being and Nothingness*, pp. 471-559.

Schroeder, *Sartre and His Predecessors.*

Introductory Questions to Consider

1. What does it suggest to you that Sartre introduces being-for-itself and being-in-itself so far in advance of any explicit mention of being-for-others? Do you think that he views the third category as on a par with the other two?

2. How does shame establish beyond doubt the existence of other people for us?

1. In what way is the struggle for authenticity a struggle against other people? How do you see Sartre here playing out once again the arguments of Kierkegaard, Nietzsche, and Heidegger against "the herd"?

2. Is it possible, in your view, to have genuinely authentic relations with other people? Or is Sartre right that the very nature of human consciousness means that all such relationships are conflicted?

3. Is Garcin (in *No Exit*) a coward? Explain.

Sartre's Being-for-Others and *No Exit*
Lecture 22—Transcript

Almost halfway through *Being and Nothingness,* Sartre introduces his third ontological category, what he calls "being-for-others." Two points: first, being-for-others he insists is on an ontological par with the other two, being-for-itself and being-in-itself. Even though the introduction of being-for-others is delayed some 300 pages, its importance and its significance in human nature is just the same as the others. So, we break our way from the Descartes view that it is consciousness, on the one hand, and it is the world, on the other. Now we have a third category, which introduces something that Descartes really doesn't talk much about at all. That is our existence with and for other people.

The second point is that the very notion of being-for-others has a slightly paranoid ring to it. If you think of the contrast, a phrase that Heidegger actually used: "being with others," that sounds cozy, friendly. It sounds non-conflicted. When you say "being-for-others," right away we get the sense of being used by others. We are there for others as an object, or we are there for others to manipulate. As you will see, these paranoid suspicions are not so farfetched, and actually fairly central to Sartre's actual view of this category. In terms of the history of philosophy, and going back to Descartes once again, we might note that there are a series of skeptical problems that have to do not just with the existence of the external world, but, as I suggested earlier, with the existence of other people. We are only aware of our own consciousness. We are not aware, we cannot be aware, of anyone else's consciousness.

There is a sense in which philosophers have sometimes suggested that in order to take other people as people, what is required is a leap of faith, believing something that we cannot every possibly prove. Of course, philosophers are not satisfied with this, so over the past 100 years or so, there have been a whole series of attempts to prove the existence of other consciousnesses.

The basic argument, as exemplified in John Stuart Mill, is like this: I am conscious, and I have a body. I notice that my body, when I am having certain kinds of feelings or thoughts, behaves in a certain kind of way, makes certain gestures, is prone to certain actions, and so on. I see other people (or, rather, other people's bodies) behaving in much the same way, exemplifying many of the same gestures and facial expressions. By analogy, I conclude that they must have a consciousness, and, furthermore, a consciousness much like mine.

This raises another set of skeptical problems, which children have played with for as long as we know. That is the very thought that maybe other people see things, think of things, differently than we do. When I say I see something green, and you say you see something green, how do I know that you aren't actually seeing something red?

This kind of skepticism is very much fun to play with. When we start looking at multiculturalism, it is a kind of skepticism which often has an important truth to it. But, to think about knowing that other people exist in terms of any such argument or inference or analogy is really wrongheaded in a very important way. First, a problem with any analogy: it is only so strong as we can verify the likeness on the two sides of the analogy. To put it differently, it works as an argument, as an inference, only insofar as we can sometimes confirm that other people's behavior does go along with other people's consciousnesses, which are like mine. That is what we can't do. The very point of the Cartesian notion of consciousness is: "I am aware of and only aware of my own consciousness."

There is a more interesting problem with this argument from analogy: that is the idea that we can know ourselves and know our own minds. What Sartre wants to say, following from the great German philosopher Hegel (whom we heard of when we were talking about Kierkegaard), is that he wants to accept the notion that we can know ourselves only with the recognition of other people.

The idea is that self-knowledge is not something which Descartes captures as: "I think, therefore I am." In fact, that is a very late arrival in consciousness and self-consciousness. As Hegel argues, we become conscious of ourselves; we become self-conscious only in confrontation with others. Hegel has a very dramatic story, which we are going to look at in a little while about how we relate to other people in accordance with our need of their recognition.

The basic idea is that consciousness, self-consciousness, and consciousness of others all come at once, as a single package. We don't, first of all, know ourselves, and then get to know other people, or think we know other people. Rather, to know ourselves, we are already presuming what Sartre calls "being-for-others." This knowledge comes not from any kind of observation on our part—not from comparing ourselves with other people, and comparing our gestures and actions with theirs. Our knowledge comes from the experience of being looked at.

Let me go back to that experience of shame, which I talked about briefly in another lecture. There is a sense in which shame is the conduit. It is a basic way of knowing that we exist and that other people exist. One notes here that our experience with other people through shame is not necessarily a happy one—thus again, the idea of being-for-others rather than the idea of being-with-others. In a way, when we are looked at, we are caught, objectified. Sartre has a number of examples of this both in *Being and Nothingness* and in his later works.

Let me, for the moment, pick one from a later work in which he writes the biography of Jean Genet, the great playwright, but also a rather perverse felon. He captures Genet in his childhood trying to understand what it is that made him into the strange person that he would become. As always with Sartre, we can expect that it is not going to be simply in terms of upbringing, in terms of the causal forces at work that are going to determine what he will become. Rather, it is going to be in terms of Genet's choices about what he will become in the context of his situation and circumstances.

The story, as Sartre tells it, is that here is this young boy who is doing what young boys often do, not paying much attention to the mature notion of private property and routing through an adult's drawer looking for something to steal. He is doing this very unreflectively, undeliberately—one might even say unselfconsciously—like the example where I am running for a bus or streetcar, and what I experience is only the streetcar or bus to be overtaken. Here is the young Genet routing through a drawer, and, if we were to phenomenologically describe his experience, what we would describe is basically just the contents of the drawer. Here is something; here is something else. Into this scene, an adult appears. The adult screams

"Thief!" As Sartre puts it, rather lyrically, the young Genet is pinned, as a butterfly to a display.

It is an experience we all have in many different aspects. It is one that captures the example in *Being and Nothingness,* in which we are also pinned in just this way. The example in *Being and Nothingness* is something equally perverse. It is the example of our looking through a keyhole. Remember we are talking in the 1940s, when keyholes weren't these small, electronic things that we have today. Keyholes were rather large holes in which one put a rather substantial key. One of the obvious things about such a keyhole is that one can look through it and see what is on the other side.

One imagines oneself kneeling down by the keyhole, looking at the scene (presumably something that is private) on the other side. If one were to describe one's phenomenology at that moment, one would describe perhaps the shape of the keyhole and the shape at the other end. It would not be a scene captured by the notion of self-consciousness, certainly not reflective self-consciousness at all. Certainly, suddenly there is a creak on the stairwell. One turns around and sees that someone has caught him in the act. At that point, the phenomenology changes dramatically. One is thrown into self-consciousness. One is thrown into reflection. One is thrown into seeing oneself as the other person sees one. Just as Genet is caught routing through the drawer, and he is labeled a thief, and his decision to accept that label is what determines his next existence. In the case where we are caught on the stairs being a voyeur, that being caught, in a way, determines who we are.

As always with Sartre, who we are is an ambiguous notion. It is who we are in the eyes of the person who has caught us. What is so painful about such a circumstance is we realize that, even if this was a momentary lapse in our behavior—in the mind of this person who has seen us, perhaps seen us for the first time—this is going to be our essence. This is who we really are: a pervert, a voyeur. We are also the way we see ourselves. We are being-for-itself. We have a transcendence. We know that this one fact, especially if this is the only time we have ever done such a thing, doesn't define us at all. Rather, I define myself in terms of my ideals and the kind of person I think of myself as wanting to be. I think of myself as a moral person, a person who respects privacy. So, this act does not define me in my own mind.

Nevertheless, I am painfully aware of the fact itself which would seem to dictate, quite apart from whether anyone else has caught me or not, that I am, at least in this instance, a voyeur.

In fact, in some cases, I catch myself. In way, this is what moral education is all about. As a child, we depend on other people to catch us in the act and tell us, "This is wrong. You should not act this way. You don't want to be a such-and-such." Once we have been through that, we have what Heidegger and many other people through the tradition call "conscience." The nature of conscience is that we tell ourselves, we catch ourselves doing or tending to do certain kinds of actions, and we stop ourselves. There is a sense in which being-for-others really is just that. There is a sense in which being-for-others is being pinned, being identified, being objectified in terms of the perceptions and judgments of other people.

Once again, we can go back to Camus and *The Stranger,* and we go to the scene where the old people are ushering into the room, and Meursault has the absurd thought that they are sitting in judgment of him. That turns out to be absolutely true, as it is explicitly true in the second part of the novel when he is actually on trial. The thesis here is we are all always on trial. We are all always in the eyes of others, even if we have internalized those eyes, so that it is our own self-consciousness which imposes those external judgments. There is a very strong tendency in individualistic societies, particularly in this one, for people to fight off the influence of other people and to act independently, and for themselves.

We have seen this in these lectures, particularly in the philosophies of Kierkegaard and Nietzsche. For Kierkegaard it is of the utmost importance that one is a Christian, not because other people are Christians, but because one has decided all by oneself that that is what one is going to do. In Nietzsche, the attack on the herd sometimes becomes downright vicious. The idea is that one is truly oneself. One can exercise one's talents and become who one is only by exercising the influence of the absurd—to put it in modern terminology, not caring what other people think.

What Sartre is arguing here—and Sartre certainly is an individualist as much as any of these others—Sartre is arguing that we cannot be indifferent to what other people think. What other people think of us is as much a part of our identity as any of the other ways in which we know ourselves—thinking of ourselves in terms of the facts of the case, thinking of ourselves in terms of our own plans and expectations. What other people think of us is a clear determinate of who we are. So, the kind of tension we talked about in the lecture on bad faith now becomes, not a two-way tension, but a three-way tension.

We talked before about facticity versus transcendence, and how we are always both, but the one tends to compromise or circumscribe the other. So, we are always pulled between seeing ourselves too much in terms of our facticity, too much in terms of our choices, plans, expectations. Now we have to expand that picture, because in addition to how we think about ourselves and what the facts would seem to make true of us, there is also this question about how other people see us. So, bad faith takes on a new dimension too.

One way we can ban bad faith is, we can accept what other people think of us as simply the truth. We can define ourselves just in terms of who we are for others. This is what Heidegger is talking about when he talks about the *das Man* self, the anonymous self—the sense in which we are not taking charge of our own existence, but simply going along with the views and roles of others. Conversely, one can be in bad faith in exactly the opposite way. One can say, as I said a moment ago, "I don't care what other people think." That is bad faith because you cannot help but take account of what other people think. Some people would say this is kind of a psychological fact. It is a psychological fact that is more true of some people than of others.

Sartre would want to counter it is not psychology, and it is not something that is peculiar to this or that individual. It is part of the very essence of being human. We are, if you like, social creatures, not in the rather benign community sense that someone like Aristotle defended long ago, but in the rather perverse and disturbing sense that we are the objects of other people's judgments. The way we identify ourselves is very much part of how we are judged by other people.

What we find here is that, as Camus discovered and as Heidegger discovers in a slightly different way, that there is a sense in which we are all guilty. What are we guilty of? If you think about the shame example, if you think about the very idea of being judged by others, we are guilty both of not living up to other people's expectations of us, or sometimes we do live up to their expectations which are very low, and then find ourselves feeling guilty for not living up to our own expectations. That is the trap that Heidegger tries to get us out of.

For Sartre, it really does take on very much the appearance of another version of the doctrine of original sin, in a purely secular way, of course. Just as we are incapable of getting out of bad faith, because we always emphasize facticity versus transcendence and so on, so too we are incapable of avoiding bad faith in the sense that we can never get straight, as we would like to, about how much we should or should not take our identity of ourselves to be in the hands and eyes of other people.

To summarize this view, Sartre comes up with a couple striking formulations. One, in *Being and Nothingness,* is that our relationship with other people is basically conflict, quite the contrary of the rather amiable sense of community that Aristotle and other philosophers have defended. What Sartre tells us is that our relationship with other people is always trying to set aside their judgments of us, or getting them to make judgments of us which are in line with our own judgments of ourselves. Consequently, we are always playing with great difficulty with other people and the extent to which we can control them and their judgments, to the extent to which they can control us and our judgments of them—and this is prone to be a very conflicted situation.

We can all think of examples, in which: "I think well of you, you think well of me; let's go have a beer." Just as often, particularly in anything in which there is the least bit of competition, there is going to be the sense of: "I am better than you; let me prove it." "No, I am better than you; let me prove it." That can take all sorts of dimensions, and we have seen it operate in every theater of human experience, and we will talk about some of them in the next two lectures.

Perhaps the most striking illustration of this, and the best slogan to sum it up, is Sartre's play *No Exit.* The phrase is: "Hell is other people," and the play itself is set in hell. It really has a kind of diabolical setting. One should add that, if it weren't for Sartre's philosophy permeating it, it could well be a piece of kitsch and not a very interesting play at all. Because it is a rather intriguing mix of, on the one hand, theatrical setting and, on the other, philosophical profundity, *No Exit,* I think, is often received as one of philosophy's most profound contributions to the theater. Anyway, the setting is hell. The three people who are its principles are dead. Sartre is an atheist. He doesn't believe in heaven and hell. He doesn't believe in an afterlife. So, one can already anticipate that the whole play is written rather tongue-in-cheek.

The three people are picked for precisely their incompatibility. One, the male of the group, named Garcin, is a man who has always conceived of himself as a hero. In fact, he has spent his life in the underground in some unnamed South American country in the Resistance, at war with an authoritarian government. He is also something of a libertine, and among his most serious defects are a kind of cruelty to women, and in particular, extreme cruelty to his wife. His situation is that just before he died he was arrested. As he was arrested, while he was running from the police, he was about to be executed when he broke down in tears. Like a small child crying for mercy, he was the very antithesis of heroic. Then he was shot. The question that plagues him is the question, "Am I a coward or am I a hero?"

This is the kind of question which has often fascinated me in terms of our conception of our dying moments. Some of it goes back to the Greeks. One also finds it in Western cowboy epics—the idea that how a person dies is in some sense definitive of his or her life. To take a more literary source, in Goethe's *Faust*, at the very end, as Faust is about to die, he repents. At that last moment, some angels come down and pick up his worm of a soul and carry it off to heaven, despite his pact with Mephistopheles. One wants to ask, does a last minute bit of repentance really undo a lifetime of, in this case, bargaining with the devil? In the cowboy, ancient morality plays, is it true that how a person dies (with his boots and his gun on, for example)—does that really say something about the life, or is it just one moment among others?

These are the sorts of thoughts that Garcin is struggling with. On the one hand, there is 30 years of undisputed heroism. On the other hand, there is this very cowardly death. So, what is he? Part of Sartre's thesis here is that as long as we are all alive, as long as we are dynamic selves in the making, there is no such thing as "what we are"—in other words, pure facticity. When we are dead, we are pure facticity. The question now for Garcin is: What is it? Is it a coward? Is it a hero? Part of the intrigue of the play is the fact that here we have a character who, on the one hand, is dead, but at the same time is reflecting and dynamically interacting with others trying to decide who he is, or was.

The other two characters are both women. They are women who are very different from one another. Estelle is a kind of high society flit. She is a coquette. She has lived her life in the eyes of men and being desired by men. She killed both her husband and her baby, which is why she is in hell, but her behavior hasn't really changed. She comes to hell rather well dressed, still very beautiful, and what she wants—as she has always wanted—is a man. There is only one man around. That is Garcin. His mind is on other matters. Then there is Inez. Inez is a lesbian and from a fairly humble, working-class background. She is not apologetic for either of those. She takes her lesbianism, unlike Sartre's homosexual in *Being and Nothingness*, as simply a fact about her, and she has no qualms about it. As for her working class status, she wears that with a kind of pride, not something to be ashamed of at all, even in the face of Estelle's high society flirtations. Inez is in hell because she murdered her lover, and also committed suicide at the same time. They are quite a trio. If we imagine a dinner party in hell, this would be it.

Garcin, while he is totally absorbed with his worries about who he is, or was, at the same time is the same macho libertine-ish fellow who was so cruel to his wife and so many other women. I might add, just as a footnote, in the first production of the play it was Camus who played the character of Garcin. Then there is Estelle who cares about nothing so much as regaining her own identity, which has to be through the recognition and desire of a man, but Garcin is the only one around. Then, there is Inez, who is very desirous of Estelle, a thought which she is unwilling to entertain.

The triangle here is guaranteed to produce conflict. Sartre's point is that it is a conflict which goes on between us all the time, although perhaps in much more subtle ways. In one of the key scenes in the play, Estelle discovers that in hell, she has no mirror. As she puts it, "They must have taken it away from her at the entrance." There are no mirrors in the room either, and for a person who has lived by her looks all of her mature life, this is a serious deficiency. Inez, at this point, steps in and says, "Let me be your mirror, dear." The symbolism here is very complex and profound. You remember when we were talking about reflection in the context of *The Stranger*, and I talked about the kind of dual image of reflection as, on the one hand, looking at oneself as if looking at another. At the same time, the idea of reflection in the mirror, and putting these two senses together in the idea of seeing oneself as another would see you, as if in a mirror.

The truth is that mirrors aren't all straight. There are all sorts of distorting mirrors, and as Inez makes very clear, looking at yourself through the conscience of another person is deeply distorting. It has to do a great deal with their prejudices and desires. Inez is filled with prejudices against Estelle's upper-class status, and more immediate desires for her. As Estelle starts asking questions, like "How do I look?" Inez starts becoming a rather uppity mirror and says at one point, for example, "Oh, is that a pimple?" Estelle, of course, freaks out. Inez says, "I was just kidding." The idea is, what if your mirror started to lie to you? What is at stake here, is how we all lie to each other—either willfully, or just in seeing people, and judging people, and dealing with people in our own terms, rather than in their terms.

The upshot of the play, therefore, is that hell is other people—precisely in the sense that if we were each aware, as Garcin tries to be several times in the play, but, of course, unsuccessfully, we might be able to satisfy ourselves with our own conceptions of ourselves. As long as we are with other people—and we are always with other people—what we are going to find is that our conceptions of ourselves are always compromised by, and determined by, other people as well. What *No Exit* gives us is a very graphic illustration of the kind of conflict that all human relationships are subject to.

In a passage in *Being and Nothingness*, Sartre points out that when we are alone, say, walking through a beautiful desert landscape in Arizona, and there is a sense in which we have this feeling "The world is mine"—although this is probably more aesthetic and reflective than Heidegger would be talking about in his introduction of *Dasein*—one can look at oneself alone in a beautiful landscape, and feeling very much at one, at home with the world, as a kind of paradigm of what it is to be *Dasein*.

But, in Sartre's example, suddenly we see another person coming over the horizon, and it doesn't much matter yet whether he or she has seen us. As soon as we see them, we understand that our world has been disrupted; that, as Sartre puts it rather graphically, our world—our personal, private unity with the world, has just been absorbed down the drain of another person's consciousness. Overly dramatic perhaps, but it is an experience that we all find familiar. We are alone, quite content with our circumstances; another person comes on the scene, and suddenly, we are thrown into viewing ourselves as the other person might view us, and that is something from that point on that we have to deal with.

Being-for-others is essentially a third consideration in the question: What is it to be a self? It is not enough to look at the facts that are true. It is not enough to simply see what I think of myself. I also have to take into consideration how others view me, and as always in Sartre, these three views are intention, and there is no simple way to find out simply who I am.

Sartre on Sex and Love
Lecture 23

> I often remark to my students that their friends are rarely such a matter of circumstance as they often suggest. ... Even if you are assigned to a roommate, you still have a number of basic choices. For example, you have the choice to like or despise that person, whether to hang out or avoid them completely. People choose their friends, and it is very interesting to ask on what grounds they choose them. ... We choose our friends on the basis of among other things, our conception of ourselves.

Sartre's analysis of human relationships as conflict suggests troublesome consequences for the understanding of one of our most tender human emotions, love. Love, as in all relationships between people, is essentially a struggle for self-definition, a struggle for authenticity. Even friendship, which people often think of as a weak or casual form of love, is essentially a struggle for self-definition. We pick people who will reinforce our own conception of ourselves. Friendship, however, is rarely exclusive, and friends do not (usually) make exclusive claims on each other. Thus, the overall determination of self-identity in the hands of any single friend will usually be considerably less than that determination in the hands of a lover.

When one has multiple lovers (as Sartre was prone to do), the overall determination of self-identity in the hands of any single lover may also be considerably less than the determination of self-identity in the hands of a single, exclusive lover. Love becomes a seductive strategy to win the other over. Because love is a strategy with an objective, not simply a "feeling," it can succeed or fail. When it fails, it readily leads to sadism, masochism, and hatred.

Sexual desire becomes the desire to turn the other into a "sex object." Reducing the other person to his or her body and bodily responses is manipulating or eliminating his or her capacity for judgment. Reducing the other person to a vehicle for one's own pleasure is also a way of manipulating or eliminating his or her capacity for judgment. The aim of sex, contra Freud and most people, is not pleasure. Pleasure is only a vehicle and can even get in the way of sex's strategy of control and manipulation. The aim of sex, in Nietzschean terms, is power. Sartre turns the twists and turns of romance into a diabolical play of wills. Hegel's "master and slave" paradigm plays a central role in his analysis. The submissive one becomes dominant as the master becomes dependent. Hegel argued that all such relationships are unstable.

> **The aim of sex, in Nietzschean terms, is power.**

Harsh as it seems, Sartre has done an important service in forcing us to open our eyes to the complexity and difficulties of our interpersonal lives. For most of Western history, the complexities of love have been buried under an avalanche of romantic foggery.

The contrast with Aristophanes, the dramatic spokesman in Plato's *Symposium*, is instructive here. Aristophanes offers us the classic parable of a single soul, split in two by the gods, each half desperately trying to find its perfect fit, its other half. Sartre, by contrast, insists that there is no such unity, no such "fit." The people we meet have been brought up differently. Even for those who are "made for each other," there is a good deal of adjustment and compromise. Relationships are never fully stable; they are, to use a word Sartre borrows, "metastable."

But Sartre maintained a romantic relationship with Simone de Beauvoir for fifty years, an apparent counter-example to his own harsh philosophy of relationships. Sartre did claim to find a true "being-with-others" in politics, not romance, "on the barricades," his primary pursuit for the last thirty years of his life. ∎

Essential Reading

Sartre, *Being and Nothingness*, Part III, and *Notebook for an Ethics*.

Anderson, *Sartre's Two Ethics*.

Barnes, *An Existentialist Ethics*.

de Beauvoir, *The Ethics of Ambiguity*.

Hegel, *Phenomenology of Spirit*, Chapter 4A (on the master-slave dialectic).

Solomon, *About Love*.

Introductory Questions to Consider

1. "Hell is other people," writes Sartre in *No Exit*. What does he mean? Why does he believe this (in his philosophy, as well as in this play)? Do you think this is true? Why or why not?

2. Can you think of a genuine instance of "being-with-others (as opposed to being-for-others")? What would this be like? Would such an instance pose an objection to Sartre? Could Sartre allow that such a relation is possible? Explain.

Advanced Questions to Consider

1. Although "being-in-itself" and "being-for-itself" are introduced quite early in *Being and Nothingness*, "being-for-others" is not introduced until Part III (p. 303). Does this mean that being-in-itself and being-for-itself are in some sense ontologically prior to being-for-others— that being-for-others is somehow derivative? If so, what could Sartre mean when he states, "it is not true that I first am and then later seek to make an object of the Other or to assimilate him; but...I am—at the very root of my being—the project of assimilating and making an object of the Other"?

2. What is the relationship between being-for-itself and being-for-others? In the final analysis, who is responsible for my emotional outlook? What does this mean in practical terms?

Sartre on Sex and Love
Lecture 23—Transcript

In *No Exit*, each character wants to impose his or her desires and self-conceptions on the others. Garcin, in particular, is torn about who he really is: a hero or a coward. To confirm the way he would like to think of himself, he has to turn to Estelle or Inez to agree with him. He turns to Estelle, and she suggests a kind of swap. He makes love to her and gives her the kind of recognition she craves as a woman, and she, in turn, will tell whatever he wants to hear. As we all know, hearing what we want to hear, from a person who tells us just because they want to know that is what we want to hear, is deeply unsatisfying and often suspicious. So, Estelle's deal won't work, and Garcin turns his attention to Inez. Inez, who has no great respect for Garcin's manliness or his worries, won't give him the answer he wants. As the play ends, we get the sense that they are going to be playing cat and mouse with his identity for all of eternity.

Also, in this play, there is an underlying, quite intentional sexual element. The fact that Estelle needs Garcin to want her. The fact that Garcin is a very macho man who would, in fact, want her very much if he didn't have other things on his mind. Inez's own desire for Estelle, and Estelle's repulsion for Inez's advances, in turn. All this adds up to a literally diabolical sexual intrigue, and Sartre wants to play on that to illustrate a number of basic truths. Notice that even if these three characters are to be in hell for all of eternity, nevertheless, they are strangers when we meet them in the play and they are just meeting each other.

The extent to which we have these sorts of identity struggles between us really depends in many ways on the degree of intimacy. Intimacy is very often thought of as a desirable thing. As you can guess, in Sartre's shift from being-with-others to being-for-others, intimacy itself is going to be a kind of threat, a very dangerous situation. We tend to think about intimate relations in terms of their desirability, in terms of their completing us, in terms of their comfort level. What Sartre wants to suggest, perhaps perversely, but profoundly, is that even such intimate relationships as love and friendship are struggles. They are not simply being with, but they are being-for, and very often in a similarly diabolical sense.

First of all, we might look at love as a kind of struggle for authenticity in Heidegger's sense. In other words, we might look at love as a struggle for being one's own person. The very concept of love undermines this. This is something that people in love have often struggled with, of being in a love relationship and being with one another, yet maintaining their own sense of identity and independence. There is a sense in which we use a very ugly term today to talk about when love relationships overstep this boundary, and take away mutual independence. We talk about "codependency," which is viewed as a quasi-pathological condition. The question is whether dependency (something like codependency) isn't present in all love relationships—consequently, not just psychologically, but ontologically they are something to be avoided.

When we look at Sartre, who talks about love not as a kind of benign relationship, but as a struggle, what we see is that it extends not just to love between lovers and spouses, but also to all relationships. Let me work my way into love from something that is in-between a relationship between strangers and mere acquaintances, and something which is full-blown intimate love affair or marriage. That is friendship.

I often remark to my students that their friends are rarely such a matter of circumstance as they often suggest. Namely, this is a roommate that I happened to be put in with my freshman year, or this is someone I happened to go to high school with, because there are many colleagues in high school and only some of them turn out to be friends. Even if you are assigned to a roommate, you still have a number of basic choices. For example, you have the choice to like or despise that person, whether to hang out or avoid them completely. People choose their friends, and it is very interesting to ask on what grounds they choose them. I think the answer comes through fairly quickly. We choose our friends on the basis of among other things, our conception of ourselves.

That is not to say that friendship is narcissistic. It does not follow that we choose people like ourselves. In fact, we might choose people very different from ourselves. For example, if I am not very intelligent and I am concerned about my lack of intelligence, I might take up with an extremely intelligent woman precisely in order to have her intelligence radiate onto me. If I am not very physically adept, I might well go out with an athlete, and make friends with athletes as a way of being part of a crowd which is athletic. Very often, we pick people who are contrasts, who are opposites rather than just like us, as friends.

The idea is that in friendship, what we do is we pick people who are going to reinforce our own conception of ourselves. So, if I think of myself as intelligent, or I want to think of myself as intelligent, whether or not I pick a partner who is also intelligent, what is going to be essential is that it is going to be a partner who somehow expands my notion of my own intelligence— either by telling me all the time how intelligent I am, or by contradicting me in such a way that I can prove my intelligence with her or him.

In other words, friendship is not just falling in with people whom you happen to like. That is a very superficial characterization. Friendship is a kind of agreement; contract, in American terms. The idea is basically: "I will approve of you in your terms if you will approve of me in my terms." Consequently, we form a kind of partnership in which the shared aim is to mutually improve each of our self-conceptions. The thing about friends is that most of us have many friends. One can make a kind of exception here. There is something which, in the 19th century, was referred to as "romantic friendship." Among the Greeks, there were stories about friends, primarily male friends, who were just as exclusive and intimate as any pair of lovers. For the most part, we talk about friendship in a very general way; I would say in a very promiscuous way. We often refer to someone as a friend, meaning we have had dinner with them once or talked to them once.

If you think about what it means to be a friend, what you understand is that friendship involves that kind of mutual identity. First of all, the mutual identity as friends, but also the sense in which we identify ourselves through our friends. The fact that we have many friends, or several friends, means that there is a sense in which this identity is diffuse, and we don't depend all that strongly on one friend for how we think of ourselves.

On the other hand, when we are talking about lovers, the picture becomes very different. Whether or not this is a universal necessity, it is clear in the Western tradition that love is conceived of as a more or less exclusive relationship. There are people who have many lovers. Sartre was one of them. By distributing one's identity among many lovers, one weakens the power of being-for-others with any one of them. By the same token, because that is true, lovers tend to be very defensive of exclusivity, and in comes a kind of double standard. We want to expand our own sense of options and identity by dealing with many lovers, but at the same time, we want to be for each of them, their only one.

The reason for that is, because with this kind of intimacy and exclusiveness, we get a kind of control. Control of what? We tend to think of love in a rather benign way. Sartre introduces love as a seductive strategy. When we fall in love—and love can succeed or fail, and with it, we can succeed or fail—what we are concerned with is how we can win over the other; for example, how we can get the other to think of us as we like to think of ourselves. Again, there is a kind of bargain, or contract, that the other thinks the same of us.

Remember back when you went on your first date, or in any given relationship, the first date. What is it like? Let's leave aside all the anxiety and the rest of it, and talk about the kind of social dynamics. First, you dress and talk in such a way as to present yourself not only in the best light possible, but the best light as you conceive of it as the kind of person you want to be. We all remember back in our teenage years when we weren't sure what kind of person that was, or the kind of person was really quite at odds with the person we were prone to be. Nevertheless, we presented ourselves in a certain way, in order to get the person we were out with to think of us that way. The other person was doing the same thing.

As the conversation proceeds, probably on fairly safe ground to begin with: Where do you go to school or what do you study? There is a sense in which we are feeling our way and trying to find new openings, new ways of presenting ourselves which appeal to the other person. To talk about seduction here might sound a bit sinister. There is a sense in which to think of it as a seduction is really just to say it is not direct—that what you do is present to the other person all the evidence and considerations that he or she needs in order to think of you in the way that you would like. It is seductive not in that it is secretive, much less that it is sinister; rather it is trying to win the other person over in a very basic sense.

As I said, love can fail. When you think about failed love, it does not just result in the end of a relationship. Instead, it turns into something else. Sartre discusses many different possibilities. If what we are trying to do when we are in love with another person, or in a relationship with another person, is win them over to our way of thinking, to take control of them, then, one natural result of a failed love is to take that attempt to control and make it explicit. What we get is "sadism."

Sadism here does not necessarily refer to cruelty, and it doesn't necessarily refer to any kind of physical abuse. Sadism, as Freud also argued, is really a kind of latent tendency in all relationships. Insofar as love is an attempt to gain control, sadism is a kind of desperate, explicit attempt to take that control. I am talking really about love just in one of its dimensions—that is, the dimension in which we talk about love in terms of dominating or manipulating the other person's view of you in a kind of straightforward way. We don't always do that.

Sometimes in a love relationship, we take a much more submissive position. One might even say that love is essentially not so much a dominating position as the submissive one. Here, what we run across is a very different kind of tendency because when we take a submissive position, it is not as if we are saying to the other person, "Make of me what you will." To the contrary, we are putting the other person in a position where he or she must please me. When this fails, it becomes explicit. Then we find "masochism," which again should not be confused with cruelty or physical abuse. Rather, it is a manipulative attitude toward the other, which replaces the more subtle mechanism which love tries to bring about.

One might also talk here about indifference. Here, we mean not just not caring, but the kind of profound and very annoying indifference that one finds, for example, in an ex-lover—someone who just now won't pay attention to you, won't acknowledge you, even as another human being. That can lead to hatred, which is a more extreme form of the same kind of hostile attitude.

In short, what we find is that love, contrary to the kind of ethereal way that we think of it, is a kind of dynamic in which a kind of mutual manipulation is essential. All of this is talking in a rather abstract sense about love. When

321

we talk about intimacy, what we often have in mind—in fact, some people would even define it this way—is a sexual relationship. As we saw in *No Exit*, there is a kind of sexual subtext, which is, in many ways, definitive of the relationship between the characters. It is not just a matter of happenstance that one is a macho male, one is a coquette and one is a lesbian. Rather, it is this kind of sexual dynamic which really makes the play move.

What are the dynamics of sex? What is sexual desire? We have all been taught in this society that it is something wrong to turn a person into a sex object. Feminists for the last 40 years have complained bitterly at the male gaze for doing this. There is a sense in which sexuality is essentially reducing the other to an object. Sartre points out that when you make love to a person—and the parts of a person which become most attractive in sex are precisely those parts of a person which are in a way the least human, the most fleshy, the least dynamic: breasts, buttocks, thighs and so on—what Sartre is pointing out here is something that on the one hand is a bit perverse.

At the same time, I think it is something worth dwelling on. When we love someone for their personality, their intelligence, their charm, why is it that sex, itself, tends to treat them in a way which really doesn't leave much room for all those traits, except in the case of a very unusual relationship? Why does sex so focus on something which is, in one way of thinking, a very basic animal activity? Of course, there are all kinds of pseudo-biological explanations for this, some of which have a lot of truth behind them. Sartre wants to say it is all beside the point. There are many biological acts that we perform—eating, for instance—but we dress it up in an enormous variety of ways, depending on our culture and depending on what the ethics and customs of the culture happen to be.

How about with sex? We often talk about sex as cutting underneath culture in a return straight to our animal nature. Sartre thinks quite the opposite. It is part of what is most human about us. It has often been commented that people have sex in a way that virtually no animal has sex. This is not true just by virtue of the biology and the way we have courtship rituals, and so on. It is a more basic sense. What it comes down to is the fact that we, in having sex, are conscious, and self-conscious, and conscious of the other. We are conscious of the other's consciousness of us. So, sex, like love, turns out to be a kind of strategy, a kind of manipulative strategy in which what we try to do is win over the other to our own self-conceptions.

What does this have to do with reducing the other to an object? Here, we enter another of those very tricky dialectics that Sartre likes to talk about. On the one hand, what we want to do it put the other in a position, possibly by giving him or her so much pleasure, that he or she will tell us whatever we want to hear, like Estelle in *No Exit*. At the same time, if we succeed, on the one hand, we have produced someone who will simply tell us whatever we want to hear, and they are not therefore trustworthy. On the other hand, we might give them so much pleasure that they won't tell us, or see us, as anything at all. They will stop making judgments altogether. That is one of the possible aims of sexual activity: in a way, to simply shut the other person up.

Again, this is only half the picture, because what we also see in sex is a kind of submissiveness, but not a kind of submissiveness that is simply: "Do what you like; I am just here for you." It, too, is, or can be, very manipulative. It is a way of getting the other person to exercise all his or her efforts toward pleasing you, and in that way, controlling what they are thinking, and in particular, what they are thinking of you. By reducing the other to a vehicle of pleasure, what you do is you manipulate. This is to say that pleasure is not the aim of sex. Pleasure is a kind of vehicle, which you use to control the other person. If you take too much pleasure in it yourself, the pleasure gets in the way. What you do, in fact, is you eliminate sex as the vehicle for just the power you are trying to attain. Make no mistake: for Sartre, sex is about power. It is a very Nietzschean view, and the aim is to see our relationships not as a simple being-with-others; rather as a kind of power play. Romance is a kind of play of wills.

What I have been saying sounds very perverse, and it sounds very perverse to me too. Nevertheless, I think what Sartre is doing is something incredibly important. What he is doing is taking something which has been buried in so much nonsense over the last 2,000 years, and given us a brutally realistic view of the kind of psychodynamics (or he would say, ontological dynamics) that are really at stake. It goes back to an earlier philosophical picture given to us by Hegel, which I have anticipated several times. It has to do with his dialectic between master and slave, or between domination and submission. In Hegel's story, two people essentially fight it out until one becomes master of the other, and the loser becomes master of the slave. Unfortunately, it is not a stable relationship. Through various attempts to either alter the relationship or escape from it, both parties leave essentially quite unhappy.

The same kind of vision is what Sartre wants to give us in his view of sex and love. We think of it as a kind of benign coupling, something that brings great satisfaction to everyone. What Sartre wants to point out is that sex and love are much more complicated, and more threatening and dangerous, than we usually like to admit. Perhaps, he would say there is no satisfaction to be gained from them. I think that is an oversimplification. Nevertheless, I think he opens our eyes to complexities that have been buried under an avalanche of nonsense over the last 2,000 years.

Philosophers especially have talked about love in very ethereal, even heavenly, ways. The metaphors that we think of when we think of love are such that they really distract us from any kind of critical attention. I know from watching young people that they must always say something like, on the one hand, "Love is wonderful, beautiful—the thing I really want to live for." At the same time, they complain about their own love relationships, and say in a profound sense—which they don't understand—that they are unsatisfied, or they are threatened in a way which they can't handle.

It seems to me, to understand what Sartre is trying to combat, one should look at some of these traditional myths and glosses. Let me pick one, which is one of my favorites. It is a piece of Plato's *Symposium*, and it is a tale told by the playwright Aristophanes. It is supposed to characterize the true nature of love. What Aristophanes tells us is that love is a product of an ancient history, in which what we call human beings were much different creatures than they are today. We were double creatures with two sets of arms, legs, two heads, and we were so intelligent, consequently, that we offended the gods. Zeus essentially threatened to split us in two. And he did. Ever since, Aristophanes says, we have been running around the world trying to find our other half. What love is, what sex is, is a kind of completion.

The idea of completing ourselves through the other, on the one hand, jives rather nicely with Sartre's conception of being-for-others. That is, we are not independent of other people. Being-for-others is an essential part of our own being. The idea of completing ourselves in the sense that Aristophanes says—making ourselves complete with another person with whom we perfectly fit—is quite at odds with Sartre's rather perverse view of love and sex.

First, to say the obvious, there is no such perfect fit. The people we meet, fall in love with, are quite different from ourselves. The analogy that Aristophanes uses in his little story is "cut in half like an apple." If you take the two halves of an apple and press them together, they fit quite perfectly. If you take two halves of different apples, which have been split rather crudely, what you find is it takes a good deal of grinding to get them to fit together. The truth is the people that we meet have been brought up differently, perhaps even in different cultures, religions, ways of thinking, different sets of habits. Any relationship, as we all know, doesn't just fit together. Even in this sort of vernacular of "we were made for each other," we have to develop a relationship over a period of time in which there is a good deal of adjustment and compromise which goes into fitting together so nicely.

Sartre means something deeper than this. It is not just a question of the amount of time and energy that it takes to fit. Rather, there is no such fit because, even in the best relationship, what we find is that there is a kind of struggle going on. While we might, at the beginning of a relationship, distract ourselves from this with sexual excitement, people often make an awful relationship, but don't see it for sometimes even years because they have managed to so distract themselves. Or, later on in a relationship, you might find all the mechanisms of distraction and denial—getting lost in our careers or friends on the side, or not paying attention to the relationship, just sitting and watching television.

If you pay any attention to your relationship, and especially in times of crisis and trouble, what becomes very clear is that there is a kind of struggle going on, even though there is a kind of adjustment and accommodation that can take place over the years that makes it seem less and less like an actual struggle. The picture is going to be the same: that we are trying to maintain our own conception of ourselves in the face of the judgments of the other person.

I would say, in correction to Sartre here, that what he doesn't take seriously enough is the fact that very often our conceptions of ourselves are not only in the face of the other, but there is a kind of cooperation that can take place on the level of actually trying to think of ourselves in mutual terms—something which Sartre alludes to, and I will come back to that in a moment. The idea that the way we think of ourselves is something which is always at risk because of the other person, is true.

You can think without much trouble, but with a great deal of pain, of the person with whom you have spent much of your life, turning to you suddenly one day and issuing the kind of criticism that never allows us to think of ourselves the same again. Or, we can imagine ourselves in a fit of rage, saying the sort of thing that not just hurts feelings but destroys relationships, precisely because we see that we have found the fault, or the fault line, in the other person's way of thinking about themselves, and we have driven a wedge in it. The point is that relationships, however stable they may seem, are never truly stable—just as in our conceptions of ourselves, we are never fully at peace with ourselves.

There is a word that Sartre borrows from chemistry. It is the word "metastability." It refers to a situation which, at a given moment, appears to be perfectly in balance. Nevertheless, a slight disruption causes the whole system to fall into disarray. The example I like here is the idea of a waiter carrying five or six cups of hot coffee, and if he balances them well, he can probably get to the table with no trouble at all. On the other hand, if there is some slight mishap, a small trip, perhaps a little curl in the rug, or if just one drop of hot coffee hits his skin, then he will flinch, he will react. That is the end of it. Suddenly, all six cups of coffee go flying into the air and we have a catastrophe on our hands.

So too, our conceptions of ourselves at any given moment might seem to be stablized and fairly fixed. We know who we are in our career. We know who we are in our friendships, and in a relationship, we might feel perfectly comfortable that we have now accommodated ourselves, adjusted ourselves to a life together. It is metastable in the sense that one hot drop of coffee might, nevertheless, throw the whole thing into catastrophe.

Once again, I don't want to endorse Sartre's picture so much as I think that it is very important to present it, and to present it in all its brutal completeness. What he does is opens our eyes to the complexities of our relationships in a way that Aristophanes, for example, seems to deny. Two things should modify this view. First of all, Sartre himself had a lifelong relationship with Simone de Beauvoir. Despite many infidelities on his part and a few on hers, and a good deal of things that most of us would think are, at best, eccentric in a relationship (such as the refusal to get married over all that time), nevertheless, they really occupy a place as one of the premiere couples— certainly the premiere philosophical couple—in the 20th century.

One might contrast it with Bertrand Russell, who, despite all his words of praise for love, nevertheless managed to go through quite a few marriages, and, by his own admission, found none of them satisfactory. So, the Beauvoir relationship is one that I would hold up as a counterexample to Sartre's own philosophy. Granted, it was filled with tensions and complexities, but Sartre showed that he was capable of, in some sense, the real thing.

The second thing to say is that Sartre did find a mode of being-with-others as opposed to being-for-others, but I guess, as we can predict from his plays and writings, it was not to be in the realm of romance. It was in the realm of politics. What Sartre claimed was the true being-with-others was something that one found in the mutuality of being under threat, on the battlefield or, more to the point, behind the barricades of a Parisian revolution. So, Sartre does want to say that there is such a thing as being-with-others, but it is only in fairly extreme circumstances. Once again, we go back to that question about human nature. Where do we find its measure? Not in ordinary bourgeois life, which Sartre despised, but in the extremities of politics and political crises.

From Existentialism to Postmodernism
Lecture 24

The truth is that existentialism is still a vibrant movement, and for that reason, I haven't spent any time at all in the past 23 lectures trying to define what it is.

Has existentialism gone out of fashion? I don't think so. Existentialism is more than a simple movement or period in history. As Sartre said, to try and define it is to freeze it—thus my own reticence about specifically defining the movement. Although the movement began in Europe, its real home now is in America. American ideas of self-improvement and mobility share much with existentialism.

Existentialism seems to have been eclipsed by two generations of philosophers since Sartre. Sartre was attacked by Levi-Strauss, a "structuralist" anthropologist, for his anthropocentrism and neglect of other cultures. Then he was rejected by a new generation of French philosophers under the banner of "postmodernism" (also "poststructuralism"). Key figures include Michel Foucault, Gilles Deleuze, Jacques Derrida, and Roland Barthes. Barthes and Foucault put forward the idea of the "death of the author," which denies Sartre's notion of Cartesian subjectivity. In Deleuze, the impersonal play of forces also attempts to replace all subjectivity. Although all these philosophers were profoundly influenced and inspired by Sartre, there has been almost a conspiracy of silence regarding Sartre's work.

First and foremost, Sartre's strong orientation toward subjectivity (and with this, most of phenomenology, as well) has been rejected.

The self, even "consciousness," as Sartre understood it, has been rejected.

The self, even "consciousness," as Sartre understood it, has been rejected. The postmodernists also reject rationality, objectivity, truth, and knowledge, as these concepts are traditionally understood. These claims are problematic, but they are also derivative of Sartre's own theories, including the rejection of ultimate rational guidelines.

In addition, Sartre's "Enlightenment project," his ideal of a "purifying reflection," and his politics of freedom have been rejected. In Sartre, there is a raging sense of rationality. Returning to the harsher views of Nietzsche, Foucault and Deleuze stress power and impersonal force as the determinant of truth and values. Derrida rejects Sartre's overly unified notion of self. The self is marginalized, fragmented, in Derrida. Nevertheless, there are serious questions about the locus of both political responsibility and morals in the postmodern reaction. The liberating project of Freud's psychoanalysis may be analogous in some ways to the "purifying reflection" of Sartre. But the emphasis on personal responsibility is a welcome rejoinder to the current cultural paradigm of victimization.

I would like to suggest that the existentialist view has much to recommend it, not just as an interesting movement in twentieth-century philosophy but as an authentic way of life, much needed as this terrible but remarkable century comes to a close. ∎

Essential Reading

Michel Foucault and Jacques Derrida in Solomon, *Continental Philosophy Since 1750*, pp. 194–202.

Levi-Strauss, *The Savage Mind.*

Supplementary Reading

Dreyfus and Rabinow, *The Essential Works of Michel Foucault.*

Kumaf, *A Derrida Reader.*

Miller, *Michel Foucault.*

Norris, *What's Wrong with Postmodernism?*

Sallis, *Deconstruction and Philosophy: The Texts of Jacques Derrida.*

1. What is postmodernism? What is modernism? In what sense is Sartre's existentialism, in particular, a "modern" philosophy? In what sense is Nietzsche, by contrast, "postmodern"?

2. To what extent is knowledge a matter of power, as Foucault suggests? What does it mean to say, "the subject is socially constructed," through power relations?

3. To what extent is there "nothing aside from the text," as Derrida has famously argued? In what sense are the world and ordinary life a text?

Advanced Questions to Consider

1. In what ways does Sartre anticipate the postmodernists? In what ways does he advocate the elimination of "the subject" from philosophy?

2. What could come after "postmodernism," i.e., what is post-postmodernism? Is the Enlightenment dead and gone, or is postmodernism possibly just another phase of Enlightenment (modernist) thinking?

From Existentialism to Postmodernism
Lecture 24—Transcript

Quite a few years ago, I was discussing an article that I had written with an editor, a friend at *Vogue* magazine. She read it through and said to me, "Isn't this existentialism?" I said, yes. She said, "I thought that was passé." Coming from an editor at *Vogue*, I suppose this judgment made sense. After all, if things don't go in and out of fashion, *Vogue* magazine doesn't have much to live for. It took me back, and I realized (as I say, this was a couple of decades ago) I had to ask myself the question whether existentialism was itself a fashion—whether it was something that had passed from France to America at a critical time in history, just after the Second World War. A couple of striking authors, mainly Camus and Sartre, had struck the American fancy, had inspired a generation of American authors who, for a short time, called themselves existentialists (Norman Mailer was an example) but then it passed on. So, existentialism belongs to the 1940s and 1950s, and after that, I have to see myself as something of a throwback.

I don't accept that, and I don't accept it just because I make a good part of my living talking and writing about existentialism. It is to me something much more than an historical phase, something much more than a period in recent philosophy, or something much more than simply a movement of the sort that one can label, stamp, can and put on the shelf. It was Sartre himself who said, when he was asked about "What is existentialism?" he said that to try to define it is to freeze it—is to treat it as no longer a living movement but as something dead, something that can be classified. I think that is quite accurate, and Sartre himself was very concerned with the idea that existentialism as a movement didn't have any definitive core, even though he himself did more than anyone to try to stamp it with his own ideas.

The truth is that existentialism is still a vibrant movement, and for that reason, I haven't spent any time at all in the past 23 lectures trying to define what it is. I have noted with some frequency some terms that keep emerging as absolutely central. Looking at Sartre, there are the notions of freedom and responsibility. Looking back to Kierkegaard, the notion of freedom and choice, again. Looking back to Nietzsche, there is a sense shared with Kierkegaard of enormous personal passion.

Through all the figures we have talked about there is a kind of strong individualistic streak—sometimes almost an individualist mania. I am thinking for example of certain aspects of Nietzsche and Kierkegaard, in particular. I would not go so far as to define existentialism in any of these terms. Existentialism, the movement, certainly vibrates around them. I think existentialism is still something very much alive. Although it started as a very European movement and the figures we've talked about have all been Europeans, nevertheless, I think its real home is in America. And I think in the United States, what existentialism amounts to is more clearly instantiated than any place else in the world.

What is that existentialism? I don't want to repeat just the same terms again, so let me say something much more general, and something, in a way, more provincial. Americans are very staunch individualists. At the same time, they are rather keenly aware (although philosophically uncomfortable with the idea) that there is a very strong sense of community that lies at the basis of American society. Americans are very concerned, as self-help books make amply clear, with the idea of self-realization and self-improvement. The very idea of picking oneself up by one's bootstraps and making something new out of oneself, to use the kind of term that Nietzsche deplored—the idea of self-improvement—really defines a good deal of American society.

The whole idea of social mobility—the whole idea of mobility in general—is something that is distinctively American, but I also think something distinctly existentialist. Even in Nietzsche, and to a lesser extent in Heidegger, where the idea of improving oneself or the idea of creating oneself is really at a minimum, nevertheless this idea of self-assertiveness, of some sense of authenticity, some sense of self-realization, comes through as a dominant philosophy. That is what I think existentialism is about.

Nevertheless, my *Vogue* editor (and friend) clearly was on to something when she noted that existentialism was passé. Certainly, if we look at the climate in Europe, it is. If we look at American universities, which often, in a kind of pandering way, follow the latest fashions in Europe, one doesn't hear too much about existentialism anymore. It is eclipsed by two generations of philosophers since Sartre, although Sartre lived long enough to see both of them. The first generation is dominated by a single figure in Paris, someone with whom Sartre's personal relationships were quite strained, but as you may have gathered from other things I have said, Sartre's personal relationships were quite strained with almost everyone. The character I am thinking about is the anthropologist/ philosopher Claude Levi-Strauss, who made quite a reputation for himself with a philosophy which is called "structuralism."

The details of what counts as structuralism, I think, is something way beyond the scope of this lecture. To begin with, it was, in fact, an anthropological insight. What Levi-Strauss was concerned with was the structural similarities which all societies shared in common. What he tried to do in his various studies of myth, ritual, and social custom was to find a system—a set of structures which were common to every society. The idea was the particulars of the different societies could be understood within that structure.

Despite his search for universals, Levi-Strauss clearly had an anthropologist's view of the world. What he attacks in Sartre is very well taken, namely the idea that Sartre really is, despite all pretenses to the contrary, not the universal picture of humanity so much as hyper-intellectual Parisian, who is taking his phenomenology as an unwarranted generalization about what human consciousness and human life is like. What Levi-Strauss emphasizes, in particular, in his studies of what he calls the savage mind—the primitive mind—is the differences between different people, and in particular, the differences in the notion of consciousness which could be accurately applied to different cultures.

Merleau-Ponty, Sartre's friend, makes a similar criticism when he asks Sartre whether a peasant in Latin America—who has never been educated, heard a radio, has no idea how people in other countries live—can be expected to have the kinds of choices, and consequently, the kinds of responsibility that Sartre is talking about. I think Levi-Strauss hits an important point, but that is only the first generation in which Sartre is attacked.

The second generation, in some ways, was more insidious with regard to Sartre. The second generation I would consider those philosophers who make up what is currently called "postmodernism." I would name, in particular, the philosophers Michel Foucault, Jacques Derrida, Gil Deleuze, and Roland Barthes. They have a number of theses in common, although here again, what we find is a group more of individuals than of collectivities. Two theses, I think, come to the fore which are in striking contrast with Sartre's philosophy.

The first is characterized in the rather stunning phrase used by both Barthes and Foucault, "the death of the author." It refers to something which has often been commented upon, often ridiculed. It is the idea that when we read books, the idea that books are written by an author is an absolute way of misunderstanding what they are about. Of course, there is a sense in which people write books, but to confuse the writer of books with the author is exactly the kind of fallacy that Barthes and Foucault are concerned about. To talk about "the death of the author" is a particularly dramatic way of bringing to life a thesis that had been flying around in literary criticism circles for quite some time. It has to do with a way to read and understand books, which is not out primary concern here. It also has to do with the idea that the subject, and subjectivity—the two key concepts in not only Sartre but the whole Cartesian tradition—have in some way been displaced and misunderstood. To read a book in terms of the intentions of an author is precisely to misunderstand it.

The second notion has to do with an impersonal play of forces, which in people like Foucault and Deleuze places an emphasis on agency, and particularly on responsibility, in Sartre. In writing about Nietzsche, for example, Gil Deleuze, in a very well known book in France, argues: in place of Nietzsche, talk about the dynamics of action. He talks instead about the impersonality of the forces— in particular, the sorts of forces that Nietzsche points to in his mythology—the Apollonian versus the Dionysian, and so on—are reactive forces of the slave versus the more aggressive forces of the master.

The idea is that we get rid of any semblance of human responsibility and decision making, and we get rid of that image that I presented in my exposition of Nietzsche genealogy in which the slave, or slaves, make a kind of brilliant decision to undermine the masters. All such talk disappears, and what we are left with is a picture that looks very much, in a superficial reading, like a treatise. That is just the idea. What these two notions together, the death of the author and this notion of the impersonal play of forces, intend to do is really kill subjectivity, and in particular, the notion of subjectivity as Sartre understood it.

I would argue that, on the one hand, something very important is going on here, but, on the other hand, I would suggest that there is a kind of conspiracy of silence regarding Sartre's own significance for both of these movements—structuralism and postmodernism—or what is sometimes in the United States called "post-structuralism." The conspiracy of silence has to do with just how much Sartre's own notion of consciousness and subjectivity informs and, in a way, forms the basis of the kind of philosophy that Foucault, Derrida, Deleuze, and Barthes want to argue. His name is virtually never mentioned in their texts. Reading, for example, *The Biography of Foucault* by James Miller, one finds Foucault sitting in a lecture with Deleuze, and saying to each other how this is really the main target against which all of their philosophy has to be directed.

Whether Sartre is the model or whether he is the target, his importance in French philosophy since his death is, I think, something which has been a very well-kept secret. But, it is not just a question of his being a target, something I will talk about shortly. I think also, if you seriously consider Sartre's view of consciousness and take very seriously the things he says about nothingness and so on, he comes up with a picture which can be very easily accommodated to the postmodernist picture.

What the postmodernists want to do when they reject subjectivity, and with it, phenomenology, is to say that there is only really a third-person way of looking at ourselves. The first person was—is—corrupt or self-deceptive. When they describe the impersonal play of forces, and when they describe a book without an author, what they are rejecting in that way is precisely that notion of consciousness which Sartre anticipated, and the idea that consciousness is not something that can be readily individuated, something readily identified. In many ways, one might say what they are confusing in Sartre is the distinction which he makes very early between consciousness and subjectivity on the one hand, and the self on the other.

The postmodernists reject both self and consciousness together, and with the third-person vocabulary, it is very often very difficult to know what, if anything, is supposed to replace them. Certainly, there is an illimitable place for the first-person perspective—namely, myself and my view of the world from my position—but it is not clear in good part of the postmodernist writing how one can account for the fact that there is such a first-person position. It is also true that the postmodernists rather famously reject rationality, objectivity, truth, and knowledge, although all these claims would have to be rather carefully stated in a longer exposition of their view. The rejection of rationality is something that goes back throughout the history of existentialism. Certainly, in Kierkegaard, the idea that rationality is not adequate to answer the questions concerning the choices we have in life is something that pervades virtually all the authors we have talked about.

Even for Sartre—whom I would say is the most rationalistic of the five authors we have discussed in detail—it is pretty clear that when it comes to fundamental choices, there is no ultimate criterion, there is no ultimate standard, there is no rational guideline to deal with. Sartre tells a story which is very famous in one of his more popular essays, about the young student who comes to him not quite sure what he is supposed to do. His brothers have been killed in the war. At the same time, he is the only one left, and he is taking care of his mother. So, he has a very real question about whether his obligation is to avenge his brothers by going off and fighting, or whether he should stay with his mother—the obligation of a dutiful son.

Sartre remarks—and I am not sure what he would have said to the individual in question, actually—but he remarks that there is nothing to tell him. The truth is what he is looking for is a criterion for the right thing to do—something objective, something rational. The truth is, that it is not as if one finds a principle and on the basis of it makes the decision. Just as we said with regard to many other aspects of human nature, it is rather the case that, first, one decides what to do, then one gathers around the principles to justify it. So, the young student has to decide whether avenging his brothers is what he will do (and consequently, whether revenge or avenging is the principle that he is acting upon), or whether he will stay with his mother, and consequently, whether filial piety is the principle upon which he is acting.

In short, what Sartre is doing is already agreeing with the postmodernists that rationality does not have the privileged place that it has had throughout the history of philosophy. With it, though this is not a primary concern of his or the postmodernists', notions of objectivity, truth and knowledge have to be put on a back burner as well, because—whatever we mean by objectivity, whatever we mean by truth and knowledge—they can't be of the sort that philosophers before Sartre, notably philosophers in the Kantian tradition, tried to make it out to be.

I think all this is, in a way, superficial. Nietzsche said when we read a philosophy we have to always ask, "What is the moral objective? What is this philosopher trying to express?" The idea is that it is always a kind of personal confession. Personal confessions can often be political confessions, too. I think one way of understanding the eclipse of Sartre, and his rejection by the postmodernists, is in terms which certainly Foucault and Deleuze have made quite explicit. That is, what they reject is what they call his "Enlightenment project." That is going to be understood in a number of different ways.

First of all, despite his queries about rationality and rational standards, it is pretty clear that in Sartre, there is a raging sense of rationality, a raging sense of monism, fitting things together. It is rather illustrative that, in Sartre's notion of psychoanalysis for example, one of the notions that he talks about is the "fundamental project." This is something that each of us has, and this is something that is supposed to replace the Freudian unconscious.

Whereas Freud says there are these forces, experiences, or effects that are somehow bubbling below the surface which are not and cannot be made conscious, and which cause us to behave in certain ways, Sartre with his emphasis on choice and purpose is saying each of us has a fundamental purpose in life. What he means is something very basic. For example, when I talked about the desire to be God, the desire to be both in-itself and for-itself—that would be a kind of fundamental project. The psychoanalytic move he makes in reaction to Freud is basically just that. To understand our fundamental project is to understand why we are acting in the way we are acting, and it has a kind of liberating effect.

Liberation is exactly what the postmodernists seek too, but they seek it in a very different way. In particular, instead of this kind of gathering together and monistic effort that goes into almost all of Sartre's discussions—despite his frequent discussions of the tension of human nature and all of that—the postmodernists rather would say what we have to get rid of is just that sense of what they sometimes call "totalization"—just that sense, that rage for unity that has preoccupied Western philosophers virtually since the pre-Socratic philosophers. This is a thesis that they get rather directly from the later Heidegger, who also came to question some of the orientation of his earlier work, which is what we discussed. The idea of rationality, the idea of a unified understanding, was very much the proposal of the Enlightenment, which had a politics attached to it. This is very much what many of the postmodernists want to reject. What I want to say is that, in many ways, Sartre had already anticipated them.

Sartre also talks in a way that suggests that there is a form of rationality which actually escapes the bounds of many of the limitations of facticity and the notions of, for example, the entrapment we impose ourselves when we talk about emotion. He talks, from his very earliest works on, about something he calls "purifying reflection." Any good rationalistic philosopher can read this and cheer, because the idea is that there is a way of thinking about ourselves—both personally and politically—which, in some way, removes us from prejudice and takes us into the realm of a kind of pure freedom. There is a real question whether this is a thesis that will stand scrutiny within Sartre's own philosophy. It is pretty clear that there is a sense, again, of this kind of uniform notion of one singular ideal which preoccupies his politics. It is the politics of freedom.

One has to say that he made a great many rather silly decisions on the basis of this politics—for example, his defense of various Stalinist regimes, including Stalin himself—for a considerable amount of time, and his sense that freedom dominates all political considerations. It is on this regard that he came to blows with Albert Camus, who had previously been a good friend. Camus published a book called *The Rebel* in the mid 1950s in which among other things he talked about his own misgivings about the leftist campaigns of which he had been a part, and, in particular, his support of dictatorships and authoritarian regimes. The idea was that freedom is not an excuse.

This rubbed Sartre very badly. In particular, freedom was not an excuse for cruelty, and for inhuman behavior. He called into question the vices of the Stalinists, in particular, and said in one of his famous essays he wanted to be neither a victim, nor an executioner, but find some way of being a good human being. The idea of being a good human being never had much weight with Sartre, nor did it have much weight with some of the postmodernists. The idea is that, for Sartre, the politics of freedom took priority over everything. For Camus, there was a much more mushy sense of what it was to be a good person, of not harming others, which took priority. On this particular fact, they ended their relationship.

The notion of power, which emerges most dramatically in Foucault, is an attempt to explain, among other things, why we have believed and accepted the beliefs that we had over the course of history. In general, philosophers like to stress rationality in the sense of gathering evidence—the best arguments for the most plausible positions. Foucault, following Nietzsche, comes up with the rather frightening prospect that what the success of theories, social movements, and even things like medicine have all come down to had to do with superior power—in particular, political power—although later in his career, he starts talking, too, about those aspects of power which are more particular to individual relationships.

Again, the notion of impersonality comes to the fore. Once again, I want to use Sartre and Camus as a way of pushing that back. The idea of thinking about our actions, whether they are individual or collective, in terms of individual explanations is exactly what the humanism of both Sartre and Camus is aimed against. It is no accident that one of the targets that the postmodernists list, and in this they follow the later Heidegger, is precisely humanism. It is a thesis which Sartre took very seriously, and when they reject it, one has to ask exactly: What is it to reject humanism?

The notion becomes very particular with regard to the concept of the self. Here again, I think a very good point is made against Sartre, but one which Sartre anticipated and covered if one looks at his philosophy in its broader scope. Jacques Derrida, in particular, has become famous for rejecting the unified notion of the self. The idea is that the self is marginalized—it is fragmented—and it becomes a very real and difficult question. In what sense can we identify the locus of responsibility?

Here we would want to talk, first of all, about political responsibility. Sartre—as I said, I think he made many foolish choices—was from beginning to end always steeped in the idea that as a writer, as a human being, he had responsibilities not just within his personal sphere, but to the world to manifest freedom, and maximize freedom wherever he could. The idea is that one took this responsibility through the choices and decisions that one makes. The question that I always have for the postmodernists is: "Where is this notion of political responsibility in their work?" Jacques Derrida, for example, has very recently defended a version of Marxism. One can ask in his defense of Marxism, again, where personal responsibility fits.

In the personal realm, there is this idea, which keeps coming through in the postmodernists, of our life and our experience—although like Heidegger, they don't like to use that word—being the result of impersonal forces. What they underestimate and what they, in some ways, deny, is what Sartre highlighted in terms of our personal responsibility for what we do, what we experience, what we are, and, consequently, the way the world is. Let me go back to the notion of Sartre's contrast to Freud. As I said when we talked about Sartre and Freud, I think while Sartre rejects Freud as his main target, the truth is that the two are much closer than either of them would probably admit. I summarize the difference by saying that wherever Freud says, "I cannot," indicating the forces of repression, what Sartre wants to say is, "I will not. I refuse," indicating a choice.

There was a book published about 15 years ago by the psychoanalyst Bruno Bettelheim, who knew Freud and, obviously, knew his German very well. He defended Freud against his own translators and interpreters, stressing that what the Freudian project was all about was a form of humanism. Many of the terms that are translated in the standard edition of Freud's works in English, in a mechanistic way, were, in fact, terms which fit much better into a kind of spiritual humanistic tradition—words like "soul," for example.

When Sartre takes on Freud for his psychic determinism and the mechanistic interpretation he puts on that, one can raise the question whether Freud might not at many points have simply turned around and agreed in terms of the psychoanalytic project, which basically is a liberating project—for Freud, liberating people from unconscious urges and the causes that made them neurotic and sometimes psychotic. For Sartre, it is liberating ourselves from wrongheaded projects—fundamental projects that are just impossible—trying to understand exactly what we are in the world by our own choices. Purifying reflection, here, becomes absolutely essential.

One asks, if all of one's behavior is essentially geared toward one fundamental aim, whatever that happens to be, where do we get the foothold to have a reflection which is not itself part of that project? On the one hand, I think Sartre has a problem here. If you say that everything has to be conceived of within the scope of the project, then the question of how there can be a reflection which is truly purifying and also free from the strictures of the project itself becomes a real problem. Nevertheless, for all of my hesitations, I think it is pretty clear that what Freud is arguing here is what we need in America now, in particular. The emphasis on personal responsibility is a very welcome antidote to the wave of victimization and the sense of blame manifest in our legal system in the explosion in tort law and liability suits.

I think the idea of purifying reflection is absolutely essential in understanding the sense in which we must try to get hold of ourselves by our own bootstraps, and understand what we are doing and why. In an age of mindless consumerism, it seems to me to be absolutely essential to ask myself as an American, "What am I doing to the planet? What am I doing to the world society? What am I doing to myself?" In short, I think existentialism is not at all passé. It is, rather, exactly what we need once we have finished with this terrible but rather remarkable century.

Glossary

Absurd: For Camus, the confrontation and conflict between our rational expectations of the world (justice, satisfaction, happiness) and the "indifference" of the world.

Aesthetic (mode of existence): Kierkegaard's conception of a life based on desire and its satisfaction.

Authenticity: Heidegger's notion of genuine human existence.

Bad faith: Sartre's conception of those forms of self-deception in which we deceive ourselves about ourselves, about our natures and responsibilities.

Being-for-itself: For Sartre, human consciousness.

Being-for-others: For Sartre, our painful awareness of other people and their effects on us through their judgments and "looks."

Being-in-itself: For Sartre, the existence of things in the world.

Being-towards-death: Heidegger's notion of human mortality and the importance of full awareness in facing death.

Dasein: Heidegger's conception of "the being through whom being comes into question," i.e., human existence.

Das Man: Heidegger's conception of the inauthentic self, the self constructed by and through other people.

Ethical (mode of existence): Kierkegaard's conception of a life based on a chosen commitment to moral principles and duty to others.

Existence (*Existenz*): For Kierkegaard, a full-blooded, freely chosen, passionately committed life; for Heidegger, that which is essentially *Dasein*. *Dasein* has no essence other than the fact that it exists, that it has possibilities and projects to undertake.

Existentialism: The philosophical movement that stresses individuality and personal responsibility, as epitomized in Kierkegaard, Nietzsche, Heidegger, and Sartre.

Facticity: For Heidegger and Sartre, the brute facts that characterize us, such as our height, our weight, our date of birth, and so on.

Fallenness: For Heidegger, a "pre-ontological" way of dealing in the world, a way in which *Dasein* fails to face up to its ontological condition

Master morality: Nietzsche's conception of a self-confident morality of virtue and excellence.

Objective uncertainty: Kierkegaard's attempt to capture those realms of human existence in which knowledge becomes irrelevant and personal decision becomes all-important.

Ontology: For Heidegger, the study of Being.

Phenomenology: In Husserl, Heidegger, and Sartre, the study of the essential structures of consciousness, experience, or *Dasein*.

Postmodernism: Contemporary philosophy that rejects the idea of the unified self and the clarifying powers of reason.

Religious (mode of existence): Kierkegaard's conception of a life based on a chosen devotion to God and His commandments.

Slave morality: Nietzsche's conception of a reactive, resentful insistence on universal principles and the protection of the weak.

Subjectivity: In Kierkegaard, the realm of personal passion and commitment. In Sartre, phenomenology, the realm of consciousness.

Subjective truth: In Kierkegaard, passionate commitment.

Thrownness: For Heidegger, our "existential" condition, the state in which we find ourselves thrown into this world, that we are "abandoned." It is the "there" in which *Dasein* finds itself.

Transcendence: For Sartre, the power of consciousness to negate and go beyond the facts of the matter.

Transcendental ego: For Husserl, the realm of consciousness.

Übermensch: Nietzsche's dramatic image of a more than human being.

Will to power: Nietzsche's conception of the fundamental motivation of all human behavior, including morality and philosophy.

Biographical Notes

Beauvoir, Simone de (1908–1986). French novelist, essayist, and philosopher and Jean-Paul Sartre's lifelong companion. The author of *The Ethics of Ambiguity* and many other works. Best known for her insightful commentaries on growing up female in a very male culture, living through the war years, and finally, on growing old.

Camus, Albert (1913–1960). French-Algerian (*pied noir*) essayist and philosopher, author of *The Stranger*, *The Myth of Sisyphus*, *The Plague*, and *The Fall* and many lyrical and political essays. Best known for his very personal expressions of humanism. His friendship with Sartre erupted with their disagreements over the Algerian War and the general question of violence as a legitimate political means.

Dostoevsky, Fyodor (1821–1881). Russian writer and religious thinker, author of *Notes from Underground*, *The Brothers Karamazov*, *The Idiot*, *Crime and Punishment*, and other novels. Best known for his deep sense of anguish and doubt regarding ultimate religious matters.

Foucault, Michel (1926–1984). French philosopher and polemicist, first categorized as a structuralist, then as a post-structuralist and postmodernist. Author of such books as *The Archaeology of Knowledge*, *The Order of Things*, and *A History of Sexuality*. Best known for his emphasis on power in the world of ideas and culture.

Hegel, G. W. F. (1770–1831). German philosopher who followed Kant as a "German idealist," author of *The Phenomenology of Spirit* and several other important works. Best known for his vision of an all-encompassing historical world-spirit that it is just our luck to finally have made fully realized.

Heidegger, Martin (1889–1976). German philosopher who followed Husserl as a phenomenologist but expanded his interests to include traditional theological and metaphysical matters, author of *Being and Time* and many other works. Best known for his notion of "authenticity," which came to dominate many existentialist concerns.

Hesse, Hermann (1877–1962). German-Swiss writer and author of *Demian, Steppenwolf, Siddharta,* and *The Glass Bead Game* (for which he won a Nobel prize). Best known for his synthesis of Western and Eastern (Buddhist) thinking.

Husserl, Edmund (1859–1938). German-Czech (Moravian) philosopher and mathematician; best known as the founder of "Phenomenology."

Kafka, Franz (1883–1924). Bohemian (Czech) writer famous for his tales of the bizarre, for instance, "Metamorphosis," *The Trial,* and *The Castle.*

Kant, Immanuel (1749–1804). German philosopher, "German idealist," best known as the author of three "critiques," "The Critique of Pure Reason," "The Critique of Practical Reason," and "The Critique of Judgment." As a moral philosopher, he has long been characterized (or caricatured) as strictly rational and "rule-bound"; thus, he becomes a point of departure for such different thinkers as Kierkegaard, Nietzsche, and Sartre.

Kierkegaard, Søren (1813–1855). Danish religious philosopher and first "existentialist." He is best known for his concept of an irrational "leap of faith" and his many religious works, many of them written under pseudonyms, emphasizing the importance of personal choice and commitment in becoming a Christian and in living a full life more generally. His philosophy has many important parallels with Nietzsche, despite their very different positions on the desirability of Christianity.

Nietzsche, Friedrich (1844–1900). German philosopher who attacked both the Judeo-Christian tradition and contemporary culture and politics with great style and passion. Author of *The Gay Science, Thus Spoke Zarathustra, Beyond Good and Evil,* and many other works.

Sartre, Jean-Paul (1905–1980). French philosopher, essayist, and literary writer responsible for naming "existentialism" and for definitively promoting some of its central themes, notably the theme of freedom and responsibility that we have summarized as "No Excuses!" Author of *Being and Nothingness* and many other works.

Schopenhauer, Arthur (1788–1860). German philosopher who followed Kant (competing with Hegel) as a "German idealist." Author of *The World as Will and Idea*. Best known for his grumpy cosmic pessimism but equally important for bringing together Western and Eastern (Buddhist) ideas.

Zarathustra (sixth century B.C.E.). Persian prophet, founder of Zoroastrianism, belated hero of Nietzsche's quasi-Biblical epic, *Thus Spoke Zarathustra*.

Bibliography

The main texts for the lectures can be found in Robert C. Solomon, ed., *Existentialism* (New York: McGraw Hill/Modern Library, 1974). Secondary texts that follow the perspective of the lectures can be found in Robert C. Solomon, *From Rationalism to Existentialism* (Wash., D.C.: Rowman and Littlefield, 1979), and Robert C. Solomon, *Continental Philosophy Since 1750* (Oxford: Oxford University Press, 1988).

Anderson, Thomas, *Sartre's Two Ethics* (Open Court, 1993).

Barnes, Hazel, *An Existentialist Ethics* (New York: Vintage, 1971).

———, *Sartre* (Philadelphia: J.P. Lippincott, 1973).

Beauvoir, Simone, *The Ethics of Ambiguity* (New York: Citadel Press, 1970).

Bree, Germaine, *Camus* (Harcourt Brace, 1964).

Calhoun, Cheshire, ed., *What Is an Emotion?* (New York: Oxford, 1984).

Camus, Albert, *Notebooks, 1935–1951*, translated by Philip Thody (New York: Knopf, 1963).

———, *The Fall*, trans. by Justin O'Brien (New York: Random House, 1956).

———, *The Stranger* (New York: Knopf, 1946, trans. by Stuart Gilbert ["British" translation]; 1988, trans. by Matthew Ward ["American" translation]).

———, *The Myth of Sisyphus*, trans. by Justin O'Brien (New York: Random House, 1955) (partially reprinted in Solomon, *Existentialism*, McGraw-Hill, pp. 177–188).

————, *The Plague*, trans. by Stuart Gilbert (New York: Random House, 1948).

————, *The Rebel* (New York: Knopf, 1956).

Danto, Arthur C., *Sartre* (London: Fontana Press, 1979).

Deleuze, Gilles, *Nietzsche and Philosophy* (New York: Columbia University Press, 1983).

Derrida, Jacques, *A Derrida Reader*, ed. Peggy Kumaf (New York: Columbia University Press, 1991).

Dostoevsky, Fyodor, *Crime and Punishment* (New York: Signet, 1968).

———, *The Brothers Karamazov*, trans. by Constance Garnett (New York: Modern Library, 1975).

————, *Notes from Underground* and *The Grand Inquisitor*, trans. by Ralph E. Matlaw (New York: Meridian, 1991).

Dreyfus, Hubert L., *Being-in-the-World: A Commentary on Heidegger's Being and Time, Division 1* (Cambridge: The MIT Press, 1991).

Dreyfus, Hubert L., and Paul Rabinow, eds., *The Essential Works of Michel Foucault* (New York: Norton, 1997).

Fell, Joseph P., *Emotion in the Thought of Sartre* (New York: Columbia University Press, 1965).

————, *Heidegger and Sartre: An Essay on Being and Place* (New York: Columbia University Press, 1979).

Fingarette, Herbert, *Self-Deception* (London: Routledge & Kegan Paul, 1969).

Gardiner, Patrick, *Kierkegaard* (Oxford: Oxford University Press, 1988).

Guignon, Charles, *Heidegger and the Problem of Knowledge* (Indianapolis: Hackett, 1983).

Hallie, Philip, *Lest Innocent Blood Be Shed* (New York: Harper and Row, 1979).

Hegel, G. W. F., *Phenomenology of Spirit* (London: Oxford University Press, 1977).

————, *Introduction to the Philosophy of History* (Indianapolis: Hackett Publishing Co., 1988).

Heidegger, Martin, *Being and Time*, trans. by Joan Stambaugh (New York: Routledge, 1997).

————, *The Question Concerning Technology and Other Essays* (New York: Harper & Row, 1977).

Hemingway, Ernest, *For Whom the Bell Tolls* (New York: MacMillan, 1968).

Hesse, Hermann, *Demian*, trans. by Michael Roloff and Michael Lebeck (New York: Harper, 1965).

————, *Steppenwolf*, trans. by Basil Creighton (New York: Knopf, 1963).

Higgins, Kathleen M., *Nietzsche's Zarathustra* (Philadelphia: Temple University Press, 1987).

Higgins, Kathleen M., and R. Solomon, eds., *Reading Nietzsche* (New York: Oxford University Press, 1988).

Hunt, Lester, *Nietzsche and the Original of Virtue* (New York: Routledge, 1991).

Husserl, Edmund, *Cartesian Meditations: An Introduction to Phenomenology* (The Hague: Kluwer Academic Publishers, 1993).

————, *Paris Lectures* (The Hague: Nijhaff, 1964; in Solomon, *Phenomenology and Existentialism*, Rowman and Littlefield, 1979).

Jeanson, Francis, *Sartre and the Problem of Morality* (Indiana: Indiana University Press, 1980).

Kafka, Franz, *Metamorphosis and Other Stories* (New York, Scribners, 1993).

————, *The Trial*, trans. by Breon Mitchell (New York, Schocken, 1998).

Kaufmann, Walter, *Nietzsche—Philosopher, Psychologist, Antichrist* (Princeton: Princeton University Press, 1974).

Kierkegaard, Søren, *Concluding Unscientific Postscript* (Princeton: Princeton University Press, 1944).

————, *Either/Or*, 2 vols. (Princeton: Princeton University Press, 1959).

————, *Fear and Trembling* (Princeton: Princeton University Press, 1983).

————, *Journals*, trans. by Alexander Dru (London: Oxford University Press, 1938; excerpted in Solomon, *Existentialism*, pp. 3–5).

Levi-Strauss, Claude, *The Savage Mind* (Chicago: University of Chicago Press, 1966).

Lottman, Herbert R., *Camus: A Biography* (Garden City, N.Y.: Doubleday, 1979).

Mackey, Louis, *Kierkegaard: A Kind of Poet* (Philadelphia: University of Pennsylvania Press, 1971).

MacInytre, Alasdair, *After Virtue* (Notre Dame: University of Notre Dame Press, 1984).

Melville, Herman, *Billy Budd, Sailor* (New York: Bantam Books, 1962).

Metha, J. L., *The Philosophy of Martin Heidegger* (New York: Harper & Row, 1971).

Miller, James, *Michel Foucault* (New York: Simon and Schuster, 1993).

Murdoch, Iris, *Sartre: Romantic Rationalist* (New Haven: Yale, 1953).

Natanson, Maurice, *Critique of Jean-Paul Sartre's Ontology* (New York: Haskell House, 1972).

Nehamas, Alexander, *Nietzsche: Life as Literature* (Cambridge: Harvard University Press, 1985).

Nietzsche, Friedrich, *The Anti-Christ*, trans. by Walter Kaufmann, in Walter Kaufmann, ed., *The Viking Portable Nietzsche* (New York: Viking Press, 1954).

————, *On the Genealogy of Morals*, trans. by Walter Kaufmann (New York: Vintage Books, 1967).

————, *The Gay Science*, trans. by Walter Kaufmann (New York: Vintage Books, 1974).

————, *Thus Spoke Zarathustra* in Walter Kaufmann, ed., *The Viking Portable Nietzsche* (New York: Viking Press, 1954).

————, *Twilight of the Idols*, trans. by Walter Kaufmann, in Walter Kaufmann, ed., *The Viking Portable Nietzsche* (New York: Viking Press, 1954).

————, *The Will to Power* (New York: Vintage, 1967).

Norris, Christopher, *What's Wrong with Postmodernism?* (Baltimore: Johns Hopkins University Press, 1990).

O'Brien, Conor Cruise, *Camus* (London: Fontana, Collins, 1970).

Sallis, John, *Deconstruction and Philosophy: The Texts of Jacques Derrida* (Chicago: University of Chicago Press, 1987).

Sartre, Jean-Paul, *The Age of Reason*, trans. by Eric Sutton (Harmondsworth: Penguin, 1971).

————, *Being and Nothingness*, trans. by Hazel Barnes (New York: Philosophical Library, Inc., 1956).

————, *The Emotions: Sketch of a Theory* (London: Methuen, 1962).

————, *The Transcendence of the Ego: An Existentialist Theory of Consciousness* (New York: Hill and Wang, 1990).

————, *The Wall and Other Stories* (New York: New Directions, 1948).

————, *Nausea* (New York: New Directions, 1964).

————, *Notebooks for an Ethics* (New York: Chicago, 1992).

Schopenhauer, Arthur, *The World as Will and Representation* (New York: Dover, 1969); abridged version (London: Everyman Press, 1997).

Schroeder, William, *Sartre and His Predecessors* (Boston : Routledge & Kegan Paul, 1984).

Sluga, Hans, *Heidegger's Crisis* (Cambridge: Harvard University Press, 1993).

Soll, Ivan. "Sartre's Rejection of the Freudian Unconscious," in *The Philosophy of Jean-Paul Sartre*, Paul A. Schilpp, ed. (Illinois: Open Court Publishing, 1981).

Solomon, Robert C., *About Love* (Rowman and Littlefield, 1994).

————, "Camus's L'etranger and the Truth," in *From Hegel to Existentialism* (New York: Oxford University Press, 1988).

————, *Introducing the Existentialists* (Indianapolis: Hackett, 1983).

————, *The Passions: Emotions and the Meaning of Life* (Indianapolis: Hackett Publishing Co., 1993).

————, "Sartre on the Emotions" in *The Philosophy of Jean-Paul Sartre*, Paul A. Schilpp, ed. (Illinois: Open Court Publishing, 1981).

Solomon, Robert C., and Kathleen M. Higgins, *For the Love of Life: The Philosophy of Friedrich Nietzsche* (The Teaching Company lecture series).

————, *What Nietzsche Really Said* (New York: Schocken Books, Random House, 2000).

Sprintzen, David, *Camus* (Philadelphia: Temple University Press, 1988).

Stern, J. P. *Friedrich Nietzsche* (Harmondsworth, New York: Penguin Books, 1979).

Tanner, Michael, *Nietzsche* (Oxford: Oxford University Press, 1994).

Thulstrup, Niels, *Kierkegaard's Relation in Hegel* (Princeton: Princeton University Press, 1980).

Todd, Olivier, *Albert Camus: A Life*, trans. by Benjamin Ivry (New York: Knopf, 1997).

Young, Julian, *Heidegger, Philosophy, Nazism* (Cambridge: Cambridge University Press, 1997).